TWELVE VIEWS FROM THE DISTANCE

TWELVE VIEWS
FROM THE DISTANCE

Mutsuo Takahashi

Translated by Jeffrey Angles

UNIVERSITY OF MINNESOTA PRESS   MINNEAPOLIS · LONDON

All photographs courtesy of Mutsuo Takahashi.

This book was originally published as *Jū-ni no enkei*
(Tokyo: Chūō Kōronsha, 1970).

The translation of this book was supported by generous grants
from the National Endowment for the Arts and the PEN American Center.

Published by the University of Minnesota Press
111 Third Avenue South, Suite 290
Minneapolis, MN 55401-2520
http://www.upress.umn.edu

Library of Congress Cataloging-in-Publication Data
Takahashi, Mutsuo.
[Jū-ni no enkei. English]
Twelve views from the distance / Mutsuo Takahashi ;
translated by Jeffrey Angles.
Includes bibliographical references.
ISBN 978-0-8166-7277-6 (hc : acid-free paper)—
ISBN 978-0-8166-7936-2 (pb : acid-free paper)
1. Takahashi, Mutsuo. 2. Poets, Japanese—20th century—
Biography. I. Angles, Jeffrey, 1971– II. Title.
PL862.A4212Z513 2012
895.6'15—dc23 [B]   2012022567

Printed in the United States of America on acid-free paper

The University of Minnesota is an equal-opportunity educator and employer.

20 19 18 17 16 15 14 13 12   10 9 8 7 6 5 4 3 2 1

Huddled on the sloping street

The hunger of the boys shined

Like the idol of some god

The miserable town, hardened beneath their eyes,

Spreads outward, rising to their height

Toward frostbitten sky, wanting to scream

Meanwhile, their mothers who have left

For so far away, cast down their eyes

With magical greatness

—"BOYS," BY TAKAHASHI MUTSUO,
FROM *ROSE TREE, FAKE LOVERS* (1964)

Contents

Note about
Japanese Names

On the cover and title page of this book, the author's name appears in the Western order, with given name first and surname last: Mutsuo Takahashi, with Takahashi the surname. In Japan, however, people place surnames first, followed by their given names, so there the author would be known as Takahashi Mutsuo. (There are no middle names in Japan.)

Commercial presses in the West that publish translations of Japanese literature have historically tended to put names in Western order. For instance, Western readers might know of the novelist Yukio Mishima, whereas Japanese speakers call the same novelist Mishima Yukio. It is increasingly the trend, especially in academic publishing, to place East Asian names in the native order so that English speakers can learn to recognize people and places by the names the natives use. For this reason, when translating this book I placed the names in the text in the native Japanese order, with surname first. The only inconsistencies appear on the cover and title pages, and I hope readers will forgive those discrepancies for the sake of cataloging.

Chart of Family Members

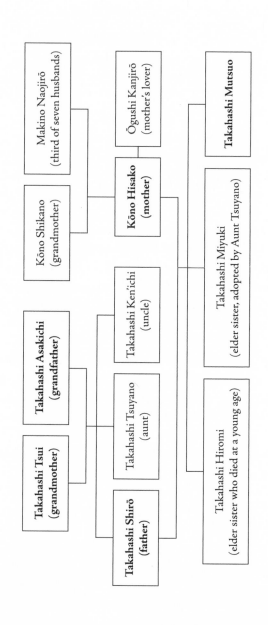

Translator's
Introduction

Takahashi Mutsuo is today known as one of Japan's most prominent living poets and most versatile writers, having published in almost every major genre, ranging from modern-style poetry, tanka, and haiku to fiction, essays, criticism, opera librettos, and even nō and kyōgen plays. Long respected in the literary world for his erudition and broad knowledge of world literature, he has been quick to draw on these resources, and for this reason his writing appeals not just to Japanese audiences but to international readers as well. As a result, he has become one of the most thoroughly translated of all living Japanese poets, with several volumes of English translations to his name. He has also become one of the most visible of Japanese poets on the world stage, frequently representing Japan at poetry festivals and readings in East Asia, Europe, and the Americas.

Takahashi's literary ascent began almost fifty years ago when the prominent critic Etō Jun (1932–1999) published a review of Takahashi's second book of poetry, *Bara no ki, nise no koibito-tachi* (Rose tree, fake lovers, 1964), in the daily newspaper *Asahi shimbun*. This collection, like the one that preceded it and the several that would follow, was unusual in that it dealt frankly with the subject of male homoerotic desire in an era when vivid descriptions of male-male desire were most often found in erotica, medical texts, or discussions behind closed doors. Takahashi's writing from the 1960s and early 1970s is often explicitly erotic; however, Takahashi couches this eroticism in the highly stylized, creative language of poetry, thus raising a subject that many might have seen as "vulgar" to the realm of "high art."[1] Takahashi was, in essence, challenging Japanese society's tendency to relegate certain "unseemly" subjects to margins of acceptability and, in the process, providing postwar Japanese literature with some of the most articulate and theoretically provocative explorations of homoerotic desire—a subject that for nearly two decades had only rarely been treated in mainstream Japanese literature.[2]

As Japan experienced its own sexual revolution and started rethinking the cultural ramifications of sexual desire, Takahashi stood out as a luminary, willing to write about homoeroticism in unflinchingly bold language rarely found in mainstream literature. It is because Takahashi was so outspoken that he quickly formed strong personal bonds with a number of prominent figures in the Japanese literary world that were also interested in nonheteronormative forms of desire. These included the novelist Mishima Yukio (1925–1970), who had written some of mid-twentieth-century Japan's most important queer novels; Inagaki Taruho (1900–1977), an experimental writer who had started writing about same-sex desire in the prewar period; and the writer Shibusawa Tatsuhiko (1928–1987), whose translations of the Marquis de Sade had been the center of a landmark lawsuit that helped determine what the Japanese government defined as pornography.

Takahashi's bold treatment of male homoeroticism was also the reason that his poetry began to earn an audience abroad. In the early 1970s, translations of Takahashi's poems began to surface in gay journals in the United States, but it was Hiroaki Sato's 1975 translation of *Poems of a Penisist*, first published by Chicago Review Press and recently reprinted by the University of Minnesota Press, that made a sizeable selection of Takahashi's work available to the English-speaking world for the first time. In an era when few Americans were aware of queer experience around the world, this provocatively titled book earned the admiration of many foreign readers, including Allen Ginsberg (1926–1997). Some of Sato's translations were then retranslated into other languages and included in journals and anthologies, helping to make Takahashi's work known around the world.

Relatively early in Takahashi's career, just as he was beginning to make a name for himself, he began writing a book of memoirs about his early life. The result is *Twelve Views from the Distance* (*Jū-ni no enkei*), a book so colorful, so richly crafted, and so vivid that it allows the reader to live within Takahashi's memories as intimately as if they were the reader's own. *Twelve Views from the Distance* is shaped at every turn by Takahashi's poetic touch, yet its restrained, quiet beauty is somewhat more subdued than the boldly erotic works he was writing around the same time. *Twelve Views* was first serialized in 1969, then published in book form the following year by the publisher Chūō Kōronsha. Lending his name to the cover of the book was no less a figure than Mishima Yukio, who declared in a blurb that Takahashi's memoirs were a masterpiece of "firm prose that shines with a dark luster much like a set of drawers crafted by a master of old." The novelist Nosaka Akiyuki (b. 1930) concurred: "I think Takahashi Mutsuo has, at the tip of his pen, a rare spirit of words, and can in the vague mysteries of the forty-eight syllables of the Japanese language make infinite, kaleidoscopic paradises appear. . . . Takahashi's damasked world is sweetly beautiful like the spirit of a dream."[3]

Twelve Views from the Distance documents the first fifteen years or so of Takahashi's life. Because he was born in 1937, the same year that Japan launched an aggressive campaign to conquer all of eastern China, Takahashi's youth overlapped with the era in which the Japanese empire descended into all-out war. In this book, Takahashi remembers the difficulties and privation of the war years, the end of the war in 1945, and the subsequent poverty and rebuilding of the occupation years—perhaps the most dramatic and traumatic era in all of Japanese history. He spent these years on the southwestern island of Kyūshū, where during the economic troubles of the 1930s there were far too few jobs for the relatively large population. It is no coincidence that during the difficult years of the Great Depression people from Kyūshū and southwestern portions of the neighboring island of Honshū were the most likely to emigrate to the Japanese colonies on the Asian mainland and to Japanese settlements in South America. As we see in these memoirs, Takahashi's mother was one of those émigrés.

Several chapters of *Twelve Views* focus on the ways that the circumstances of Takahashi's family intersected with events on the international stage. Early in the book, he mentions that his father died from pneumonia. His illness and death were the result of many long hours of work in a metal factory, and Takahashi sees him as a victim of the war, one casualty of the rapidly militarizing Japanese empire. Takahashi's mother left for China in the early 1940s in search of opportunity and a better way of life in the colonies, and as we see in *Twelve Views*, her departure became one of the major events that shaped Takahashi's life for years to come. During her absence, Takahashi was left to live with his poor, rural grandmother who becomes another of the central figures in this book—a woman who lives through tenacity, toughness, and a self-centeredness that is endearing and shocking at turns. Living with them was also an uncle, who served as a pivotal figure in Takahashi's development. This uncle was both frightening and alluring at the same time, a powerful, attractive role model in a family that had no other young men. Once again, however, fate intervened, and he was sent to the battlefield in Burma, where illness claimed his life. Takahashi has written much about this uncle and his attraction to his masculine virility in the poetry he wrote in the late 1960s and early 1970s, around the same time as *Twelve Views*.[4]

Because Takahashi spent his youth in rural, poor southwestern Japan, he was far from Tokyo, Kyoto, Osaka, and the other metropolises that have tended to shape the ways that people in the West—and even in Japan—talk about Japanese culture. There in the poor countryside of Kyūshū, superstitions, folktales, premodern beliefs, and prejudices lingered well into the modern age, even as they were dying out or taking on new forms elsewhere. As a result, the descriptions of his early life recorded in this book sound very different from the descriptions of the lives of many of his fellow countrymen who lived in cities and other rural areas elsewhere. Nowadays, the small, rural city of Nōgata, where Takahashi lived with his grandmother, and Moji, the port town where he moved with his mother after her return from China, look like many other small Japanese towns, with the same types of stores and apartment buildings one finds elsewhere throughout the country. Still, in the late 1930s and 1940s, both were distinctive places, and Takahashi fills his descriptions of them with details rich in nuance and local color. He lovingly describes the outskirts of Nōgata, the layout of his grandmother's rickety home, the clusters of houses around the pond by her house, the Korean settlement beyond the graveyard, and the shrines scattered across the nearby countryside. Similarly, the descriptions of the dusty streets and rocky shoreline of Moji evoke images of an era before today's asphalt roads and concrete ocean–break walls. The uniqueness of place is strengthened by Takahashi's account of the quirky and distinctive culture of the people who populate the book's pages. Among them one finds an old lady who speaks to the spirits of the dead, a crazy lady who is tied to a pole outside allegedly "for her own good," schoolboys who play homoerotic games every chance they get, a drunkard who runs through the streets brandishing an ax, and a charming girl who picks up pieces of sea-polished glass on the seashore. The descriptions of these often amusing characters breathe life into Takahashi's evocations of wartime Japan, giving them a depth and richness that bring these memoirs alive as a piece of literature.

In *Twelve Views from the Distance*, Takahashi captures the full range of his mental world as a boy. Chapters shift between events in his youth and family to detailed descriptions of his childhood games, friendships, school experiences, and feelings. In this, Takahashi's memoirs are much like the masterpiece of modern Japanese literature *The Silver Spoon* (*Gin no saji*) by Naka Kansuke (1885–1965), an author whom Takahashi once called one of the greatest influences on his own early style.[5] Naka's memoir, published in 1913 and praised by novelist Natsume Sōseki (1876–1916) as "unprecedented in the depiction of the world of a child," also describes a boy who grows up away from his mother, living a life that is so introverted that he had little do with his peers until entering school.[6]

The vignettes in this book are clustered around twelve different themes, each forming the backbone of one chapter. Takahashi included an afterword in the first edition of the book that explained the organization of the chapters:

> The title *Twelve Views from the Distance* serves as somewhat of an explanation. Each of these twelve individual views from the distance is a single mirror, independent of the others. I wanted these twelve mirrors, when brought to conclusion, to form a circle so that they would reflect off one another, illuminate one another, and create a world through the interplay of their light and reflection. . . . Perhaps it would be better to say that this was

my hope for these chapters rather than the grand design behind them. One of the reasons I ignored the occasional overlap and duplication in the content of these twelve chapters is that overlapping and replication are themselves special characteristics of mirrors.

The remainder of the 1970 afterword consists of a series of acknowledgments to various colleagues at the advertising agency where Takahashi was employed when he wrote the book. He has requested that I not include the original afterword in this translation, since the list of names has been rendered largely irrelevant by the flow of time. Instead, he has written a new afterword, which has been translated and included at the end of this book.

The passage quoted above suggests that Takahashi manipulates his past, examining childhood events from different perspectives in order to evoke different adult meanings from them. Indeed, in the first chapter, "The Snow of Memory," Takahashi argues that memory is not static and unchanging; instead, memories warp and distort like a scene seen through an old window of yellowed celluloid. The process of remembering, Takahashi argues, is a creative process in which one recalls, reconstructs, and reenvisions the past, allowing it to take on different shapes depending on its context. To put it another way, one's view on one's past—and perhaps even one's identity as a whole—is constantly being reshaped by a continual, ongoing dialogue between present and past. Because of this, Takahashi's recollections are always narrated from the vantage point of the present, as he looks backward across the distance of time. In the new afterword, Takahashi remarks that this book is very much a product of the specific moment in his life when he sat down to write this book, and he doubts that he could possibly write the same work now.

This view of memory and the self as a shifting, morphing entity appears to owe much to postmodern thought in which the self, rather than being the origin of meaning and experience in humanist terms, is organized only through a performative activity in which separate, often conflicting meanings, voices, and experiences are organized to form a vision of the self that changes based on particular circumstances and moments in time. In his discussion of the nature of memory, Takahashi states that memory—the building block of the self—involves a negotiation of textual fragments that are reworked, distorted, or even implanted from outside. By looking at his youth reflected in the twelve mirrors of these chapters, Takahashi contests the concept of the individual as a linear being organized by unique experience and chronological time. By paying attention to the distortions present in his own act of viewing and remembering his past, he has, in one sense, written an archaeology of his own development. The self he has created in this stunning autobiography is the product of a concerted engagement with the ever-escaping ghosts of the past.

ON THE TRANSLATION

Because Takahashi's memoirs are so full of specific references to the culture of wartime Japan, they pose some significant challenges to the translator. Whenever it seemed feasible, I have tried to leave terms referring to elements of Japanese culture in the text. To give some simple examples, I have chosen to use the word *tatami* instead of the more explanatory "straw mat," or *shōji* instead of "wooden lattice door covered with paper or frosted glass." In doing so, I hope to invite readers into the world of the Japanese text to meet Takahashi and his family in their own territory. At the end of the book, readers will find a glossary listing some of the Japanese terms sprinkled throughout the text, along with some basic cultural information that might aid in understanding.

There are many times Takahashi felt it necessary, even in his original Japanese text, to explain elements of the culture that surrounded him as a boy. For instance, in the chapter "Heaven and Hell," he describes several games that he and his schoolmates played as little boys, adding detailed explanations regarding the rules, which would be necessary even for contemporary Japanese readers unfamiliar with the local games of northern Kyūshū. There are, however, some places where supplemental information was necessary to make certain elements of the text under-

standable to anglophone readers. For instance, in the same chapter Takahashi plays off the fact that someone who is "it" in a game of tag is called a
"demon" (*oni*) in Japanese. This word leads him to begin reflecting on how
the adults in his early life treated him as an outcast demon, damning him
to hell over and over again by passing him from one family to another.
To help English readers follow these word associations, which would be
obvious to all Japanese readers, I have worked in an extra sentence or two
of explanation.

Another place where I have employed the strategy of subtly working in necessary cultural information is in the chapter "Tales of Long Ago,"
in which Takahashi talks about the stories he learned as a child. Most of
these are stories well known in variant versions to contemporary readers.
As a result, when Takahashi points out the idiosyncrasies of his grandmother's own version of the story of Mount Kachikachi, for instance, contemporary Japanese readers would immediately recognize how it differs
from the standard versions they heard as children. English readers, however, are not likely to be familiar with the story, so I have incorporated an
occasional sentence or two to help English readers understand the points
Takahashi was making about his grandmother's version. In doing so, I
have tried to be as unobtrusive as possible, and Takahashi himself has
given me his blessing to make these minor augmentations for the sake of
reaching an English-speaking audience.

Dialect poses one of the most difficult problems for translators, and
many of the conversations, songs, and stories that fill this book are written in the distinctive dialect of rural, northern Kyūshū that Takahashi
spoke for the first twenty years of his life. As a translator, I feared that
rendering these passages in northern Kyūshū dialect into, say, the dialect of some other economically disadvantaged, marginal area, such as the
Appalachian mountains in America or the countryside of Ireland, would
lead to a profoundly misleading impression that somehow Kentucky or
County Cork were culturally akin to Kyūshū. Instead of using a dialect
of English that might sound jarring, awkward, or perhaps even inhibit
understanding on the part of some English readers, I tried to find a relatively neutral language that would, on one hand, sound colloquial enough
to remind readers that these passages were spoken, but that, on the other,

would not be too closely associated with one particular place to form unnatural correspondences.

There are places in the text where Takahashi points out double meanings or particularly unusual usages in the Kyūshū dialect of his characters. In many of these cases, Takahashi himself has added an explanation for the benefit of readers of standard Japanese who might not otherwise understand. I have rendered these explanations in English, often with the small addition of some romanization to help readers who understand Japanese and are interested in seeing exactly what he is talking about.

One final point worth noting has to do with the tenses of the verbs used in Takahashi's memoirs. Typically, Japanese authors will slip from the past tense into the present tense when talking about certain things in the past, simply because the use of the present gives a sense of greater immediacy and impact, creating the illusion that the landscapes and events are unfolding right in front of the reader's eyes. Takahashi sometimes uses that effect in *Twelve Views* when describing places and scenes. For instance, in the beginning of the second chapter, "Grandma's House," Takahashi uses the present tense as he walks the reader through his grandmother's home, describing the layout of the grounds and interior. The impression one has from reading the Japanese is that the sights of the house are unfolding one by one in the author's imagination, and he is sharing them directly with the reader as he sees them in his mind's eye. English typically tends to stick to either the present or the past and not switch between the two; however, since one of the major themes of this book is the nature of memory and the distances involved between viewing subject and viewed past, in many places I have tried to reproduce the verb tenses in Takahashi's original. The slippage back and forth between past and present tenses may feel somewhat more experimental than it does in the Japanese, since such slippages are not uncommon in Japanese storytelling. I hope that the reader will look kindly on those tense shifts, seeing them as part of Takahashi's exploration of the nature of memory.

NOTES

1. On the aesthetic and political dimensions of Takahashi's early poetry, see Jeffrey Angles, "Penism and the Eternal Hole: (Homo)Eroticism and Existential Exploration in the Early Poetry of Takahashi Mutsuo," *Intersections: Gender, History and Culture in the Asian Context* 12 (January 2006). Accessed at http://intersections.anu.edu.au/issue12/angles.html.

2. Japanese literature in fact has a centuries-old history of writing about male homoeroticism, but there have been significant ebbs and flows over time in the frequency and approaches that the Japanese literary world has used to write about the subject. See Gregory Pflugfelder, *Cartographies of Desire: Male-Male Sexuality in Japanese Discourse, 1600–1950* (Berkeley: University of California Press, 1999); Jim Reichert, *In the Company of Men: Representations of Male-Male Sexuality in Meiji Literature* (Stanford, Calif.: Stanford University Press, 2006); and Jeffrey Angles, *Writing the Love of Boys: Origins of Bishōnen Culture in Modernist Literature* (Minneapolis: University of Minnesota Press, 2011).

3. Takahashi Mutsuo, *Jū-ni no enkei* (Tokyo: Chūō Kōronsha, 1970). Promotional blurbs.

4. Several of these poems have been translated by Hiroaki Sato in Mutsuo Takahashi, *Poems of a Penist* (Chicago: Chicago Review Press, 1975; Minneapolis: University of Minnesota Press, 2012).

5. See Takahashi Mutsuo, *Tomodachi no tsukurikata* (Tokyo: Magajin Hausu, 1993), 262.

6. Quoted in Iino Hiroshi, "Gin no saji," in *Nihon bungei kanshō jiten*, vol. 5 (Tokyo: Gyōsei, 1987), 74. For an English translation of Naka's famous memoirs, see Naka Kansuke, *The Silver Spoon*, trans. Etsuko Terasaki (Chicago: Chicago Review Press, 1976).

TWELVE VIEWS FROM THE DISTANCE

The Snow of Memory

I have a photograph.

This photo, which has browned with age, is taller than it is wide and has roughly the same proportions as a playing card. In it stands my mother. She is leaning on a waist-high set of shelves against the wall of what appears to be the interior of a photography studio. She is wearing a coat of iridescent material over an under-kimono decorated with a striped pattern, and her hair is up in the rounded *marumage* hairdo traditionally worn by married women. On her right is a little boy with his hair cropped close. That is me as a boy, probably three years old. I am seated on top of the shelves with my back against the wall, and I am wearing a white turtle-neck sweater under a three-piece suit that looks too grown-up for my age.

Here and there, little flecks of black and white are visible against the background of the suit. You can see them on my jacket, vest, and pants. These little flecks look like snow. The white flecks remind me of snow-flakes falling from the sky to the earth below, and the black flecks look like dull flecks of snow that have fallen to the ground and become soiled. Beside me on top of the shelf is a black vase. Even though it is almost the same size as my head, it is positioned so that it looks as if I am holding it in my right hand. Inside are several branches of a plum tree covered with blossoms. Come to think of it, the petals of the plum blossoms also look like snowflakes floating in the air.

As I recall, snow was falling that day. Mother had been urging me to go out. When I slid open the wooden doors of Grandmother's house and went outside, the sky hung down heavily over me. At the same time, however, part of the cloudy sky seemed to be swollen with light, almost like the insides of a frothy, spoiled egg. Snow was gently falling from the spot where the heavens harbored the light, but when the flakes reached the dirty patch of earth in front of our house, they simply disappeared. Likewise, when they fell in the water beyond the embankment on the far side of our yard, they turned the color of the sky and vanished in the murky water.

We went along the road by the embankment, passing the houses of the Kawahara and Kaneko families, and then we turned. When we reached the main road, my playmate Kakko-chan from the Hashimoto family jumped out, pointed at Mother's rounded hairdo, and started jeering, "Look, a bride! Look at the newlywed!" I seem to remember she was wearing black rayon work pants and a jacket covered by an apron.

We climbed into the rickshaw waiting for us in front of the Hashi-motos' house. First Mother got in; then I climbed onto her lap. Once we were situated, the rickshaw driver threw a worn-out fuzzy quilt over my lap. He lowered the hood of the rickshaw in front of us to shield us from the weather, then started to pull the rickshaw forward.

In the center of the hood of the rickshaw was a celluloid window that allowed us to peek at the world outside. From where I was seated on Mother's lap, the window was directly in front of me, but it was too high to see much more than sky. The celluloid of the window had turned slightly yellow and taken on an irregular warp, perhaps from weathering the wind and rain. Through the warped window, I watched the yellow snow fall in a twisted trajectory toward the earth.

The rickshaw climbed up and down hills, crossed railroad tracks, and passed through streets lined with houses. From Mother's lap, I felt the warmth of her body and, along with it, the quick movement of the rickshaw rolling forward. Each time the rickshaw rolled up an incline, down a slope, or across a flat stretch of ground, I sensed the change of direction through the jolts in her lap. Meanwhile, I watched the snow through the plastic opening. As we moved, its downward path appeared to shift through the warped window. When the rickshaw stopped tempo-rarily but did not change direction, I could tell we had come to a railroad crossing. As I watched the movement of the snow falling in its warped trajectory outside the window, I heard the gasp of a steam whistle from a boiler car stopped at the switch on the tracks. The sound of the whistle seemed to mingle with the movement of the snow.

The photography studio was located on the edge of a red-light district in the coal-mining town of Nōgata in northern Kyūshū. By the time we got there, it must have been late morning, probably about ten o'clock. The driver lowered the poles of the rickshaw so that we shifted forward and down. After he raised the hood, the driver lifted me in his arms from where I sat unstably on Mother's knees and stood me on the ground. The door of the photography studio was a cracked glass door, splattered with mud. To hold the cracked glass in place, someone had pasted patches of the kind of Japanese paper ordinarily used on sliding doors. The patches were cut in the shape of cherry blossoms. Despite the mud and patches, the mirror-like surface of the glass reflected a deep, silent vision of the falling snow. The ground was speckled with black and white snowflakes.

There were no other customers, perhaps because of the snow. We were probably the first ones to come that day. The photographer brought a brazier with hot coals for us to warm up, but the studio with its high ceilings, wooden walls, and spacious interior did not seem to grow any warmer. As I trembled in the cold, the photographer seated me on top of the shelves by the wall and positioned Mother beside me. He then lifted the cloth at the back of his big box camera—the cloth was black on the outside but lined with red inside—and peered through the lens. The reason I look so bullnecked in the picture is that the dusty room was so cold. By the time the photographer ushered us outside, the snow had started to accumulate, hiding the ground from view.

Why do I remember these details so well after all these years? I remember because Mother disappeared soon after the day we went to the photographer's studio. Her disappearance probably superimposed itself over my memories of the falling snow—a quite unusual event in Kyūshū— and produced a clear image of the scene in the dark depths of my unconscious mind.

I also remember with great clarity the day she disappeared. It was one of those days in early spring when the breeze still had a slight chill to it, when the wind had grown so calm that it could easily lull you to sleep before you even knew what was happening. Mother was wearing her iridescent coat over her *yagasuri* under-kimono that day, just like before. This time, she was also clutching to her breast a little package wrapped in a folded, purple cloth. Mother never wore makeup, but for some reason that day she smelled of the sweet, dusty powder women sometimes use to whiten their faces. I remember thinking that she smelled like someone who had put on her best clothes in order to go someplace special.

"I'm going into town for a bit. Be good, and wait for me like a big boy."

As far as I remember, I only nodded. I don't think I said anything at all. She began walking.

Grandmother's house, where we were living at the time, was next to a pond lined with an embankment. The road that went alongside it passed the earthen plot of land in front of Grandmother's house. Two doors down, the road disappeared behind some houses but then reappeared a little beyond that. For a little while it followed the embankment along a low hill, but as it curved around the far side of the hill, it once again vanished from view. From there it gradually descended between some steel factories, crossed some railroad tracks, and continued through town.

I stood there watching Mother. She disappeared for a moment behind the houses, then reemerged on the other side, becoming part of the distant landscape. I watched until she disappeared for good, hidden by the bank of the hill. No, that's not entirely true. I continued to stand there even after she had disappeared from sight. Mother did something unusual as she disappeared—she looked back over her shoulder, turned, and looked back over her shoulder again. Each time, she waved at me.

I don't think there was anyone else home when she left. I know it sounds strange to say that she left me all alone, but in my memory, at least, there wasn't anyone else there. When Grandmother returned home that evening, I asked her, "Grandma? Isn't Mommy back yet?"

"She'll be back soon."

But three days passed. Ten days passed. Still, Mother did not come home.

"Isn't she back yet?"

"Be a big boy. She'll be back in no time at all," Grandmother answered me as she turned the handle of her stone mill. A month later, Mother still had not come home.

Then after three months, a big package arrived for me in the mail. It was from Mother. Inside, I found some chocolate, hard candy, a toy paper parachute, and some picture books. That was when Grandmother finally told me the truth.

"Your mommy went off to China."

I threw the paper parachute into the air, but it got stuck on a branch of the persimmon tree beside the storage shed. I had the strange feeling that Mother was not in some far, faraway place called China, but that she simply was no longer anywhere at all. The rainy season was just drawing to a close.

2

When I think back on these memories, it was the day that I gazed at the snow through the window of the rickshaw that marks the crucial turning point when Mother started to disappear into the distance. In a sense, my earliest memories are on the far side of that snow. When I think back on them, I do so through that snowy veil.

The snow of memory ... It is not always white. Just as the snow falling that day looked yellow through the celluloid window of the rickshaw, the snow of memory turns yellow and browns with age. For that reason, the photographs of the deep snows of yesteryear that we retain in our minds are also yellowed and brown.

The snow of memory does not necessarily fall downward in a straight line. Like the falling snow that seemed to twist in midair as I watched through the celluloid window, the snow of memory often falls in a warped path. Indeed, the images of long ago that we retain in our memories are just as contorted.

The warping of memory also arises from the fact that memory and secondhand stories tend to intermingle. Before we know it, their patterns cross over and blur together so thoroughly that we can no longer distinguish which is which. All of my memories before my third birth-day are that way. For instance, I can remember Mother putting me on her back when I was two and walking down the stone staircase behind Grandmother's house, but I am not sure if that is my own memory, free of outside interference, or if Grandmother told me about that and the image she helped construct simply took on the form of a memory. Perhaps both are true; perhaps stories and memory have supplemented one another to form a single image in my mind. I am not sure.

If this is the case, then the first type of memory, namely, pure rec-ollection, isn't the only thing one might call memory. Wouldn't it also make sense to think of a second type of memory, which is built on stories gathered from outside, and a third type, in which recollection and story supplement one another? I suppose you could call each of these a sort of memory in the sense that all of these things work together to form images in the mind. For instance, my "memory" of the date I entered this world, December 15, 1937, is clearly a memory of the second type.

It is all too easy to create memories. When Mother told me her tales, my own imagination mingled with what she told me to form new memories. In all actuality, I do not know whether or not it was snowing the day she left, yet in the story she told me about that fateful morning I make the snow fall.

The night before I was born, her abdomen had begun to experi-ence a lingering, sluggish pain, but the real labor pains were not quick to come. Nonetheless, she went out to the neighborhood public bath. There at ten in the morning, in the steel-producing town of Yahata, the bath was quiet, even though it was the busy month of December. Sinking into the clear, hot water, she looked up at a high window and watched the snow gather on the crossbeams. The space outside the window was filled with falling snow—so much snow that it seemed that it was light itself that was falling. When I think about this, I have the feeling that somehow I can return to my unborn state. There, inside the capsule of my mother's uterus, strained and waiting to give birth, I can almost sense the light outside.

There is another "memory" that must have also come from Mother, considering that there is no way I could possibly remember the scene that took place that day. It takes place soon after my father's death. I am lying on a futon suckling at someone's breast. The woman lying there with the infant at her exposed breast is pale. Her head has slipped from the pillow so her neck is craned toward her chest, and she is breathing with great difficulty. Near her pillow, a two-year-old girl with big eyes leans against a low writing desk and intently plucks at the white blossoms in a nearby vase.

Suddenly, someone begins knocking fiercely at the front door. The pounding on the door continues for a while, then moves to the sliding wooden door beyond the place where our bedding is laid out. A sliver of light shines through the crack between the sliding wooden doors. I see the shadows of people pass back and forth across the light. Beyond the shadows, it is snowing.

The flowers the little girl is plucking off are cherry blossoms. The blossoms must be relatively fresh; if not, they would have fallen from the branch and the petals would have scattered. This means this memory could not have taken place any earlier than mid-April. In the southern island of Kyūshū, the snow falls only once every ten years or so, and when it does, it is no more than a light dusting of flurries at best. A mid-April snowfall hardly seems likely, but even so, I make the snow of memory fall outside the sliding wooden door. The snow is probably something I added—an association created from the cherry petals the girl is scattering and from the brightly glinting granules of powdered medicine spilled by the pillow.

The woman with the child is, of course, my mother, Hisako. I am the baby suckling at her breast, and the girl plucking at the cherry blossoms is my older sister Miyuki. Mother had given both of us a big dose of sleeping medicine and then taken a large quantity herself. She was barely breathing.

My grandparents arrived. They were the ones who had been knocking so fiercely at the front door. They had found it strange that the front door was latched from the inside and that the sliding wooden doors were shut in the middle of the day, so they borrowed some tools from a neighbor and pried open the door. That was when they discovered what had happened. They called a doctor immediately.

Because my older two siblings, Hiromi and Miyuki, were both girls, I was the first little boy born into the family. Mother had more or less given up on her ability to have a boy when I happened to come along. People tell me my father was so thrilled to have a boy that he acted as if he had become a father for the first time, carrying me, his tiny son, with him wherever he went. I was not an attractive infant. Someone once told me he had said, "Gosh, if his own daddy thinks he's so ugly, I can only imagine how funny he must look to others!" Even so, he could not resist taking me around with him. He was in seventh heaven.

On March 29, 1938, only 105 days after my birth, he took his last breath. The previous year, open hostilities had broken out between Japan and China on the Asian mainland. The effects of the war were felt even in the little tin factory where my father worked. His factory was part of the Yahata Steel Manufacturing conglomerate, which in turn was one part of the big industrial zone that stretched across northern Kyūshū. One after another, the factory workers were sent off to war, and by March 1938, there was a considerable labor shortage. My father died of acute pneumonia exacerbated by overwork. This was a few years before sulfonamide drugs, effective in countering pneumonia, became available.

Toward the end when my father was losing his lucidity, Mother slid my little body into bed with him. He had been so pleased about my birth that she wanted to send him into the next world with the touch of his first little boy as his last memory. That was probably the only form of consolation she could provide. He played with me for a little, but after a while, he pushed me away as if he was in too much discomfort. He turned his back to me and, before long, stopped breathing. People tell me that Mother was so overwhelmed by the enormity of his death that for a while she lost all desire to respond to or even hold her frantically wailing children.

The day after his death my older sister Hiromi, who had seemed to be suffering from some sort of flu, died from meningitis. My mother placed her daughter, only four years old, side by side in the same coffin as her thirty-year-old husband. People tell me that Mother did not shed a single tear when she took me, still little more than a newborn, on her back and walked to the crematorium, leading my sister Miyuki by the hand.

Due to these circumstances, my grandparents strongly urged

Mother to give up Miyuki. Grandfather kept telling her she should send Miyuki to live with Aunt Tsuyano, his favorite daughter, who would adopt Miyuki as her own. This suggestion was initiated by my aunt and Grandmother. Grandfather was not ordinarily a very demanding person, but he took the opportunity to make up for it in assuming the role of the patriarch and putting pressure on his daughter-in-law in her time of grief.

"Give Miyuki to Tsuyano. That's the best thing to do. If you don't, you're no longer welcome here in the Takahashi family. Just leave Miyuki and Mutsuo and get out." This unreasonable demand came right on the heels of the sudden deaths of her husband and first-born daughter. In the face of her father-in-law's despotism, Mother had chosen to kill herself and what little remained of her immediate family.

Her attempt at murder-suicide ended in failure, yet for me this failed ending could be seen as a sort of symbolic death. Perhaps it would not be terribly inappropriate to dot this scene of death with the snow of memory like the scene of Mother just before my birth. In a sense, both of these memories of birth and death are on the far side of the faded, brown snow in that browned photograph of mine.

3

Although I imagine myself as an infant on the far side of the snow of memory, I am not the only one there. Mother is there as well, and she is in the guise of a young girl. As the snow begins to fall more heavily, her form begins to melt into the rapidly falling snowflakes, and I realize I can no longer see her. Still, I am able to transform myself into her without any difficulty. In the illusory world of memory, the young Hisako and I are not necessarily two different people.

My mother, Hisako, is only three years old and is strapped onto the back of her mother, Shikano. Her face is pressed against the nape of Shikano's neck, right where several loose strands of hair have fallen from her hairdo. Hisako's soft, flat nose catches the sweetly sour aroma of her mother's oily skin and the sweat trickling from her neck to her shoulders.

Suddenly, Hisako feels pressure on her back. A moment later, her body, still tied to the back of her mother, is facedown in a horizontal position. The weight on her back grows even heavier, and little by little it grows more oppressive. Because she is lying facedown, she cannot see what is pressing so heavily on her. Underneath, her mother's body seems to make a creaking sound. From where she lay, Hisako tries her best to look in front of her. On the other side of her mother's collapsed hairdo, she can see bunches of kindling gathered for firewood. No doubt, there are sticks and kindling underneath her mother, too. The creaking she heard was probably her mother's body rubbing against the sticks. Hisako wants to cry out, but her mother is silent—she must not raise her voice. This thought passes through her young mind. Beneath Hisako, her mother pants heavily.

The weight on Hisako's back suddenly disappears. Her mother gets up, and Hisako becomes vertical once again. She hears a door squeak, and as her mother turns in that direction, Hisako sees a man in a crew cut and striped kimono step across the threshold. Right then, she also catches a glimpse of snow falling in the garden beyond him. Hisako and her mother are in the dark shed where the kindling and firewood is kept.

Hisako was the child of Shikano and her third husband, Naojirō. According to the family register, she was born on November 15, but it seems that in reality she was born in September. As with Shikano's first and second husband, her parents did not approve of her liaison with Naojirō, so Hisako was actually born before the marriage, while her mother was still using her parents' surname, Kōno.

Naojirō was a migrant worker from Tamashima in Bizen, and he was often on the road for work, even when Hisako was born. When he was home, he would pour drinks for himself. When he had consumed one *masu* of sake, he would sing the song "Farmers, do not make a fuss, the barley is ripe" in a low voice hardly more than a mumble. When he drank two *masu*, he repeated the same song, and when he had finished three, he fell over on the *tatami* flooring, and his breath would grow quiet as he fell asleep. When Hisako was three years old, Naojirō died. He was on the road when he passed away. Soon after his death, Shikano married for the fourth time. Her new husband was Naojirō's friend, and so he was already close to Hisako. Nonetheless, their close relationship was short-lived. He died two years later.

It is unclear if the memory of the snowy day in the firewood shed was from the time when Shikano was married to Naojirō or the husband who followed. Even though Hisako was still a child, it seems unlikely her mother would carry her around on her back much past the age of five. It seems clear that the man who left mother and child lying on the firewood was neither Naojirō nor her next husband. If it had been one of them, there would have been no reason for him to knock her down while she was carrying their daughter or to violate her there on top of the woodpile.

Shikano was not only beautiful; she was born in the Year of the Rabbit, which meant that she was given to physical passion. Her relationships with men were on the theatrical side, and even when she was married to Naojirō and her next husband, she continued to have secret affairs with men. I imagine it was probably one of those paramours who forced his way into the memory of the young Hisako that day, remaining lodged there, with the memory of her mother's warm body pressed close to hers.

After the death of her new husband, Shikano quickly entered into her fifth marriage. This time, she went with her daughter to live at the home of her new husband's large family, but her mother-in-law, brother-in-law's wife, and sisters-in-law made her life so miserable that she fled with only the clothes on her back.

Shikano's family, the Kōnos, had more or less fallen into ruin by that point. The Kōno family had lived on a stretch of land in Shinnyū village in Kurate-gun along the Inunaki River. The Inunaki River is one tributary of the Onga River, which is one of the largest rivers in northern Kyūshū. In the past, the Kōnos had been middle-class farmers and had even served as the leaders of their village, but in the generation before Shikano came along, their fortunes had started to decline. To make matters worse, the family manor burned down soon after Naojirō's death, and Shikano's mother went insane, sealing the fate of the family once and for all. From as far back as Hisako could remember, her grandfather would spend all of his time seated in front of the kitchen range. When the tiny girl went to say something, his face would budge ever so slightly and he would rebuke her, telling her in his heavy Kyūshū dialect not to speak so loudly.

After her fifth marriage fell apart, Shikano settled down with her daughter in an earthen storehouse that had survived the fire at the burned manor. The older members of the family had already died, and the patch of earth where the main house had once stood had been turned over to the helpers. Shikano was living a miserable life without a chopstick or bowl to her name when she entered into her sixth marriage, but that marriage also eventually failed.

Then came her seventh marriage. His surname was Maruyama; he was younger, and he was a complete good-for-nothing. Their life together was an unending repetition of the same pattern: the couple would fight, Shikano would run away from home, and Maruyama would beg her through tears to return. Unable to rely on her husband but equally unable to cut the ties between them, Shikano decided to take a job as a money collector at the electrical company that had recently extended its services through the countryside of northern Kyūshū.

With the income that Shikano earned, Hisako was able to enroll in a school for girls. She also sometimes pilfered a fifty-*sen* coin from her mother's collection bag to go see movies in town. When she was thirteen years old, she was an ardent fan of the swashbuckling actor Onoe Matsunosuke, or "Mat-chan with the eye" as he was called. With one of her braids hanging in back and one dangling in front over her chest, Hisako cut the figure of a lively schoolgirl.

Suddenly, Shikano fell ill. As she lay in bed, she ate as much of whatever she most wanted to eat—sushi, eel over rice, and so on—but one month later, she was dead. She was diagnosed with gallstones and peritonitis. Hisako was left behind at the tender age of fifteen. Shikano's older sister and her husband, the Nakaharas, tried to take her in, but Maruyama insisted he was her stepfather. It was decided that they would continue their life together just as before.

At first, Maruyama acted like a proper adult. As time passed, however, temptation got to him and he tried creeping onto Hisako's futon. The upright young girl let out a loud scream. "If that's the way you're gonna act, go buy yourself a whore! Just go buy yourself a whore!"

"Too bad you don't take after your ma a little more . . ." Suddenly growing more timid, Maruyama grumbled this to himself and crept back to his own bedding.

A family meeting was called at Hisako's request, and it was decided she should go live with the Nakahara family; however, the Nakaharas were even worse than Maruyama. Under the ruse of keeping her things safe, they took all the money Shikano had saved for her daughter's dowry, as well as all her furniture and clothes. Hisako was treated as little more than a maid.

That was around the time a request came from the Takahashi family for her hand in marriage. The Takahashis, a poor family, had wandered into the area from Yame-gun, further west in Fukuoka. The father had managed to save up a little money by doing plastering and other odds and ends for the building and repairs office of the Mitsubishi Mining Company while tending vegetable patches in his free time. They had two sons and one daughter, and the eldest son had recently reached the age when he was beginning to think about marriage.

Although their fortunes had declined, Shikano's family, the Kōnos, had once been village heads. Moreover, Nakahara was the head of the personnel section at the Mitsubishi Mining Company. For those reasons, Nakahara refused the marriage, stating that the backgrounds of the families were too different. He continued putting up this show of refusal for a while, but later he went back and asked them to take Shikano off his hands.

Mother never told me whether on the day of their marriage it was snowing or not, so my "memory" of those events is unclear. If it were up to me, however, I would like the snow to fall that day as well. It would seem appropriate if that night, after all the wedding guests had gone home, after her sister-in-law had prodded her saying, "The groom is waiting for you in bed," and after my seventeen-year-old mother crawled onto the futon with her new husband, the only sound that greeted her ears was the silence of the falling snow gathering on the thatched roof above.

4

A year had passed since Mother's disappearance.

One morning a young relative of mine, Non-chan, came to the house. She was dressed in her best clothes, much like Mother that day when we went to have the photograph taken. She definitely had the appearance of someone dressed up to go somewhere special. I had associated going away with countless little flecks of black and white snow, but that day there was no snow falling. It was as warm as the day Mother had disappeared. About a foot over Non-chan's head two yellow butterflies flitted around one another in midair.

Non-chan took my hand and led me into a train. She had not said anything to me, but I clearly understood we were about to go meet Mother who had disappeared so many months before. Non-chan sat with her back to the front of the train, while I sat across from her, quietly looking out the window.

We took the Chikuhō line from Nōgata, transferred to the Kagoshima main line at Orio, and took the newly completed underwater Kanmon tunnel connecting the northern tip of Kyūshū to the city of Shimonoseki on Honshū. By the time we arrived in Shimonoseki, it was probably past two in the afternoon. The newly built station was still heated with steam, giving it a wintry smell that evoked nostalgic memories. As we passed in front of the station dining room, I smelled a thick omelet frying in a skillet.

Shimonoseki is a long, narrow port town with many slopes that all descend to the sea. As we rushed from the new station to the hotel where I was sure we would find Mother, we took a flat road that crossed many of these sloping streets. Each time there was a break in the clusters of warehouses and the other buildings that lined the roads I caught a glimpse of the sea, which was an unusually deep blue.

We found ourselves in a flagstone-covered square near the pier where the ferry from Korea arrives in Shimonoseki. The square was surrounded on three sides by buildings, and on the one that faced the sea there was a hotel named Fujikichi. We went inside. A woman wearing a white cook's apron quickly led us to the third floor. She said something to another lady by a bay window. The lady had been holding up a newspaper that hid her face, but when she heard the woman from the hotel, she folded the newspaper and looked our way.

The light of noon flooded through the window so that the seated lady seemed to float in the backlighting. She was wrapped in a cloak of light, as if she were some mystery woman from far, far away. She looked at me and smiled.

"My little Mut-chan."

The lady crossing her legs in the wicker chair was Mother. Reflections from the sea far below filled the room with tiny droplets of light—droplets, not little flakes of snow. The shimmering light danced over her calves.

She was wearing a pale aqua, sleeveless Chinese-style dress decorated with a small navy-blue clover pattern. She was smoking a cigarette, and there was a ring with a deep green piece of jade on the ring finger of the hand that held it. As my gaze traveled from her ring finger to the palm of her hand and her forearms, her skin seemed to grow ever paler. I could not help noticing that the blood vessels, which were of a lighter green than the jade, seemed to press up against her skin.

Perhaps these subtle changes were from her year in the cold climate of northern China. There, the cold penetrates to the bone, even when you wear three layers of woolen socks on top of one another. Or perhaps these changes were due to the shady days she had spent there—days full of things at which others could not even guess. Whichever it was, during her time in China she must have experienced snowfalls so deep and heavy they would dwarf anything she had ever seen in northern Kyūshū.

After leaving me, Mother had gone across the Korea Strait, through Korea, and across the Yalu River into China. Her destination was the mansion of a Japanese gentleman by the name of Ōgushi Kanjirō who lived in Tianjin. Ōgushi-san was from Saga in northwest Kyūshū, but he had gone to China at a young age. Once there, he began doing an extensive business in buttons and other decorative accoutrements. In the process, he amassed what appears to have been quite a fortune. It was when he was in his fifties that he met Mother, who was then working as a parlor maid in a Japanese-style inn located in Shimonoseki.

Based on the stories Mother told me later, I can call up a thorough image of the house where they lived in the Japanese concession of Tianjin. The house was an unnecessarily spacious Japanese-style building in what was more or less a malformed square. From the front, it appeared to be a one-story house with unusually high eaves, but the inside was roomy, with three stories. Outside, about where the second story would be, there hung a large sign with gilded lettering that read ŌGUSHI KANJIRŌ BUTTON SHOP, spelled out from right to left in a horizontal row of Chinese characters. The front part of the ground floor was a shop with buttons lined up all in rows, while the back part served as offices. The Ōgushi family and their servants lived on the upper floors.

Mother served both as Ōgushi-san's secretary and his children's nanny; she was given a cheerless room on the third floor as her living quarters. All of the rooms on that floor had originally been used to warehouse merchandise and other things, but one of the rooms had been cleared out for the newly arrived resident. There was one window, and beneath that only a desk, a chair, and a bed. Even so, I imagine Mother gave the room a feminine, flamboyant flair in no time at all.

Making the excuse that he wanted to make the rounds of his storage rooms, Ōgushi-san often snuck to the third floor in the middle of the night. Mother had to take great pains to greet her lover silently, without raising any noise. The private rooms of Ōgushi-san and his wife were directly below.

Breakfast was served in the dining room on the second floor, and the entire family ate there, including the servants. Ōgushi-san sat in the seat of honor at the rectangular table while his wife and Mother sat opposite one another. Right next to him were his second and third sons, but the eldest son sat next to Mother. Finally, the other servants sat in a row off to the right and left. This lineup was frequently put in disarray by the fact that the second and third sons wanted to sit by my mother's side. All three of the Ōgushi boys were far fonder of my mother than they were of their own.

Mrs. Ōgushi always treated Mother as an older sister might treat a much younger sister. Still, who knows what their real feelings were? Sometimes when Ōgushi-san had some business that kept him away from the breakfast table, his wife would scold her children when they wanted to sit by Mother. The two women would sit with silence reigning between.

It seems that at some point during her stay in China, Mother became pregnant with his child and snuck off to a doctor in the French concession for an abortion. Mother hated even the slightest traces of sexuality. As if her shame were not enough to keep her quiet, this all happened during the war when abortion was still considered a form of homicide. Her relationship with Ōgushi-san and the abortion were topics that were strictly off limits, but somehow I managed to find out about her transgressions. Perhaps when I saw her fair-skinned hand with that large jade ring and pronounced veins, I was able to sense all that had befallen her that year, even though I had not witnessed any of it directly.

I imagine that the abortion probably took place soon after she came to the Ōgushi household. If so, it would have been toward the beginning of spring when the final snowflakes of the season were falling and melting on the pavement, over and over again. In fact, it might be the case that the entire reason Mother went to China was to abort the unwanted product of their earlier liaison in Shimonoseki.

This is how I imagine the scene. The apartment of the outlaw doctor, who lives in a state of self-imposed exile from the outside world, is on the third or fourth floor of a six-story building. Mother is lying on a simple bed next to the wall, opening her eyes, which are bleary from exhaustion after the procedure. On the opposite wall is a double window that opens outward, and below that is a simple triangular cupboard on which the doctor has laid his surgical tools. A square metal basin sits on top of the cupboard. Inside, a bloody fetus takes its final shallow breaths.

Mother sees this. Behind the bloody fetus, black velvet curtains hang from the ceiling, covering most of the double window. They are mostly drawn, but there is a slight gap between them. Outside, she can see snow falling. Because the double panes of glass are meant to keep out the cold, the snow looks warped, just as it did through the celluloid window in the hood of the rickshaw that day we went to the photography studio. Steam is rising from the stove in the corner of the room.

The bloody fetus Mother gazes at is not just a newly aborted child. It is also me. She had decided to be a woman rather than a mother, and as proof of this choice she had sacrificed her fetus—she had sacrificed my blood. . . .

"Look! It's your mom, go on!"

When Non-chan said this, I began edging nervously backward,

away from the window that looked out over the sea and that spilled the reflection of the silvery waves into the room. My eyes were still fixed on Mother.

"What a funny boy! Are you shy?"

Non-chan looked at Mother and smiled. Neither Non-chan nor Mother realized it, but during the year of her absence Mother had become someone else, someone who was a complete stranger to me.

After that, Mother came to live with us in Grandmother's house. When I entered grade school at the publicly funded Citizens' School, we moved to be near my school in Kamenko, and together we stayed in the house of an old lady everyone called "the single granny," who made her living selling cheap candy. For some time, I tried to figure out how to restore the old image of my mother and me that remained in my memory from before her disappearance. I had to figure out how to apply that image to this woman, who had become an unrecognizable stranger.

Still, despite my efforts, the mother within me—the mother from my past who resides on the far side of the yellowed snow of memory—never returned.

Grandma's House

I spent several stretches of my youth being passed from one person's house to another, but other than that, most of my early childhood was spent at my grandmother's home. "Grandma's house." Strange that I should think of it as hers instead of Grandfather's. For most of the time I stayed with them, Grandfather was alive and in good health. He was not one of those men who married into his wife's family, moved in with her, and took her surname. In fact, the name that appeared on the wooden nameplate above the door was his name, "Takahashi Asakichi," although it was written in worn-out letters that had faded away almost completely. Next to that, Grandmother's name, Tsui, was written in small, humble letters. The reason that I think of their house as Grandma's is that when I remember their home, her presence seems far stronger than his.

In my memory, everything looks just like it did when I was a little boy: next to the pond is the main house with its thatched roof. In front of that to the right is a separate building for cooking and the bath. This little building has a slate roof and only goes up as far as the lowest eaves of the main house. Following the path around the pond, I come to a field, then pass the row house where the Kanekos and Kawaharas live before I reach the main house. If I pass between the main house and the separate building for the kitchen and bath, I emerge by the Kubos' house, our neighbors on the right side. At some point, someone had placed some boards between the thatched roof and the slate roof as a sort of simple, makeshift roof, so as I walk from the Kawaharas' house to the Kubos',

I pass beneath the planks. Between the main house and the Kubos' is a urinal that someone made by burying a pot in the ground. Every time I pass by, a whiff of stale urine assaults my olfactory senses.

As a young boy, I spent most of my time in the main house with the thatched roof and the neighboring building with the slate roof, but strangely, when I remember it, Grandmother's house is always closed, so I wander around outside. To the left of the door with the nameplate is a *tobukuro*, a wooden box built into the wall. Burned into the roughly hewn wood of the *tobukuro* is a decoration that looks like wood grains. To the left, along the outside of the house, are four frosted glass doors decorated with patterns that look like ferns. Underneath the glass doors is a raised platform. Sometimes, there are piles of firewood under that, while at other times there are chickens milling about. Whenever the chickens are there, there is a screen pinned up between the platform supports to form a makeshift coop. To the left of the glass doors is a storage room built against the main house, but the rusted latch on its ill-fitted wooden door is always down and in the locked position.

When I look at the main house from the front, that is all I can see; however, behind the storage room and the main house is a small garden enclosed by a crude, rectangular bamboo fence. Growing in the garden are some persimmon trees—both sweet and astringent ones—plus some other trees I do not recognize. Apart from them, there is little else there. The garden is always muddy and smells of earthworms. Coming the full way around the house, I arrive once again at the main door labeled with my grandparents' names. This sliding front door, coated with splashes of mud that come all the way up to waist level, is the entrance to the house—a place that holds a special place in my memories.

I still clearly remember the interior of the house. Inside the front door is an entryway of bare earth, which has grown hard and is smooth from repeated sweepings. On three sides, including the side with the door, the walls are rough and made of red earth packed around straw, which is still visible here and there in the earthen wall. A farmer's almanac is hanging square in the middle of one of the walls, which are otherwise bare. Three sliding *shōji* doors mark the boundary of the entryway. In front of them is a box for nails that my grandparents use as a step into the inner part of the house. When Grandmother and the others went out to work, they would use the nail box as a stool as they put on their leggings and *jikatabi*.

As I step onto the nail box and open the sliding paper doors, I enter a dining room four and a half *tatami* mats wide. Sitting there is a hexagonal dining table with a hole in the middle. The table remains in that same position all year round. In the winter, we spread out a cloth in the hole in the table and put a portable charcoal brazier in it. The family sits around the table to eat, rest, and talk to guests. Beside the table stand a washstand and a cabinet with a hinged front door and screen-covered openings. In our dialect this sort of cabinet is known as a *hairazu*, which literally means "won't let in a fly," while in standard Japanese it is known as a *nezumiirazu*, "won't let in a mouse," because the screen allows air to flow through while preventing vermin from getting inside. On top of the cabinet is an old wall clock that ticks away the time. When the time is right, the gears creak as if in pain, and the clock strikes the hour.

To the left of the dining room is a nine-mat sitting room. The back of the room has a closet and an alcove, each of which occupies half of the back wall. Next to the closet are some sliding *fusuma* doors that hide another six-mat room. Beside the alcove, there are some sliding *shōji* doors that lead to a veranda that runs along the back of the building. Between the veranda and the outside is another set of sliding doors, these made of glass. When night would come, we would shut the wooden *amado* outside the glass doors.

At night, we would pull out our futons and place them in the sitting room near the eating area. Our futons were cheap and heavy, and although they were stuffed with cotton, they were still as hard as a board. We would put our comforters right on top of them, without any sheets in between. There were no coverings to keep our comforters clean, just a black lining at the end. One difference between our comforters and others was that ours had a black lining at both the top and the bottom. In other words, the top could also be a bottom, and the bottom could also be a top. Grandmother and Grandfather would crawl under the covers feet first, each facing opposite directions, and they would sleep in that peculiar way, face to feet.

When Mother was home, she would spread a second futon by the closet and the alcove, and I would sleep with her there. When she was gone, however, I had to crawl in with my grandparents and sleep with them. Their bedding was far harder, colder, and heavier than Mother's. I yearned for her to come home quickly just so that I could sleep on her pleasant, comfortable futon.

When I slide the closet door open, it has a horizontal shelf down the middle, dividing it into an upper half and a lower half. On the upper half is a big, black-lacquered Buddhist altar. Inside the hinged double doors of the altar are the memorial tablets for my father, Shirō, my sister Hiromi, and my maternal grandmother, Shikano. There is also a five-inch statue of the angry-looking deity Fudō Myōō cast in iron, and a three-inch statue of Shakyamuni made of wood and covered in gold leaf. These things are lined up in no particular order. Later on, we would add the memorial tablet for my uncle Ken'ichi. Outside the altar and on the wall above the closet there hangs a dark brown picture of my father in a black frame. This picture was drawn by the portrait artist in town. In the portrait, my father is wearing his kimono with the family crest, a hanging wisteria blossom. His eyes are open wide as if he is surprised, staring at me, the little boy below.

There are no flowers or decorations in the alcove. The space is occupied by two chests of drawers whose only redeeming feature is their sturdiness. One of the chests shines with a harsh black luster, and in one of its small drawers, underneath the pile of *furoshiki* that we had received as gifts on special occasions, is the place where Grandmother hides the single thing that gives her life meaning: the bankbook for the savings account she keeps at the post office. In fact, there is a special lock just for that drawer.

The six-mat room beyond the *fusuma* belongs to Uncle Ken-chan— that is, my paternal uncle, Ken'ichi. His room was entirely off limits to me, and for a long time the only glimpses I got of it were brief peeks I managed to sneak from outside the door when Mother or Grandmother went in to do some cleaning. In the short moment as the *fusuma* slid open and closed, I saw only a few things—the silhouettes of the trees in the garden beyond the glass doors at the far end of the room, the *kasuri* kimono hanging from the wall above the glass doors, and the low desk on the ground where he kept his ink stone. What left the most distinct impression on me was the scent that struck my young nostrils. In the moments his room was open, I caught the mixed aroma of ink, books, and sweat—the aroma of melancholy youth. When my uncle came home in the evening from his job at the railroad, he immediately shut himself in the room behind the *fusuma*. He would only come out to eat dinner, and as soon as he was done, he would retreat once again behind the closed doors.

Straight from the front door through the *shōji* and across the dining room, there is a small room that leads to the toilet on the far side of the wooden doors. This room has a sliding wooden door and is only about two *tatami* mats wide. Although tiny, it is lined with five-gallon canisters, a chest, and an earthenware pot in which we keep rice, barley, and miso paste. Grandmother would leave wave patterns on the surface of the rice and barley with her rough hands. This was her bit of wisdom—if anyone took any, she would know right away. The boards of the wooden sliding door are warped and shine with a black luster. On winter evenings, cold drafts would blow mercilessly through the cracks.

The toilet is outside the wooden walls in a six-foot corridor that extends straight back, away from the house. On the left side of the corridor are a urinal and a seated toilet, each of which takes up about three feet of space. At the end of the corridor is a big, green container full of slightly dirty water for washing our hands. The thin hand towel hanging above is also dirty and flutters in the draft. There are often big spiders that stick to the wall by the toilet without moving.

In order to get into our storage area, I have to go out of the house. I put on Grandmother's big wooden clogs, walk out the door, and walk along the veranda to get there. The doors to the storage area are never closed properly. When I push on them and slide them back in the door pockets, the light pours in, making the scythe, hoe, mortar, and hatchet shine where they lie among the winnow, bamboo baskets, and wooden mortar. Even when I was very young, I knew the metal in these tools that gave us our daily bread also was capable of killing people. When Grandmother's younger brother was only eighteen years old, his parents sent him out to buy some land, but someone slashed him to death with a short sword while he was out in the hills.

There are two side-by-side doors that lead into the cooking shed and the bath. Immediately inside is an earthen cooking range. I used to sit there quietly and watch Grandmother absentmindedly as she put out the coals after cooking our rice. She would manipulate her metal chopsticks to pull the live embers from the range and put them in a pot so they could burn out safely. Next to the range is a long, narrow pot shaped like a pitcher, complete with a handle and spout. In it, Grandmother keeps some of the dye that married women used to use to color their teeth black in the old days. The reason she had it, however, was not that anyone in our family dyed their teeth. She would pour some into the enamel sink and mix it with hot water to dye her gray hair black. Perhaps that was why the pillow she always used—a cylindrical cushion tied on top of a piece of wood the shape of an inverted boat—always had a dirty scent about it.

In the bath is a glass window. When I was bathing in the evening, I would hear the croaking of the frogs through the steam-clouded window. They always sounded to me like they were imitating the lowing of the cows. I would also hear the voice of the *yosshoi* bird coming from the far side of the pond. It would call out with its distinctive cry—*yosshoi, yosshoi*—and even though it scared the wits out of me, I was also captured by a certain melancholic nostalgia.

Outside, the moon grows cold, and the cemetery above the field between Grandma's house and the Kawaharas' home grows quiet once again.

2

Grandma's house was in the countryside of Shinnyū, across the railroad tracks from the outskirts of Nōgata. If you were to go a little more than six miles from the city of Kita-kyūshū along the Onga River, that is where you would find Nōgata, right in the center of the Chikuhō coal field.

No longer able to eke out a living in the mountains of Yame-gun in western Fukuoka prefecture, Grandmother Tsui and Grandfather Asakichi decided to come east to Nōgata where the mining industry was booming. I imagine that it was probably Tsui, who was known for her gutsiness, who came up with the idea to leave Yame-gun and drag her husband east. That could not have been much after 1912, the year the Meiji emperor passed away and the Taishō emperor stepped onto the throne.

Tsui had left her home in the countryside of Tagata, located in the plains of Yame-gun, to become a bride at age eighteen. She walked several miles to her new husband's home in Hebaru, a little community located deep in the mountains. She had never met her husband before the marriage ceremony. She told me that when she met him the first time, she thought, "My goodness, this joker's only got one eye!" Asakichi had been married once before, and apparently when he saw Tsui dressed in her bridal outfit, he spoke right out and said, "My other wife was a real looker, but this one's got a nose as big and round as a rice dumpling." In other words, neither thought the other was perfect. Grandmother often told this story, laughing as she removed the hot embers from the stove and placed them in the pot to cool.

In less than a year, Asakichi had discovered the bride with the dumpling nose was not only beautiful but also a solid companion, the likes of which he could hardly hope to find elsewhere. Perhaps it was because he worked like a dog and never complained, but Tsui took over the reins of the household for the shy and retiring man. When I was little, I remember that whenever Grandfather needed to get her attention, he would cautiously call out to her, "Hey, sweetheart" in a hesitant voice. Grandmother would respond sharply, "What?! You're bugging me." Their conversation was certainly brusque, but in it there was still the strange love and affection that develop over long years together as man and wife.

When my grandparents went to the Chikuhō mines, business was up, but the prosperity did not necessarily extend to all the people who worked there. The miners, as well as their families, were like slaves bound to the prison of long row houses where they lived. If they tried to run away and were captured, the company would exact extreme punishments, sometimes even killing them. For instance, there was once a couple who met in the mines and became lovers. He was what was called a *sakiyama*, someone who digs the coal, and she was an *atoyama*, someone who transports the coal after it is taken out of the ground. The two ran away together but were caught. They were put outside on public display alongside a road; the man's genitals were beaten to a pulp, and a burning stick was shoved into hers. They were accused of not just running away but also of having illicit sex. This story shows how horrible life was for the miners. In fact, there are many stories like this about life in the mines during the first decades of the twentieth century.

Perhaps because Asakichi was blind in one eye, the couple never had to go into the mines. Tsui helped him avoid dangerous work by finding a job for him at the building and repair facilities. Although he didn't get paid well there, she was able to steer him away from danger. He was not a carpenter or plasterer; he was a gopher who did all sorts of humiliating work—carrying lumber, mixing gravel, and doing other menial things.

He was scraping together a minimal salary doing these things when he and Grandmother started planting little plots of vegetables. They planted them here and there in little bits of unoccupied land: in the slopes next to embankments, in the narrow strips of land next to roads, in the places where people threw away their coal cinders, in the tiny plots of land beside cemeteries. . . . All these vegetable patches were so tiny that no one bothered to notice them, but if put together, they would have added up to quite a sizeable plot. My grandparents sowed barley, planted buckwheat, raised beans, and grew pumpkins in their gardens. They took their harvest and put it in canisters, packed it in chests, lined it up in wooden boxes, and stashed it in their storage room. They produced enough that they could eat all year long without running out of food. In fact, there was even enough so that they could sell the surplus to women in company housing and thus earn a little extra money.

After waking up at four in the morning, my grandparents would stoke the kitchen stove and creep around to the vegetable patches while it was still dark. After sunrise, they would come back, rush through breakfast, and go out to work all day at the building and repair facilities. After work, they would stop by the yard where the coal was dressed to see what coal they could glean; then they went back to the vegetable patches to work some more. Finally back at home, they had dinner and dedicated themselves to the evening chores.

Tsui did her best to keep costs down as much as possible while working her fingers to the bone. That was the wisdom that got her through life. Even when I was an infant, she would say to me, "You can't control outside folks that much, but folks don't know what goes on inside your house; that's where you can save as much as you like." She said this so often that it became a stock expression in our home.

By the time Uncle Ken'ichi was born, the couple had managed to save a nice little nest egg through all their hard work and scrimping and saving. (Ken'ichi was the last child in the family, born more than ten years after their first son Shirō and daughter Tsuyano, both of whom had come with them from Yame-gun.) It was probably around then that the family stopped moving from rental to rental and finally settled in the single-family home with the thatched roof that I came to know as "Grandma's house."

That was the same house where my grandparents welcomed Mother into the family as a young bride. The morning of the wedding, a light snow was falling. Mother was at her own home hurriedly tying up her hair when she heard a voice calling, "Hisako-san!" When she looked outside, she saw the man who was to be her father-in-law at the end of the street. He was pulling a cart piled with lacquered sake barrels and the multilayered stacking boxes used for special celebrations. Her future mother-in-law was there, too, her hair tied up in a *marumage* hairdo, the sleeves of her crested kimono tied back, and her right hand sticking straight up in the air and holding an umbrella.

"Hisako-san, now be sure and come early this evening!" her future mother-in-law cried loudly.

Mother often told me this story when I was little. Where else would you find a mother-in-law so eager to welcome her daughter-in-law into the family that she would tell her to rush on over? Grandmother was probably proud to be able to bring her new daughter-in-law into the house that they had managed to buy after so many long, hard years of labor. The house represented the fruit of all the sweat she and Grandfather had spilled over the years. When I think about how the house became theirs largely due to her scrimping and saving, I realize that perhaps it is not entirely inappropriate to call it Grandma's instead of Grandpa's house. In a sense, she really was the master of the household.

3

There, in the house, I was known as *obāchankko*—Grandma's little boy—a phrase that makes it easy to imagine just how attached to her I was. This expression, however, has a rather prissy, high-class air about it. Perhaps in my case, it would have been more appropriate to use a more down-and-dirty expression like *babasango*, which is closer to the dialect of the poor, southern part of Japan from which I had come. Most of the years between the time I stopped suckling and the time I entered school, Mother was away working in Nakatsu, Shimonoseki, and even Tianjin, China. As a result, I spent more time living with Grandmother than with her.

Since Grandmother worked outside the home all day, I would stay either home alone or with neighbors. Grandmother would come home during her lunch break, warm up lunch, feed me, and then go straight back to work. I would sometimes chase after her crying as she left, but she would console me, "You're a good boy, now. Don't cry." If I still wouldn't stop, she would make a scary voice and say, "If you don't stop crying like that, I'll have to throw you into the pond water. Then a *kappa* will come and pull your guts out of the hole in your backside!" And with that she would leave. I would wail in a loud voice, and gradually my cries would transform into convulsive sobs. All alone, I would eventually feel the tears retreat like a tide going out to sea.

Night, however, was a different story. After we finished dinner, I was able to get all the love I wanted from Grandmother. She was the one who bathed me. The sink was about one and a half feet from the ground, and when the water spilled, it would splash on the cement floor, making a dramatic noise. As she washed me, she would turn on the water so it gushed out vigorously. Meanwhile, she would roll up the corner of a washcloth and swoosh it around the inside of my ear, saying, "Kids who've got soft earwax grow up to be stinky little boys. If you don't wash under your arms real good, your friends won't like you and they won't wrestle with you." After saying this, she would put soap on the washcloth and scrub my armpits until they became sore. At night, when we were lying on our futons, she would tell me over and over again the stories of Otsuru the Pilgrim and The Old Lady Whose Head Was Smashed in a Single Stroke.

I looked forward to the evenings when Uncle Ken'ichi was on duty at the railroad yard and Grandmother would take me to the crew room in the station to deliver dinner to him. I remember how the evening primroses would bloom along the watery ditch parallel to the railroad tracks, which were in turn surrounded by burnt wood. I called out, "Grandma! Grandma!" every time something crossed my mind, even something small and silly, but she responded to each of my comments in an attentive, grandmotherly way.

When I was walking with her and we would run into one of her acquaintances, they would usually say, "My goodness, your grandson has really started to look like your poor deceased boy, Shirō." She would respond happily, "I'm looking forward to seeing how he turns out."

At the same time, Grandmother was also doggedly determined to save every tiny thing she could. At breakfast and lunch, she would serve what she called "rice," but in actuality there was more barley mixed into it than rice. After all, barley was much cheaper. For dinner, she would serve rice dumplings in soup. After she crushed the wheat into flour in her stone mortar, she didn't separate the bran. Instead, she just mixed it, bran and all, with water to form the dumplings, hoping not to waste a single morsel of food. She would comment with an air of self-satisfaction, "Crunchy—rice dumplings in soup's good if you make it this way, don't you think?"

When it came time to harvest the *daikons* from the vegetable patches, we would eat side dishes made of *daikons* for one or two months. When we harvested beans, we would eat beans and barley mixed with rice, bean soup, boiled beans, and all sorts of other dishes made with the legume. In her head, she had a complete plan for everything she would make throughout the entire year—all the main dishes as well as the side dishes. Although she did not know how to read, write, or use an abacus to do math, she could do all the calculations in her head to figure out exactly how much of each kind of food she would need for months on end. Grandfather praised this ability, calling it "Grandma's mental math."

In those days, it was expected that men would turn the management of the household over to their wives, but Grandfather did not just stop there. He also allowed his wife to take the initiative in the building and repair facilities, in the vegetable patches, and in even the financial planning that got them through hard times. "Your Grandmother sure is a great grandma," he would say to me while seated in front of the dining table. Then he would fall silent, absorbed in packing his pipe full of tobacco.

Perhaps Grandmother felt something was lacking in her husband. She took another lover named Ōsugi-san who was slightly younger than she was. The gossip on the street was that Uncle Ken'ichi was actually his son. Perhaps it was not a big deal for her to have an extramarital affair. After all, in the culture she grew up in, after the village festivals women would often go home with men they did not know and spend the night with them. Even Grandfather, who usually acted terribly grown up, would sometimes grab a neighbor woman from behind and start humping her like a dog to make everyone laugh.

Ōsugi-san lived about eight blocks down the road from Grandmother's house. His home was in the shadow of a small hill with a cemetery. Whenever she found herself with a few free minutes, Grandmother would go over to see him. She would talk about him in front of her husband, "Ōsugi did this, Ōsugi did that," never seeming to give it much thought. Grandfather was Grandfather—he didn't seem to care too much.

Grandmother apparently borrowed some money from Ōsugi-san. To tell the truth, he was an indolent good-for-nothing who idled his days away, never doing any work at all, so no doubt the money came from his adopted daughter Haruko. This unfortunate girl, whom Mother and Grandmother both affectionately called "Haa-chan," was sent away from home multiple times to work in other people's houses as a maid. Somewhere along the line, her father even sold her into prostitution. Eventually, she contracted tuberculosis and died. On her deathbed, she held on to my mother's hand, simply because there was no one else who would stay with her.

When Haa-chan died, Ōsugi-san also began to grow weak. By the time of the ceremonies commemorating the forty-ninth day after her death, he was unable to get out of bed. All of a sudden, Grandmother stopped visiting him. Mother was still in the area at the time. She hadn't yet returned to work after leaving her job in Nakatsu and taking care of Haa-chan. She decided she would be the one to take care of him since she could not stand watching him wither away without anyone to care for him. She went every day, attending to everything from his meals to far more personal needs. Grandmother clearly did not approve. She warned her, "He'll get you sick too. You shouldn't get too close."

As Ōsugi-san grew weaker, he would clasp Mother's hand and say, "I'm so sorry, thank you for everything." Sometimes, he thought of Grandmother. He would grow agitated and denounce her—"She's not a real human being"—and then break into a fit of frenzied coughing.

Then one morning, Mother took me to Ōsugi-san's house as usual. The old man lay cold in his bed. In the light that passed through the paper *shōji*, I could see that his sunken cheeks were covered by salt-and-pepper stubble, even though Mother shaved him every morning. Death spots had already appeared on his small, narrow nose.

Mother told Grandmother right away. Her reaction to the news about her former lover's death amazed us all. She immediately hired a neighborhood man to help her husband pull a cart to Ōsugi-san's house. Right away, they set off, the two men in front and her pushing from behind. Casting contemptuous glances at the corpse the whole time, she piled all the things of value in the house onto the cart and took them home—everything from the household goods and clothing to the dishes, pots, and pans. Next, she went back and sat down beside the newly deceased man as if nothing had happened and told Mother go make the rounds to announce his death. As the guests crowded into the room to make their condolence calls, Grandmother held her hands to the corners of her eyes to hold back the tears, like a commendable woman. "We did our best to take good care of him and Haa-chan. We all felt so sorry for them." And with this, her voice choked up.

Was this only a performance? I am not sure. Whatever the answer, both the grandmother I saw before the guests arrived and the grandmother who acted so virtuously afterward were one and the same person. These two sides came together to form a single person—the whole of my grandmother as she really was.

4

After Mother came home from her year in China, the two of us moved into a small three-mat room she rented from a ninety-year-old lady. The home was in the neighborhood of Kamenko, just about five blocks away from Grandma's house. Right away, I started attending the Citizens' School, but in the second semester of school that year we moved to the port of Moji, located on the shores of northern Kyūshū. Finally, the umbilical cord that had connected me to Grandmother was cut. That was the first time that I had ever lived so far from my grandparents.

In the dialect of northern Kyūshū, the word *walk* has a special meaning: to take a trip back to the place where you come from. After Mother and I moved to Moji, we would "walk" to our village about once a month. That was during the last phases of World War II and the beginning of the postwar period, when food was too scarce for people to be generous. Grandmother did not even try to hide her stinginess, even from us.

If we arrived late in the evening, I would complain that I was hungry. Grandmother would nod and say, "There's some soup from the rice dumplings left at the bottom of the pot. Go ahead and drink it up." I would lift up the charred, wooden lid of the pot and look inside to find only a half-inch of cold, leftover soup at the bottom of the pot, which she had patched over and over. There was not a single rice dumpling left inside for me.

If we stayed two or three days, Grandmother would tell us, "Our rice supply is getting low. Time for you to go home to Moji." She would lift my little body onto her shoulders and carry me the one and a quarter miles to the train station. She would plunk me down onto the wooden bench, then leave, without ever turning to give a backward glance. One time when Mother was not there, Grandmother took me to the station and left me sitting alone. It was snowing outside the station, and as I sat shivering on the bench Mother ran up to me, tears in her eyes.

All of this might sound harsh, but I am sure Grandmother loved me. Grandmother would usually see us off when Mother and I went home. The road followed an embankment all the way into town. She would watch us walk along the road until the turn where a small hill would shade us from view. When we reached that spot, I would send up a loud wail and start to cry. I remember I would look back over my shoulder over and over again as Mother pulled me by the hand. The sunset over the valley behind us always looked so beautiful.

Although I knew Grandmother loved me, after we moved to Moji, I found myself feeling as if she no longer existed at all. I suppose it was a habit of mine to think that way. Just as I had believed that Mother no longer existed once she left for China, I also found myself believing that Grandmother had just disappeared, and I told myself I had been deceived when I had seen her.

Grandfather did not leave nearly as strong an impression as Grandmother, but I do remember that his shows of stinginess were on par with hers. Once when I was really young, I was eating a cake that I had received from one of Mother's friends, when Grandfather snatched it away and popped it into his own mouth. In my surprise, I didn't say a thing. Another time, he was sitting with drawn-up knees and eating a piece of fish all by himself. Wanting to have some too, I started babbling, "Grandpa, Grandpa . . ." Without even looking up, he said, "When this little guy lived with his mother at Hachiman, he lived high on the hog. No need for him to eat this." With this, he glared at the fish with his one good eye and peeled the small bones from the fillet.

Later, when Grandfather heard that Uncle Ken'ichi had died from illness on the battlefield, he underwent a subtle change inside. When he was at work—repairing the company dormitories in Otateyama or elsewhere—he would put part of his lunch in tissue paper and bring it home to me. Then around the time Mother and I moved to Moji, another change took place in him: he seemed to be taken ill with a strange sort of regret. This disease of regret came in waves that peaked about once a year. When it did, he would stay in bed late, even though he usually got up at four in the morning. When he finally got up, he would sit in front of the dining room table and would hardly budge. He would pack his pipe with shredded tobacco and sigh deeply.

"Ahhh, Shirō's gone, and Ken'ichi's gone, too . . ."

"Ahhh, is there anyone as unfortunate as me . . . ?"

"Ahhh, I hope Amida comes from paradise to take me away soon...."

He would continue in this vein for three months or so. When he was in really bad shape, he could keep this up for half a year.

When I was in third grade, Grandfather lost the ability to move his legs. The room in back where Ken'ichi had once stayed now became his sickroom. When we "walked" back to see him and Grandmother, I lit a stick of incense at the Buddhist altar, then slid open the *fusuma* to visit him in bed. He said to me, "Your daddy, Shirō, died so young. You poor thing! You're the most unfortunate guy in the whole world," and he started weeping out loud. Then he took the wallet from under the bedding and pulled out five hundred yen in bills. He pressed the money into my hand, telling me, "Go buy yourself some books."

The money was from the survivor's annuity given to my grandparents after my uncle Ken'ichi's death. I felt terrible receiving the little money Grandfather had—after all, he could barely move anymore—so we started coming less often. That just made Grandfather cry all the more: "These days, I don't have any money to give Mutsuo, so he's not coming anymore." Grandmother scolded him loudly, "No, the problem is that you *are* giving him money. That's the reason Mutsuo doesn't come!"

It was not much longer before Grandfather passed away, but I did not hear about it until two months later, when a distant relative told me. At that time, my aunt Tsuyano had divorced her husband and brought her twelve-year-old son to live with Grandmother. I imagine the reason my aunt didn't say anything to us was that if she had, she would have had to share his assets with us. To this day, I still do not know the exact date he died.

In fact, I don't know the exact date of Grandmother's death either. After Grandfather died, my aunt sold the house and moved elsewhere with Grandmother, settling in the tiny community of Fukushima in rural Yame-gun. Not long before Grandfather passed away, Grandmother also lost sight in one eye, just like her husband, but she continued to live for more than a decade before she finally passed away. Her death came suddenly. They tell me that the morning she died, she got up and cooked a pot of rice first.

I later learned that the home I recall so fondly as Grandma's house burned to the ground. The person who bought it was careless and let a fire get out of control, even though it was the middle of the day. In my mind's eye, I can picture the fire that reduced the home to ashes. As the flames reached the straw-thatched roof, it no doubt burned with ferocious intensity, coloring the persimmon trees, the stones of the cemetery, and the water of the pond a brilliant crimson.

When the fire incinerated Grandma's house, it also reduced a certain part of my early youth to ashes. In a sense, the fire represents a funeral pyre for my grandparents. Grandmother did live several years after Grandfather died and the house burned down, but she was no more than a thin shadow of her former self, as if she already had one foot in the grave.

Tales of Long Ago

1

The gears in the dining room clock wheeze into position like an asthmatic trying to catch his breath. The chime sounds ten o'clock at night. Grandfather stands from where he sits beside the dining table and pounds two or three times on his lower back with his right fist. He goes to the restroom, sliding the door open twice, first to leave, then to return. Next, he slides open the *fusuma* to the main sitting room.

From the other side of the door, I can hear his voice saying, "Paradise, paradise." For my elderly grandparents who spent the entire day at work, the short time from the moment they stretched out on the floor until they fell asleep was the ultimate in pleasure—it was paradise for them.

After Grandfather goes to bed, it is my turn. Grandmother hustles me to the bathroom, where I hastily urinate. She reproaches me, "Didn't you wash your hands?" but I cannot be bothered with that. The corridor that leads to the bathroom is little more than a breezeway with boards nailed to supports, so in winter it is cold and dark. Beyond the washbasin at the dead end of the corridor is a high mound of dirt completely covered with a dense thicket of grassy *sasa*. The plants are so thick it seems like they will eat me up completely.

The *sasa* is constantly whispering outside, making its rustling sounds. On dark nights I used to be terrified of the thicket of *sasa*, which seemed to wriggle in the blackness, but I was even more terrified of the

sasa when the moon's reflection would shatter on the surface of its countless shiny leaves.

Grandmother has spread out for me a brown flannel night coat
decorated with a checkerboard pattern. I put my arms through it, and she
ties the belt that hangs at the side. As soon as she finishes the knot at my
back, I quickly dash into the sitting room.

There, Grandfather's breath indicates that he has already fallen
asleep on the futon, which is as hard as a board. I snuggle in beside him
and whisper quietly in his ear, "Grandpa?" If he still does not respond,
I shake his chest, covered in a light, warm undershirt. "Grandpa, you
asleep?"

"Yeah," he answers, eyes still shut. His response comes from far
away. Once again, he is already slipping away to the distant land of sleep.
Meanwhile, Grandmother gets into bed, entering the opposite end by his
feet. As I mentioned previously, it was their strange custom to sleep on
opposite sides of the same futon, head to foot.

I go to Grandmother, crawling through the darkness of the quilts,
which have grown warm from the heat of their bodies. The warmth is
enough to make my head ache. During the winter, Grandmother would
wrap my cold feet in the band of cloth she would keep around her stomach
to stay warm. Right by my chest is the hot-water bottle that Grandfather
uses to warm his feet. It is wrapped in an old *furoshiki* that has practically
turned into rags from so much use, but the warmth of Grandmother's
body through my wrapping feels much more natural and pleasant than
the bottle.

I tell her where I feel itchy. "It itches over here. There's another itch
over there, too." She puts her hand down the collar of my night coat and
rubs all over my tiny back. Because she has worked constantly since she
was young, her hands are stiff and big, and their surface is as rough as a
piece of lumber that has not been planed smooth. As her rough hands rub
my back, I feel great satisfaction.

I coax her, "Grandma, tell me a story."

"Well, now, what story do you want to hear?"

I knew that in the world of the bedclothes, which were warm from our bodies and smelled faintly of grime, she was no longer the same Grandmother who would frighten me so much during the day. She had transformed into the kind of sweet grandmother who would listen to anything her grandson had to say. The bed was the one place where she could finally relax her nerves, which were ordinarily on edge throughout the day. There in bed, she revived that most primitive of customs: passing on to her grandson the old stories she had been told when she was a little girl.

The first story she told me when I was little was probably the story of Mount Kachikachi. It started, "There once was an old farmer who was married to an old lady." Most versions of the story talk about a farmer who chases a *tanuki* from his fields, but then the destructive, mean, shapeshifting *tanuki* takes revenge by hurting the farmer's elderly wife. The old couple has a rabbit friend who decides to help them. One of the tricks he plays is to light the cruel *tanuki*'s house on fire. When the *tanuki* hears the rabbit's pieces of flint clicking together, he asks, "What is that *kachikachi* sound?" The rabbit responds, "That's the *kachikachi* bird of Mount Kachikachi." Eventually, the rabbit conquers the nasty *tanuki* through a combination of strength and trickery.

In Grandmother's version of the story, however, it was not a *tanuki* who was the villain of the story but a monkey. For that reason, we knew the story as "The Rabbit and the Monkey." And in Grandmother's version, the monkey did such terrible things! In one refrain, he puts the old lady in a mortar and grinds her body with a pestle: "He crushes the old lady's head with a first stroke. He crushes the old lady's head with a second stroke." The monkey changes his appearance so that he looks like the old lady. Then he cooks the corpse of the old lady into soup and feeds it to her husband when he returns. The old man says, "I've never tasted anything so delicious in my whole life," and eats until there is nothing left in the pot. Later, when the old man learns he has eaten his own wife, he weeps, "The monkey made me eat her, ohhhhhh, ohhhhhh. . . . The monkey made me eat her, ohhhhhh, ohhhhhh."

Sometimes after the story of the Rabbit and the Monkey, Grandmother would tell me about her younger brother who was killed as a young man. His name was Nii-tan, and when he was eighteen, he had a bunch of friends who were chivalrous, Robin Hood sorts. He set off alone to buy a mountainous patch of land when a group of men cut him down cruelly in the hills. All of them, however, died soon afterward as a result of Nii-tan's curse. This ending was a lot like Grandma's story of Mount Kachikachi, in which the cruel monkey suffered an untimely death as a result of his cruelty.

What could Grandmother have been thinking as she told me that horrifically bloody story over and over again? I was not yet even three years old. There were many times when fear kept me awake, long after her breath had grown quiet and slow with sleep. I would be left awake, lying in bed and listening nervously to the ticking of the pendulum of the clock in the dining room.

I would shut my eyes tightly in the hopes of falling asleep more quickly, but instead I would see visions in the reddish darkness under my eyelids. The blood congealed on the white hair of an old woman . . . the blood staining the tip of a big pestle . . . the blood spreading on Nii-tan's chest under his *kasuri* kimono . . . the blood oozing from the mouth, nose, and ears of the assailants who had died from my great-uncle's curse . . . these images would take turns appearing before me, disappearing, and reappearing again. Somehow, however, I would manage to slip into a deep sleep.

2

When I got a little older, Grandmother changed the story she told me at bedtime. She now started telling me the story of Otsuru the Pilgrim, based loosely on the eighteenth-century play *Keisei Awa no Naruto*. The play is about a young girl who is abandoned by her parents when she is three. She goes on a pilgrimage to pray that she might find her parents when she unknowingly encounters her mother, who is named Oyumi.

When Grandmother told the story, she would sometimes say the lines with great dramatic effect. For instance, in the section where Oyumi is asking the name of Otsuru's father, Grandmother played Otsuru's part, practically weeping as she stretched out the vowel sounds: "Ohhhh! His naaaame . . . is Tokushima Jurōbeiiiiii . . . from Awaaaaa. . . ." A few moments later when Otsuru is describing her sadness at not having a mother, Grandmother would pause dramatically and give her voice great inflection: "When I see the other children . . . Their mothers are doing their hair for them. . . ." No doubt Grandmother learned how to perform this way from the itinerant storytellers she had heard as a little girl.

The story involved a counting song that begins "One, *saa no yōnoē*," and then throughout the song the refrain is repeated: "Two, *saa no yōnoē*" and so on. *Saa* is a word that does not mean anything and is just used as filler as one gets ready to do something or move on to something. The other word was not familiar to me. I asked, "Grandma, what does *yōnoē* mean?"

"It means the time when dawn comes." It was later that I realized that Grandmother herself did not know that this was also just a meaningless expression used in popular ballads and lyrics to fill in space. Because she spoke Kyūshū dialect, this word, which is relatively common in songs elsewhere in Japan, sounded foreign and unfamiliar to her. Because she mistakenly explained it as meaning sunrise, every time she repeated these words in the song, I imagined that dawn had come once again, filling the sky with its brightness.

Grandmother would alternate back and forth between the lines of the song, which she performed in a singsong voice, and her explanation of the story, which she delivered in her heavy Kyūshū dialect. Meanwhile, she would constantly interrupt herself and question her own narration. Put together, the whole thing would go somewhat like this:

> *One, saa no yōnoē. There is Otsuru the pilgrim, the lone traveler with a walking stick and straw hat, scooping up water. (Now, is that how it goes again?)*
>
> Years before, her father and mother had left her with her grandmother as they went out to search for a sword their lord had lost. The grandmother took good care of Otsuru, but the grandmother suffered many hardships and died. Otsuru was little, but she dressed herself up like a pilgrim and went out to search for her mother and father.
>
> *Two, saa no yōnoē. (Wait, what was number two again? I forgot.)*
>
> When Otsuru stood in someone's doorway, groups of men chased her out. When she tried to sleep under someone's eaves, groups of children poked at her with sticks. Those were the

hardships she endured, but she still continued wandering, asking about her parents.

Three, saa no yōnoē. Look, look, there is Oyumi. Otsuru comes up from below. (Now, is that how it goes again?)

Otsuru stood in the doorway and asked for charity as she always did. The person who came out was her mother, Oyumi. Oyumi spoke to the pilgrim.

Four, saa no yōnoē. Welcome to our little place. Have you brought your parents with you? (Now, did I get it right there?)

Oyumi asked Otsuru, "Are your mommy and daddy with you?" Otsuru shook her head.

Five, saa no yōnoē. No, no, I am traveling alone. I want to see the faces of my mother and father. How I want to see them!

Oyumi asked Otsuru, "What is your father's name?" and "What is your mother's name?" Otsuru answered what her grandmother told her just before she died: "His name is Tokushima Jurōbei, from Awa. My mother's name is Oyumi." Oyumi was surprised, but she refrained from saying, "Oh, my daughter, my daughter!" Instead, she took out some money from her clothes and gave it to Otsuru.

Six, saa no yōnoē. I work hard for this money, but please take this little bit as an expression of my feelings. (Is that how it goes?)

The tears welled up in Otsuru's eyes, and she said, "Auntie! You are so kind, as if you were my very own mother. You aren't my mother, are you?" But Oyumi still had to find her lord's missing sword, so she said, "No, I'm not. Your mother is still far away," and she rubbed Otsuru's head to comfort her.

Seven, saa no yōnoē. Weeping, weeping, Oyumi stands up. Otsuru stands as tall as she can. (Is that it?)

"Well, I need to go," she said. Oyumi steeled her heart. How was she able to act so cold-heartedly as she watched her very own child weeping and weeping?

Eight, saa no yōnoē. She has come over mountains, come over rivers, come over valleys, come such a distance to this place. (Is that it, now?)

There was no sense in going through a long good-bye. Weeping, weeping, Otsuru began walking away. Oyumi wanted to embrace her daughter, who was moving farther and farther away, but she restrained herself.

Once we got this far, Grandmother's commentary would disappear, only leaving the counting song and her own self-questioning.

> Nine, saa no yōnoē. Taking her by her nine-year-old hand, she leads her to the entrance of her own house. (Now, is that the way it goes?)

Then, after singing, "Ten, saa no yōnoē," for some reason she continued: "Will Tokushima Jurōbei from Awa unknowingly kill his own daughter on her pilgrimage?" The alliteration was off. Later, I learned that the first part in which he declares his name should be "Jurōbei from below the Tokushima castle," and the part where he says "kill his own daughter on her pilgrimage" should be "send his own daughter," but Grandmother's version of the song was about death.

There were other mistakes in Grandmother's version. The part where she said, "Otsuru the pilgrim, the lone traveler" should be "dressed like a pilgrim, she searches for her mother and father." "Look, look, there is Oyumi" should be "Before her eyes, Oyumi stands up and puts out some white rice as an expression of her feelings," and "Welcome to our little place" should be "Welcome to you on your pilgrimage." Also, the refrain, "Can this really be happening?" was Grandmother's own invention to fill in the passages she had forgotten. For instance, in the first part, the song is "asking along the way"; the third part is "and she walks forward," and the fourth part is "Are you traveling together?"

I imagined the tenth night coming to an end when Grandmother said, "Ten, saa no yōnoē." Meanwhile, the day came to a close for us as Grandmother ended her song. Once we had finished, I always asked, "Grandma, what happened to Otsuru?"

"She got killed. Her father cut her down with a sword." In the original play, her father who does not know her true identity comes back and cuts her down in order to steal her money. All of his years living in the underworld, trying to track down the thief who had stolen his master's sword, had corrupted him as well.

Otsuru's death came all of a sudden in Grandmother's version. There was no preparation for or explanation of what had happened. The god of death had simply borrowed the form of her father, appeared like the wind, unfurled his blinding sword, and then disappeared. The only thing left behind was the blood-covered corpse of the innocent girl who had fallen over without so much as a word.

I would look at Grandmother reproachfully, and she would grow flustered and sing the same tune again, this time without the *yōnoē*. "*She gave birth to so many children. Will this one look like Bungorō? (Is that the way it goes?)*"

"Grandma, what does that mean?"

"It means her mother, Oyumi, wanted to give birth to her dead daughter Otsuru again."

What a strange, incoherent tale of karmic change. And then there is the strange rhythm of the lyrics, which had too many syllables. I realize now that she had forgotten the words and was filling in the blanks by making something up, but perhaps at the same time the final line represented a charm to purify the curse left by the bloody finale of the counting song.

This song is one of a long line of legends that describe yearning for one's parents. Such stories have been around since at least the story of Master Kumawaka in the fifteenth-century *Tale of the Great Peace*. I suspect the sad, longing-filled song of Otsuru the Pilgrim was one way in which Grandmother was acting out her sympathy for me—the grandson who had lost his father and whose mother had gone far away, entrusting him to an elderly couple. I cannot say with any certainty that was what was going through her mind, but it all makes sense thinking about it now.

There were times when Grandmother would follow this song with the ballad-like song of a pilgrim. The lyrics went like this:

> *Kimyō chōrai*, lordly flowers
> I come to a temple with flowers
> And as I stare long and hard at them
> The open lotuses do not scatter

But it is the buds that scatter
Somewhat like that little child
But I will not weep, I will not cry

Kimyō chōrai is a set expression used in supplications to the gods. "Lordly flowers" (*hanado-sama*) is probably a mistake for "flowered hymns of praise" (*hana wasan*), an expression that refers to songs of praise written in Japanese instead of the traditional Chinese of the sutras. Could the song be about a lamenting mother? Here is what I imagined. . . . A mother has lost her young child to an unforeseen death and goes to pray at a temple for him. She arrives right as the lotuses—the flower of death as well as the flower of the Buddhist paradise—are in full bloom in the temple pond. She is lost in thought, gazing at the lotus flowers, when a gust of wind blows through the garden. The petals do not scatter, but the hard bud of one of the unopened flowers breaks at the stem and falls. The mother sees this as a symbol of the fate of her young child, and she leaves the temple grounds, aware of the impermanence of life. . . .

Maybe Grandmother was trying to teach me about the impermanence of life, even though I was only four or five. Indeed, there is nothing in life that is permanent and unchanging. The red face of the morning sun transforms into the white bones of evening, and young children grow up to become elderly men and women.

However, I cannot help but wonder if the impermanence of life was the only reason that the children in her songs always died. It would not be surprising if sometimes the fetus of an unwanted child that someone had "thinned out" would come floating downstream behind the home where Grandmother was born. Also, I imagine that sometimes, in the mountain village where Grandmother went as a bride, famine would prevent women from producing enough milk for their children, leaving the children to die of starvation. Both Grandmother's birthplace and her husband's town were as poor as dirt, so such tragedies were not unheard of.

What I am trying to say is that there is a part of me that believes that when Grandmother was telling her folktales, chanting her pilgrim's ballads, and singing her songs, she was singing her own personal requiem for the souls of those unborn infants wandering the earth. That is how kind she was, even as she lay there on her futon.

3

The afternoons were especially long during my early childhood.

When afternoon came, Grandmother would return home to feed me lunch, then go back to the building and repair facility where she worked. I would run after her crying, but I would stop in the garden even before the tears dried and stiffened on my cheeks. I would stand and watch the butterflies dance toward the nearby graveyard, or I would go underneath the fig tree at the edge of the water. I would also sometimes watch the black-and-white striped dragonflies lay their eggs on the surface of the water. Grandmother had taught me that when they stuck their tails into the water, they were trying to put out the flame in their backsides.

One time, our neighbor Kawahara-san, who lived in the row house next to Grandmother on the other side of the garden, came out of her house and called to me, "Mut-chan, what happened?" I didn't answer. She withdrew into her house for a moment, then came out carrying a wet towel. I turned my face upward, and she wiped away the traces of my tears.

"Oh, poor baby." She looked into my eyes again and said, "Will you help Granny here spin some thread?" (In Japan at that time we would refer to all old ladies as Granny, not just our own grandmothers.)

I did not say anything, just nodded my head. She walked in front of me, and I followed.

Granny Kawahara had sent her only daughter to Shimonoseki, so she was alone with her husband, who went into town to work during the day. She had a flowerbed planted with azaleas and camellias. Beyond that was a little path, and beyond that was the pond. There was a little veranda along their garden. She would sit and do various chores, such as mending clothes and removing *soba* husks to put inside pillows as stuffing.

When she ran out of thread for her mending, she would have to spin another bundle, and she enlisted me to hold out my hands and support the thread as it came off the spinning wheel. At first I would move my hands dramatically to keep in time with the movements of her spinning, but soon I would grow tired and my hands would begin to hang listlessly.

"Oh-ho, so you're tired, eh?" She would humor me. "How about I tell you a story? Now, what would be a good story?" This was an established ritual that we went through all the time. My answer was the same every time, and Granny Kawahara knew it.

"The story of Ishidōmaru!"

"Ishidōmaru? Well, then, okay!"

Granny Kawahara's storytelling style was much simpler and more refined than Grandmother's. Whereas Grandmother would stick in words in dialect like *jatta* meaning "was," she would use the standard Japanese *datta*. Whereas Grandmother said, *serashita* for "did not do," Granny Kawahara would say *shinakatta* in standard Japanese. The two sets of words did not have different meanings, but the difference made a big impression on me. Even though I was little, I was keenly aware of how much more polished Granny Kawahara's language sounded. Her speech had the feel of a citified daughter who had married into a country home. As a result, I was very fond of the way she would narrate her stories.

There was a song called "The Hymn of Karukaya Dōshin" associated with the Ishidōmaru legend, much like there was a counting song in the story of Otsuru the Pilgrim. The song begins like this:

Chikuzen, Chikugo, Hizen, Higo
Ōkuma, Satsuma—these six provinces
Were governed by Katō Saemon Shigeuji
Who excelled in both letters and martial arts
Through experiencing jealousy, he came to know
The impermanence of life and entered the *bodhi* way
Leaving his wife behind in their old home
He immediately left his province and post
And took up residence on holy Mount Kōya
While inside the womb of his wife Chisato
Lodged the boy Ishidōmaru. . . .

But Granny Kawahara would not sing the song. Instead, she simplified the hymn for me and narrated it in words. She had a mild case of palsy, so her hands would shake as she was reeling up the silk filature. Her face would also shake as she told me the story of Ishidōmaru.

In her version, Shigeuji was a noble from the province of Chikuzen, not the governor of all Kyūshū as in other versions. His retainers, wife, and concubines took care of his needs, and so he lived without any wants whatsoever. One day, he peeked into his wife Odai Chisato's room and caught sight of a snake slithering in from the *fusuma* on the opposite side. The *fusuma* was the barrier that separated Chisato's room from the room of his second favorite, who was one of his concubines. The snake moved closer and closer to the pillow where Chisato was taking a nap. Shigeuji's breath caught in his throat. Right then, another snake crawled out from her disheveled hair. The two snakes lifted their curved heads into the air, stuck out their forked tongues as quickly as flames, and crawled over one another. When Shigeuji peeked in his concubine's room, she was also sound asleep. . . .

At that point, I would invariably ask, "What were those snakes?"

"Both women were jealous of one another. Their jealousy took the form of snakes, and the snakes wanted to fight each other. You see, when they were awake, it looked like the two ladies were on friendly terms, but when they fell asleep, their true feelings came out as snakes."

"Oh . . ."

"And so when Shigeuji saw that, he realized what a bad thing he had done. After all, it was because of him that they were feeling so unhappy and jealous inside. And that's why he decided to become a monk."

"Oh . . ." I nodded, but as I look back on it now, I am not sure how much I really understood the idea of jealousy transforming into flesh and becoming a snake. The image that remained with me was that there were slimy, twisted, disgusting serpents coiled up inside people who were elegant, refined, and beautiful on the outside. I imagined there must be snakes like that lodged deep within the guts of all people. It seemed to me that must be where people's souls reside.

In the story, Shigeuji becomes a Buddhist monk and leaves home, taking the new monastic name Karukaya Dōshin. Meanwhile, Chisato gives birth to a beautiful baby boy, whom she names Ishidōmaru. For the sake of both her and her newborn, she sets off to look for her missing husband. During the autumn of the year that Ishidōmaru turns thirteen, the priest Kōbō Daishi appears to him in a dream and tells him his father is living in one of the many monasteries on Mount Kōya. Ishidōmaru sets out with his mother and, after a long trip, arrives at the base of the sacred mountain. At that time, women could not set foot on Mount Kōya, so Ishidōmaru leaves his mother, who is sick and tired from the journey, in an inn at the base of the mountain and sets up for the top of the mountain alone. . . .

"Why didn't his mommy go, too?"

"Women weren't allowed. They said women were unclean and didn't let them climb the mountain."

"So what did his mommy do?"

"She waited for Ishidōmaru to come back, but she died in the meantime."

This little conversation was a ritual that we repeated over and over again more times than I could count. Even though the answer was always exactly the same, warm tears would well up in my eyes every time, blurring my vision to the point I could hardly see.

Ishidōmaru climbs Mount Kōya all alone and goes around the 990 temples at the top, but he doesn't find anyone who seems to be his father. He is crossing an unlit bridge one evening when a tall monk crosses from the other side. As they pass one another, the long sleeve of Ishidōmaru's kimono brushes against the sleeve of the monk's robe. Ishidōmaru suddenly queries, "Father?" but Karukaya did not forget the strict rules of his priestly status and simply answers, "I'm not your father." He leads the boy to one of the graveyards where the monks are buried and points to one of the gravestones, saying, "That is your father. Offer a prayer to him."

When Ishidōmaru finishes praying, Karukaya tells him it is time for him to go home. The boy goes down the mountain weeping, but when he reaches the bottom, he learns of his mother's death. He gives her the best funeral he can muster, then goes back up the mountain. He tells Karukaya what had happened and begs him, "I've become an orphan. Please let me become a disciple of the Buddhist teachings with you." Karukaya shaves Ishidōmaru's head with his own hands, initiating him into the priesthood. They spend the rest of their lives together, calling one another master and disciple instead of father and son. In the end, they were deified, becoming a set of father-and-son Jizōs. . . .

As a testament to her skillful timing, the bundle of thread would usually end right as the story was coming to a close. I would continue to hold my hands outstretched even after she had finished winding the thread onto a spool. I savored the lingering atmosphere of the story as if enjoying the lingering flavor of some deliciously sweet treat. The story of Ishidōmaru was sad, but it was equally bittersweet, and so I was happy to enjoy its peculiar flavor over and over again.

4

Through their narratives and melodies, these stories and songs tilled their way into the still, soft flesh of my heart, like oxen drawing sharp, heavy ploughs through soft soil dampened by the noiseless showers of early spring.

In addition to Grandmother's story of Otsuru the Pilgrim and Granny Kawahara's tale of Ishidōmaru, one of the stories I remember best is the story of Anju and Zushiō, which Mother told me after she returned from China. All three of these stories have something similar at their core, and so like the characters Otsuru and Ishidōmaru, the little girl Anju and the little boy Zushiō were especially close to my heart.

The story is about a little boy and girl from the nobility who are separated from their parents and sold into slavery. There were two sections of this tale that were especially poignant to me when I was little. One was the scene in which slave traders trick the two children and put them in a separate boat from their mother, who is going north. As their boat pulls into the rough sea, the helpless children weep in fear and call out heart-rending good-byes to their mother as she retreats into the distance. The other was the scene toward the end in which Zushiō, who has succeeded in getting free, regained his rightful place in life, and even managed to become a governor of the same province where he was once a slave, hears a blind old woman on the side of the road. She is singing a song as she chases sparrows away from a pile of millet. Zushiō realizes the old woman is his long-lost mother—the same woman for whom he has been searching for so many years.

But there was something in this story that did not appeal to me, namely, the ending. After Zushiō meets his mother, he weeps tears of love, and as his tears drop on her eyes, they miraculously restore her lost eyesight. For some reason, I did not like this overly simplistic ending at all. The parting at sea is the painful moment when tragedy befalls them, and the meeting on the side of the lonely island represents the moment when the tragic wound of parting is finally sutured together. The narrative flows swiftly in a single direction from the separation to the conclusion. So why was it necessary to have all that happiness after they manage to find one another? The part about the tears and the repetitious ending "How auspicious! How auspicious!" struck me as something that someone had tacked on artificially. Without it, the whole story would have been a tragedy.

What I am trying to say was that by the time I was five I was already most attracted to stories involving tragedy, and of those tragedies, I was most attracted to ones involving separation and wandering. That was partly because, somewhere in my young heart, I felt that fate had dealt me a tragic hand; it was because of my own lot in life that I was drawn to stories of tragedy, separation, and wandering.

The story of Otsuru the Pilgrim has to do with a mother and daughter who are lost to one another, and the story of Ishidōmaru is about a father and son who are separated. Both stories involve a search, and in this respect these stories are not completely unlike my own early childhood. Still, the reason I wanted to hear the story about Otsuru over and over again isn't just that I identified with the main character. Likewise, the reason that I wept whenever Ishidōmaru left his mother at the base of the mountain was not just that I identified with the young man in the story.

I was touched by the ways that the dice of fate directed these young boys and girls across the tragic game board of life, but at the same time these boys and girls appealed to me because there was something so beautiful and pure about them—something as light as a rainbow. The characters in these stories struck me as angelic beings flying through the clear heavenly vault of these tales.

Angels . . . I suppose I thought of them as something like western-style angels—pure beings that appear before us ordinary people, treading lightly as they guide us through the paths of our own human fate—even though they have their own fate to deal with, just like all regular human beings. Neither Otsuru nor Ishidōmaru ever seem to be weighted down by the burden of the flesh. That was the reason Otsuru died partway through her pitiful search. That was the reason Ishidōmaru died and was deified as a manifestation of the bodhisattva Jizō. That was also the reason that I could not abide Zushiō after he abandoned his angelic pathos and adopted a clumsy, heavy earthliness. I wanted him to die at the very moment of the long-awaited reunion with his mother.

In later years, I heard many other stories in addition to these. At some of the festivals I went to as a boy, the storytellers had mechanisms with a lens that we could peek through as they told their stories and held up illustrations. It was there that I heard for the first time the famous story of the double love-suicides at Akashi. Standing just outside where those storytellers told their tales, I overheard the story of the cow maiden. In picture books, I read the sad fairy tales of Ogawa Mimei and *The Little Mermaid* by Hans Christian Andersen, and I buried myself in *bunraku* plays and Greek tragedies, but none of these captured my imagination like the stories the old ladies recounted to me during my youth. I could not help feeling that as I encountered all the other stories, the guardian angels of the wandering boys and girls I had learned about in my youth were still with me, guiding me. I unconsciously superimposed the characters of Otsuru the Pilgrim and Ishidōmaru on the characters of the other stories, even though they had no part in them. I remember seeing images of guardian angels watching over little boys and girls in the kinds of illustrated books used in the West for catechism. In my case, there were two—perhaps even four—guardian angels watching over me, guiding my fate during my earliest years of life. Otsuru, Ishidōmaru, Anju, and Zushiō. Liberated from any earthly attributes, the souls of these four characters soared through the tragic skies of my childhood, blessing the heavens with their benedictions. And it was all thanks to those old, uneducated ladies that I was able to see them, so sad and so joyous, in their flight.

One of those old ladies—my grandmother—lost sight in one eye toward the end of her life due to an accident in the fields. By that point, Grandfather had died after a long bout of paralysis, and Grandmother, pressured by my aunt, had sold the home by the pond where she had lived for so many years. On one of the rare occasions that I visited her after she

moved with my aunt and her husband to Yame-gun, it became clear that
the one eye she had left could not see very well.

"Welcome! Who are you?" she asked in her heavy Kyūshū dialect.

"Grandma, it's me, Mutsuo!"

She smiled and said, "Ohhh . . . Mutsuo?!"

The other old lady, Granny Kawahara, who had lived next door to
us, was left all alone after her husband died. She rented all the well-lit
rooms to other people and moved into a room on the other side of the
pond. It faced a mound topped by a shrine dedicated to Inari, the fox god
of harvests, and so it was as dark as a cellar.

After Grandmother moved away, I hardly went back to her neck of
the woods anymore. Plus, I was in middle school by then. There was one
time, however, that Mother and I did have something to do at the Nōgata
city hall, and we decided to stop in to visit Granny Kawahara on the way
home. Her room was like a storage cellar. It was no bigger than four and
a half *tatami* mats, and it was illuminated by only the pale light of a single
bulb. Her clothes and household goods were scattered everywhere, and
her bedding was spread out on the floor in the middle of them. From
where she sat on her bedding, she turned to gaze at us with the same look
as in the old days. She looked terribly small. She spoke to us, gesturing
with her hands in the air. She struck me as looking a little like a witch,
perhaps because of the pots, pans, and portable clay cooking stove around
her on the *tatami*.

But what a friendly, personable witch she was! She knocked on the
wall and asked the girl next door to go buy some ice candy. I have no
idea how she paid for it. What income could she have possibly had? As
Mother and I sat there eating the ice candy and feeling bad about all the
trouble we had put her to, her face grew soft as she said, "I remember how
Mut-chan would listen to that story of Ishidōmaru over and over again.
His eyes always got full of tears. Boy, oh boy, you sure have grown up!"

I do not know what happened to her after that. No doubt she, like
Grandmother, withered away and died, more like a tree or a plant than a
human being. Still, to this very day, her angel Ishidōmaru, who came to
life through her stories, continues to live inside me alongside Otsuru, the
guardian angel born of Grandmother's songs.

Spirited Away

1

The time a young soul spends in sleep is a magical time of nonexistence. The scent of the threadbare covers give me a slight headache, but I wrap myself in them and listen to Grandmother tell her bedtime stories in a voice that speaks on and on without pausing. Then, all of a sudden, I cease to exist. As I disappear, even time itself stops. Later, in the morning, I rediscover myself lying in bed. I cannot tell whether the time I spent away was long or short. After all, a time that does not exist has no such thing as length.

Through the magic of that time in which I do not exist, I enter into being once again. In the first moments of my new existence, I am always alone, curled up in the warm darkness under the covers. My head is tucked away, hidden inside. There in the warm, dark bedding each morning, I experience a certain happiness that is also tinged with a touch of loneliness. Perhaps this feeling stems from some distant memory of being inside my mother's womb. In order to prolong this happiness, I snuggle down even farther into the covers and close my eyes tightly to shut out the light sneaking in.

I close my eyes, but it is still impossible to close my ears. The sounds of morning invade my ears, which are wide open and vulnerable. I hear the reverberations of metal striking metal from some early-to-rise worker in the Kanchiku Ironworks located just on the other side of the pond outside. . . . I hear the sounds of Grandfather who is standing outside in front of the house gargling. . . . I hear the greetings and small talk about

the weather from Grandmother and the neighbors passing by . . . one
would say in her heavy Kyūshū dialect, "The sun's out today, how nice!" . . .
the other would respond with equally heavy dialect, "You're out working
hard so early this morning!"

The nearest sounds are the prayers at the Buddhist altar, which
Grandmother keeps inside the closet in the same room where we sleep.
There are two rings of the bell, one right after another. Next, the sound of
fingers clicking the beads of a rosary. Then praying voices. Grandmother's
prayers are extremely simple. She would mumble to herself for one or
two seconds, hardly letting the words escape her mouth. After that, she
would say her set expression, "Please keep us safe from harm," and lower
her head.

Sometimes the prayers are much longer and contained the names of
lots of different Buddhist deities:

> . . . Protecting us in the Hōzōgura
> Lord Fudō Myōō of Kiyama
> Lord Jizō of Naka-aruki
> Lord Kannon of Hiroi
> Lord Kannon of the thousand arms
> Goddess of Awa Island
> Oh generations of enlightened ancestors . . .

The voice belongs to Mother. Each time I would hear her voice, which
sounded so much younger than Grandmother's, I would feel perplexed
for a moment; then I would remember the person I had slept with last
night was not Grandmother but my own mother, who had come back
home. Her voice invokes an unfurling vision of what is just outside the
covers where I lay snuggled.

No doubt she has placed some incense on the bottom ledge of the
altar and some votive lights on the upper ledge. She has also draped the
rosary she had bought at Mount Kiyama between her index and middle
fingers and is rubbing its big beads between the palms of both hands. The
biggest bead on the rosary is a different color from the rest and in it is a
tiny peephole. If you look inside, you see a picture of a tiny world, round

and enclosed like a womb. At the bottom is a row of mountains. The sky above them is rosy with dawn, and floating in the middle is a big image of a Buddhist deity. Around his shoulders are trails of auspicious clouds inscribed with Sanskrit letters.

I imagine the scene outside the bed. The votive candles tremble slightly with the sounds of the rosary and the words of prayer. The tips of the flames stand up, stretching, stretching as high as they can go. The trembling flames majestically illuminate the walls inside the altar, from which the gilding has worn half away. The light flickers over the contents of the altar—the memorial tablets of my father, sister, and maternal grandmother and the small statues of Shakyamuni and Fudō Myōō—which have grown sooty from candles and incense. Just the flickering of the candles seems proof of just how much the buddhas, gods, and ancestors appreciate the prayers Mother offered to them.

As I lie in the futon summoning up an image of Mother praying at the household altar nearby, I envision the walls coming off the altar, leaving a wide open expanse of the rosy sky of dawn exactly like inside the rosary bead. Then, as Mother summons up the spirits of the different deities, they line up in the order she calls out their names. In spite of the fact that Mother's prayer was nothing more than a string of names—or, rather, precisely because they were nothing but names—my eyes fill with a vision of the buddhas, gods, and my ancestors lining up together in their proper places as I listen to the prayers.

Fudō Myōō, the frightening deity surrounded by fire, and Jizō, the bodhisattva who guided children and travelers along their way, stand in the foreground. The Kannon of Hiroi and the thousand-armed Kannon—two different versions of the bodhisattva of mercy—stand slightly farther away, along with the great Shintō Goddess of Awa Island. Standing in back of them are generations and generations of ancestors from both Mother's and Father's sides of the family. The closest blood relatives are in front, but behind them are long, long lines of people. The closest people in these lines are the size of beans, but as the lines of ancestors continue into the distance, they shrink to the size of poppy seeds, then to simple dots, and in the end, they disappear altogether. The buddhas, gods, and ancestors who appear in this vision were the spirits that protected me throughout my youth.

Mount Kiyama was a little more than an hour from Nōgata. To get there, we would take the Chikuhō train line, go to the final stop at Haruda, transfer to the Kagoshima main line, and then go two more stops. There was a large Buddhist temple dedicated to Fudō Myōō located there. In the expansive temple grounds was a pitch-black hall known as the Hōzōgura or Repository of the Buddhist Law. People would shut themselves in this hall and engage in rites to purify their bodies and spirits—rites that were kept as secret as the Eleusinian mysteries. When I was little, my family left a paper image of me there in a purification ceremony, thus ensuring that I remained strong and healthy. That is what Mother was referring to in the first line of her prayer when she said, "Protecting us in the Hōzōgura."

The mystical power of that same introductory line also seemed to apply to Lord Jizō of Naka-aruki. If one were to get on a bus at Nōgata going toward Fukumaru, in less than an hour one would arrive at the Seitai Bridge. Walking from there, one would encounter a series of clustered houses, respectively known as Shimo-aruki, Naka-aruki, and Agari-aruki. The word *aruki* means "walk," whereas the words *shimo, naka,* and *agari* mean "lower," "middle," and "upper," respectively. Clearly these words had been given to each of the clusters of homes based on where they fell along the road. The Jizō statue she was referring to was housed in a temple in Naka-aruki. It was known as the Nail-Pulling Jizō because it was believed it could remove the aches, pains, wounds, and illnesses afflicting the body, and for this reason many locals came to pray before it. Mother had left a paper image of me there too, and so this statue also protected me during my childhood.

The Kannon of Hiroi was sometimes called the Ocular Kannon because it was known for healing diseases of the eyes. Mother once took me to the little shrine where the statue was housed. To get there, we walked from Grandmother's house until we reached the shrine in the middle of the hills. The building itself was in the middle of a bunch of trees like the trees we would use for brushwood, and it was weathered from the rain. When we walked around the back, there was a mossy basin filled with dirty rainwater. Damselflies circled around the basin, landing on the water and sticking in their bottoms to put out the fires in their behinds. Mother told me, "People say if you put this water on your eyes, you'll be able to see better," so I wet my fingertips with the tepid water and placed it on my eyelids as she instructed.

I do not know which particular deity Mother was referring to when she spoke of the thousand-armed Kannon. Whenever she said the word "thousand-armed," she would say *sente* instead of *senju*—the way the word is supposed to be pronounced. She was misled by the fact that the character meaning "arm" or "hand" has two readings, *te* and *ju*, but she did not have enough education to know which way it was supposed to be read. Each time I heard her praise Sente Kannon, she would call up in my imagination an image of a great purple Buddha surrounded by countless hands. I imagined Kannon to be purple because of the ink stamps Mother had collected during a vacation she had spent in Kyoto. Many tourist sites have inkpads and rubber stamps that portray images of buildings, statues, and other things associated with the site. Tourists bring blank books and fill them with ink stamps from the temples, thus creating a scrapbook of the places they visit. Several pages into Mother's book of stamps, she had a big purple one from Sanjūsangendō in Kyoto, a temple famous for its hundreds of images of the bodhisattva Kannon, each with countless hands. As I looked at the stamp Mother had brought home, the arms of the statues looked like wings to me. No doubt, Mother went there with her lover Ōgushi-san. I cannot help but wonder if every time she reverentially intoned the name of Sente Kannon she was not thinking of some summer day she spent strolling down the cool hallway of Sanjūsangendō with her boyfriend.

The Goddess of Awa Island had a peculiar association for me. When I heard this name, I tended to think of spinach beets, which are known in Japanese as *fudansō*, or literally "the plant of no refusal." Ironically, Mother would often refuse this shiny, dipper-shaped root when it appeared in her soup. The beets would be the only things she took out of her soup bowl and gave to me. As she did so, she made a strange face and said, "This is because I'm making a wish to the Goddess of Awa Island." I wonder what she was wishing each time she refused the plants of no refusal.

I was terrified every time I heard the tale of the Goddess of Awa. The story went that she was cursed by her husband, who was also a god, because she came down with some kind of disease called "the disease of red and black blood"—probably some sort of venereal disease. As part of her curse, she was placed in an empty boat and cast onto the great plain of the sea. She floated down the coastline, passing through seven different bays, and in the process she suffered so much that she was transformed into a goddess.

And then there were my ancestors. They would come to the living, threaten them, console them, and give them advice. They did not want the living to respect them as if they were dead; they wanted the living to receive them in the same way they received living people. As for their part, the living also were not eager to treat them as strangers who had come from the realm of the dead; they wanted to petition the ancestors with wishes, vent grudges, and discuss matters as if they were invisible, rich relatives.

Because of Mother's lot in life as a young widow, these buddhas, gods, and ancestors were especially important to her, but of course she did not have an exclusive monopoly on them. Mother and Grandmother did not always get along terribly well, but Grandmother also sat in front of the same Buddhist altar and prayed to the same spirits.

There were other spirits, too—ones that Mother did not specifically invoke—and those spirits were everywhere. There was a spirit of the threshold at the entrance into the main house; therefore, it was forbidden to step on it while wearing anything on our feet. In the cooking area, there was a god of the kitchen range, and this god hated dirtiness more than anything. There was a goddess of the lavatory. She was beautiful, but she was also blind and spent the entire year doing a handstand. As a sign of respect to this goddess, we would do our business in the lavatory facing backward, but no one, not even Grandmother, could explain why.

The gods, the buddhas, and the dead were not the only things around us that had spiritual power. There were worms in the ditches and at the bottoms of the pipes that led from the sinks outside, and if you were to urinate in those spots, the sensitive young reed between one's thighs would begin to swell up visibly. When toads came creeping out during the day, they brought news of misfortune to the family, and when dragonflies bent their thin wings and flew into the pale purple sunset, they were carrying the spirits of the dead on their backs. When the day would draw to a close, we would hear the cries of the *yosshoi* bird from the far side of the pond. The bird, I was told, was on the lookout for naughty little children as well as children who would not stop crying. If it found one, it would snatch it and take it away. A little more than a mile from Grandmother's house was a neighborhood called Hachiryū where shape-shifting *tanuki* were known to transform themselves into bamboo baskets and change size. People around there would often say, "I saw a *tanuki* basket the day before yesterday," and "Me, too! Why, I saw one just yesterday!"

Yes, when I was little, the spirits surrounded us, and we carried out our lives in their midst.

2

Something strange happened to me when I was little, before I was old enough even to remember. To put it in Mother's words, I was "spirited away." Actually, it happened not once but twice. Both times were when Mother was living and working in the singles dormitory for the Mitsubishi Mining Company.

The first took place one afternoon during the time of year when the days were growing long. Mother had finished cleaning the rooms of the young residents and taking in their laundry from the clothesline when she realized I was nowhere to be found. This did not especially worry her. I would often put on the hand-me-down vests I received from the residents, slip on a pair of the big women's clogs that Mother and the other maids wore, and go play at the offices of the company. It was only around a thousand feet away.

Not especially worried, Mother started making preparations for supper. In addition to the usual rice, grilled fish, and boiled vegetables we always had, she would often try to add an extra little something that would show her attention to detail—perhaps some egg whites cooked with broth or boiled spinach if it were in season. One by one, the residents would come in, smelling like young men who had been hard at work. The first thing they would always ask was "Where's little Mutsuo?" Sometimes the first resident who came in would pick me up and hold me on his lap.

That day, the first resident who came in asked about me as always.

"He must have gone over to the offices to play."

"Nope, I didn't see him over there."

That was when Mother grew alarmed. She went outside the wooden fence around the dormitory, cupped her hands around her mouth, and yelled, "Mut-chaaaan! Mutsuoooo!" That was always how she called me to come home. First she would call me with my diminutive nickname "Mut-chan," and then if there was no response, she would always call out my whole name "Mutsuo" with no suffixes attached. No doubt she drew out the final vowel to make her cry flow across the cabbage fields and resound in the deep blue skies of twilight.

There was no response. She ran over to the pond by our home. Once she confirmed I was not at Grandmother's house, she rushed two doors down to Granny Tejima to ask her to pray for me. Granny Tejima offered up an entreaty to Fudō Myōō and Jizō, the protector of young children, and then made the following proclamation in an austere voice: "Your little boy is sleeping peacefully in the arms of a young woman."

Late that night, I still had not shown up. Mother was unable to sleep. She was wide awake with worry when all of a sudden someone knocked at the door. When she opened it, she found a young maid standing there, her face stained with tears. The maid had started working at the dormitories only a month before. I was sound asleep in her arms, making quiet breathing noises. She had gone back to her family's home for the first time in quite some time, and she had decided to take me along with her.

She had intended to be back by dinnertime, and so she had not bothered to tell my mother, but her family held her up at home; then on the way back, the bus broke down. She had wanted to call, but of course there were no telephones along the country roads through the mountains. The nervous young girl was so worried that she burst into tears, but there was no way for her to communicate with Mother or anyone else. Still, the protective god of children had been right: I had been sleeping peacefully in the arms of a young woman. Perhaps it is not exactly right to say that I was spirited away. It was a person who had taken me away, and the spirits had simply protected me. The spirits were not the ones at fault.

The next disappearance happened one spring afternoon. (I have a vague recollection of what happened that day, so I suspect it must have taken place about a year after the other incident.) I put on Mother's wooden clogs and left the dormitory through the kitchen door to walk into the hazy landscape of spring.

The misty landscape seemed to flicker as the shimmering air rose from the fields and hills. The springtime rays of the sun filled the air like warm mother's milk. In one spot in the tranquil landscape, a middle-aged man from the Kōda family was hoeing his fields. I went up to him to talk. He stopped his hoe and took a break, and we stood there talking together like two adults.

It was a little later that Mother realized I was missing. She remembered what had happened a year earlier, so she was much more worried this time. She ran outside, her apron still hanging from her waist. This time, she probably did not call out "Mut-chan" then "Mutsuo." It was still daytime. Those cries were better suited to twilight, when the shadows grew as dark as the deep green shoots of a green onion.

She asked Kōda-san, who was still hoeing his fields, "Have you seen my little boy, Mutsuo?"

"Sure did. Just a few moments ago he was here. We stood here and talked just like adults for a while, then he went on his way."

"Which way'd he go?"

"That way." Kōda-san took the towel from where he had tucked it in the back of his pants, wiped the sweat from his brow, and pointed west.

In the west was the graveyard where my family was buried. On the other side of the hill near the graveyard was Ōsugi-san's home, the man with whom Grandmother was having her affair. There was also the earthen storehouse of Kōno Chikasuke, one of Mother's distant relatives who happened to live in relative comfort. Beyond that were several hills and even farther beyond that were the six slopes of Mutsugatake shrouded in bluish mist. At the base of Mutsugatake was Tsurugi Shrine, which served the Kurate district.

"Thank you very much." She bowed to Kōda-san and hurried off, guessing that I was most likely at Ōsugi-san's house.

Ōsugi-san had brought a box of papers onto his veranda, which faced onto the road and got lots of sun. He was organizing his papers, having perched his reading glasses on the end of his nose.

Mother called out to him. "Has Mutsuo been here?"

"Nope, he hasn't."

She set off running. She heard Ōsugi-san yell, "Hisako-san, has something happened? Hisako-saaaan!" But she was too preoccupied to answer. She ran to the cemetery and rushed over to the corner. There, she came to the stone that marked the spot where the ashes of the Takahashi family had been laid to rest. She placed her forehead first against my father's gravestone, then her maternal grandmother's gravestone and muttered a prayer for protection: "Please don't let anything bad happen to Mutsuo."

As she was praying, she suddenly heard the gentle sound of a group of children playing. She stood up and went in the direction of the voices.

A little ways down the hill from the Takahashi family grave was the grave of Kōno Tasō, one of Mother's relatives. Because of Tasō's womanizing, his entire family had fallen so deeply into ruin that it was hard to believe they had ever been people of standing. The only sign of their former wealth was a magnificent granite stone carved with characters stating that several generations of the Kōno family were buried there. Grouped around the stone were the graves of his children, some of whom had grown up and some of whom had died young.

Still frightened half to death by my disappearance, Mother approached the little ruffians who were carousing in the graveyard where her closest relatives were buried. There I was, the son she had been looking for, in the middle of the ring. I was kneeling down, my eyes shut, and my hands were pressed against one another as I prayed intently. The other children were climbing on the stones, making mud pies, and making fun of me as I sat there in prayer.

Mother grabbed my hand, and as we walked down the hill from the graveyard, she asked, "Mut-chan, how on earth did you get here all alone?"

"Daddy and Hiromi came to me. They told me, 'Come, come,' so I did."

That is what Mother told me, anyway. I don't really remember what explanation I gave for my disappearance. All I remember is talking to Kōda-san on the side of the road, praying in front of the gravestones, and the other children gathered around me. All my other memories of that day have vanished completely.

If it is true that my deceased father and older sister Hiromi came to me, I wonder why they didn't guide me to their graves and instead took me to the nearby graves of my relatives. Perhaps it was not my own relatives who guided me there at all. Maybe it was some other spirit entirely.

I have been loved by many different kinds of spirits. In the graveyard near Grandmother's house, where the people in the graves had little or no relation to the Takahashi family, I would also speak to the departed. I would pile seeds from the tall grass on fragments of roof tile, then crush them with a rock. As I did so, I would speak to the dead. They were my playmates for entire days at a time.

3

"There's a crazy lady at the Tejima place."

The shouts came from outside the frosted glass windows that looked out over the veranda. A moment later, someone ran by. Without bothering to put on my shoes, I jumped to the front door and ran out the front of the house.

From the window of the kitchen where Grandmother cooked our meals and from the front door of the Kubos' house next door, there was a clear view of the water in the pond twinkling brightly in the midday sun. Next to that was Granny Tejima's house. As soon as you stepped into their yard, tall thick fig trees blocked out the sunshine and the view of the water. The yard always had a cool aroma that suggested moss, centipedes, earthworms, and other earthly things.

There was a young, barefoot girl there, dressed in a long undergarment. Someone had tied her to one of the fig trees with several red cords of the same type one would use to tie a kimono closed. The cords had been tied end to end to make a rope long enough to bind her to the tree. The undergarments she wore were soiled with spring dust, and her hair, face, and limbs were dirty. She looked young, hardly older than twenty. Both of her hands hung limply at her side, and her fingernails were bluish-black with dirt. She gazed at everyone with big, black eyes that seemed like empty spots until the children said something to tease her. Then she grew angry and kicked dirt at them with her bare feet, acting like an angry cow on the loose.

Grandmother had come to the Tejima's well to get some water. As she led me home, I asked, "Why was that person tied up? Did she do something bad?"

"A 'wind' got into her. They say that's the way to chase it out."

"A 'wind'?"

"It's a fiery ball that floats up from dead people."

There in the countryside, people believed that a drifting soul, which they thought of as a kind of wind, could get into a person's body. If it did, the wind could make them lose their sanity or even give them tuberculosis. The kind of wind that could make a person crazy was considered especially depraved, and so country people would tie mad people outside to expose them to the rain and the dust. This form of treatment was intended to punish the evil spirit, not the poor person who had lost his or her mind. If anything, the country folk thought they were being kind to the insane person by doing this.

The rain fell, the dust blew, and the days progressed ever further into spring. Before long came the day each year when the pilgrims would dress in white and file by as they made their rounds to the temples and shrines. The crazy girl's undergarments were just about as soiled as they could possibly be, and the hem had turned into a muddy mess. The front hem had ripped suggestively in two, revealing her legs, which were covered with patterns of grime. She would sometimes let out a piercing laugh, but when the old pilgrims wearing their traditional white arm and leg coverings came to stare at her, she did not grow angry as before. When a young woman dressed in her finest clothing would pass by, she would grab at the flamboyantly colored sleeves with her fingers and her bluish-black fingernails and shriek, "Look! Is that silk crepe? Rayon? *Manken?*" *Manken* was a made-up word, and the absurdity of her question made her sound truly crazy.

When the gods and buddhas helped her improve a little, someone took her away. Grandmother said to Grandfather, "It looks like Tejima-san isn't going to get any more money to take care of her." That statement was not entirely fair. The money Granny Tejima got to take care of the crazy girl wasn't her only source of income.

Right in front of the fig tree where the crazy girl had been tied was the room where Granny Tejima kept her Buddhist altar. It was a gloomy, empty room about ten mats wide. Granny Tejima did not think of it as a regular room; she called it the *hondō*, or "inner temple," as if it were the main building of a Buddhist temple. In the institutionalized world of Buddhism, the highest-ranking temples of their individual sects would ordain priests with the authority to mediate between the worlds of the living and the dead, but Granny Tejima had no need for official status. She had earned her position as a go-between directly from the spirits themselves. The spirits had chosen her, and in response to their call she had gone out into the cold and lived the life of an ascetic for some time on a rocky outcropping. In her eyes, her *hondō* was even more legitimate than the sanctuaries you would find in real temples.

The *hondō* was always dimly lit and smelled of old, damp *tatami* mats, plaster, and incense. On three sides of the room was an eclectic assortment of statues of Buddhist gods and Shintō deities. There was a stone statue of Jizō wearing a red bib, a stone statue of the fiery Fudō Myōō that had been painted with bright colors, a glass case enclosing a crooked statue of the Goddess of Awa Island with her face painted starkly white, a shiny golden statue of Shakyamuni that was missing a hand, and a statue of Kannon whose paint and gilding had worn away or peeled off. There were statues of Sanbō Kōjin, the fox god Inari, and even the see-no-evil, hear-no-evil, speak-no-evil monkeys. These idols were lined up against the wall in no particular order. In front of them were artificial flowers in gold and silver, different kinds of cakes, a wooden drum, and a gong, all of which lent an air of legitimacy to her temple.

Whenever something happened, Mother would scoop me up and run to Granny Tejima's *hondō*, and there the old lady would listen to Mother say what was wrong. She would either nod or shake her small head, which was covered with wiry, white hair smoothed into place. Next, she would turn her back to us and face the buddhas. As she did so, the small, stooped lady who did not ordinarily stand out as any different from the persnickety old ladies you might find anywhere, straightened her back and suddenly took on a magnificent, dignified look.

She struck the wooden drum and rang the bell at intervals, summoning up the spirits residing in the darkness behind the statues. Her speech fell into the classical patterns of five and seven syllables, and this rhythm struck me as quite beautiful:

> ... Your power is not to be wasted
> For you we are thankful
> From this moment today
> We beg you for your kindness
> We humbly beg your pardon
> We ask you to make yourself known
> We ask you for your forgiveness. ...

She continued to entreat the spirits for their forgiveness since she had awakened them from their peaceful slumber; then she delivered an impassioned plea for them to accept her prayers.

When the flame of the great candle burning in front of the statues grew thin and stretched toward the ceiling, we knew the spirits had forgiven us and accepted her prayers. The spirits would borrow the mouth of the old woman and speak through her, declaring their will in sad, rhythmic cadences:

> ... Oh how pitiable
> Oh, how touching
> You have beseeched me
> You have called upon me
> From here on out
> Please beseech me!
> Please rely upon me! ...

After the spirits spoke, Granny Tejima would close her prayers with a recitation of the Heart Sutra or the Kannon Sutra, then turn to us and start talking to us about more worldly affairs, saying things like "So-and-so's bride is really lazy and won't even wash her underclothes" or "So-and-so from such-and-such a place committed adultery with so-and-so from over yonder." During the prayers, Mother had wrapped some change in a cloth, and as they spoke, she slid the bundle across the *tatami*. Never pausing for a moment, Granny Tejima would stretch out her hand, take it, and squirrel it away into her sleeve.

Once, soon after Father died and Mother moved from Yahata to Nōgata, Mother's aunt from the Nakahara side of the family did something terrible to her. Mother picked me up and ran to Granny Tejima's. The summoned spirit was that of my maternal grandmother, Shikano. The spirit grew angry that her younger sister had been cruel to Mother and proclaimed, "Something unusual will befall the Nakahara family within a year. Just sit back and wait. Wait, just as if you were patiently taking a ride on a boat." When the spirit had finished, Mother picked me up in her arms, and we left.

Before long, Mother forgot all about the spirit's proclamation, and a year went by. The daughter of the Nakahara family married into the family of a distant relative and gave birth to a little girl. The fingers on one of the baby's hands were completely motionless, as if they had been stuck together with glue. As she grew, it became clear that she was severely mentally disabled. Other than looking at her own mother and cooing happily, she showed no sign of being aware of the world around her.

Mother was now deeply sorry for having borne a grudge. The grudge was against her aunt, not her daughter, with whom Mother was relatively close. And what crime could the daughter's daughter, no more than a newborn, have possibly committed? There was no going back now, however. Shikano's spirit had sworn revenge, and sure enough, the revenge had taken place.

Grandmother's extraordinary stinginess was another thing that Mother repeatedly complained about at Granny Tejima's. This complaint from my devout mother was also answered somewhat after the fact. The summer I was in third grade, we went back from Moji to visit Grandmother's house. We found her wearing a patch over one eye. When we asked what had happened, she just responded, "I lost sight in the same eye Grandpa could see out of." She joked, "Between the two of us, we'd have one set of eyes," but she would not tell us the particulars of what had happened to make her lose her sight.

When Grandmother went out into the fields, Granny Kawahara from next door ran in. She had been waiting to tell Mother the news.

Grandmother had gone into the fields one day recently to harvest the barley when she stuck herself in the eye with an ear of barley. They had tried a local folk remedy and crushed bagworms from the persimmon trees and dripped the juice onto her eyes, but her eye did not get any better. At Granny Kawahara's suggestion, Grandmother had finally started to think about going to consult with the spirits, but she was too stubborn to go to Granny Tejima because of her closeness to Mother. In the end, an acquaintance introduced her to a faith healer in town. When the healer was praying on her behalf, the spirit of my father appeared and said, "You are much too stingy with your grandson, and so that's why your eye got poked out—it was punishment. If you don't fix your ways, I'll poke out your other eye, too!"

Granny Kawahara shook her head back and forth on her half-paralyzed neck and made a rather nasty smile, saying, "Your grandmother had better give you something next time, eh?"

Sure enough, soon afterward, Grandmother packed up about four cups' worth of uncooked rice and gave it to me, saying, "You've come a long ways, so take this home and make something with it." The war had ended only a short time before, so four cups of rice was a tremendously valuable amount. She had obeyed the spirit's warning even though her stinginess ran to the very marrow of her bones.

When I look back across the distance of the years to my childhood, one of the things I see is my poor grandmother scrimping and saving on food and her own son poking out her eye in retribution.

4

Soon after entering elementary school, I joined a group of women, including Mother, that Granny Tejima was taking on a religious pilgrimage to Mount Kiyama. This was not the first time I had gone there with Mother. Still, this was an important trip for her. She took a *furoshiki* and draped it around her neck like a sling for a broken arm. The whole way there, she cradled a statue of Fudō Myōō in it. Mother was a great believer in the power of the Fudō Myōō that was located in the waterfall within the sacred grounds of the mountain. Before the trip, she had taken what little money was in her postal savings account and asked a stonecutter to carve a statue of the deity for her, and now she was bringing it to donate to the temple. That evening, she gave her statue to a monk who immediately enshrined it near the waterfall.

The next day, everyone woke up early to go stand underneath the waterfall and pray as the water splashed over their heads. The waterfall was little more than a trickle that had been diverted from the mountain streams to a high crag in the rocks, and from there it fell to the ground below. That morning, however, the sight of the water falling through the crisp, early morning air had an especially gallant beauty about it.

As the water fell, it narrowed into a thin stream before striking the rocks below. Mother and all the others wore nothing but a wrap around their waists. Meanwhile, I squatted in the stream about thirty feet below and played with the tiny little river crabs in the water. When I stuck out my fingers at them, the crabs lifted both pincers and came toward me to fight. I was able to pick them up if I pressed down on the shell on their back with my index finger, then quickly grasped them at the base of their pincers with my thumb and middle finger. The four legs on each side of their bodies would wiggle busily in the air for a moment and then suddenly grow still.

As I was squatting in the water with my head down, I suddenly heard a strange voice. "*Namu amida butsu, namu amida bu, namu amida bu.*" The voice began repeating the Buddhist incantation faster and faster. First the final syllable disappeared, but as it grew quicker and quicker, it turned into little more than the syllables *dabudabudabudabu*, then *budabudabuda*. Next, the voice started quickly repeating the name of the deity enshrined there: "*fudōfudōfudō.*"

I looked and saw Mother standing directly under the waterfall, water splashing off her shoulders, and Granny Tejima beating her exposed back with the flat of her hand. The other ladies were gathered around them and were praying intensely with their eyes tightly shut. The strange voice was leaking from none other than my own mother's mouth.

Mother herself did not even seem to be aware of what she was saying. As her prayer went through its various transformations—*Namu amida bu* turning into *dabudabu*, then *budabuda*, then *fudōfudō*—she seemed to be indicating that the spirit of Fudō Myōō himself had entered her weak body and possessed her. At that moment, some burning, smoldering transformation was taking place inside. Her eyes were shut tightly as if she were in pain. As a result, the only thing she could see was the vision unfolding in her mind's eye. Meanwhile, her entire body was trembling.

Granny Tejima showed no mercy, however. She slapped Mother's back again and insisted, "If you just keep saying '*fudōfudō*,' we don't know which one you're talking about. Which Fudō are you? Where are you from?"

Mother's lips, which had completely drained of color, trembled all the more. Her teeth chattering, she started all over again. "*Namu amida bu, namu amida bu . . . dabudabudabu . . . daddaddadda . . . tattattattatta . . . takitakitaakitaaki . . .*" The strange word she was saying was *taki*, meaning "waterfall." She was declaring that the Fudō Myōō of the waterfall, which she worshipped with such reverence, had come down and possessed her, taking hold of her thirty-year-old widow's body.

An unruly and violent spirit had forced its way into the body of my closest relative in the world—my own mother—and taken possession of her. The sun had risen high in the sky and was pouring its light directly down on her so that she seemed to radiate a dazzling light. For me, who was still no more than a young boy, the sight of this spirit possession was as embarrassing as it was blinding. I could not watch. I ran behind her into the depths of the forest where the sound of the waterfall grew quiet, becoming no louder than the wind singing in the pine trees. I could hear the furious beating of my heart in my chest.

Later, at the cafeteria where we ate our lunch and that evening at the lodgings where we spent the night, neither Mother nor I mentioned what had transpired earlier in the day. Granny Tejima and the other ladies who had come along also appeared to avoid the subject, perhaps out of consideration for the awkwardness that had transpired between Mother and me.

The next morning, after a somewhat late breakfast, the group set out to continue their pilgrimage to the main statue of Fudō Myōō within the temple. Ordinarily, Fudō Myōō is portrayed as a powerful, muscular spirit surrounded by a halo of enormous flames that spill out in all directions; however, the statue in the temple was nothing but a single blaze of fire. The angry shoulders that supported his fiery halo, the hands that grasped his treasured sword and rope of steel, the open thighs that stood with feet planted firmly atop a craggy rock—all of these were made to look like fire transformed into flesh. The entire statue was fashioned out of fire. I cannot help but wonder if the statue, which burned so red and brimmed with such angry, masculine vigor, didn't somehow take the place of a man for my young, widowed mother. Perhaps it even represented the entirety of the masculine sex itself. The statues of Fudō Myōō in the waterfall, in Hōzōgura, in the main hall of the temple, in the lodgings, alongside the pilgrimage route, and along the roads through the mountains were all similarly frightening. There were statues of Fudō Myōō everywhere.

As we traveled on our pilgrimage from one Fudō Myōō statue to the next, Granny Tejima finally broke her silence and became the first to talk about what had happened the day before. "Hisako-san, just a little longer. It'll just be a little longer."

"Granny, what do you mean, 'It'll just be a little longer'?"

"Lord Fudō came down and possessed you yesterday. When I was young, the exact same thing happened to me. Before long, you'll be hearing the voices of all sorts of deities speaking to you."

Mother was silent. Her silence made it clear how uneasy she was. Granny Tejima did not say anything else.

When we returned from Kiyama, Mother started purifying herself by pouring cold water over her body early each morning. When it came time for the second semester, she and I moved to Moji. As I lay in bed early each morning in our new home in the port town, the sound of cold water striking Mother's flesh would mingle with the clatter of the horse-drawn carts and the notes of the tofu vendor's whistle.

When the war came to an end, Mother's lover Ōgushi-san was forced to leave China and came to stay with us. It was around that time she stopped purifying herself with cold water, but before long, that relationship also came to an end. After Ōgushi-san left, the spirit of Fudō Myōō never again descended into her body.

On Mother's Back

1

My early memories of happiness and of the war are, strangely enough, both linked to my mother's back. I am not trying to say that happiness meant war to me, or that the war was a happy time. If anything, the situation was quite the opposite. Our happiness and the war were as diametrically opposed as heaven and hell, and Mother's back represented the diverging point between the two. In other words, Mother's back was the fork in the path—one side led toward paradise while the other led toward the fiery depths.

Probably the earliest of my well-formed memories is the experience of Mother carrying me on her back when I was two. She is carrying me step by step down the stone staircase behind Grandmother's house. She has her arms behind her back to support me, and in one of her hands she is carrying a small metal pot. With each step, the rough metal of the pot brushes my ankle and sends a cool chill through my leg.

The path branches in three directions at the bottom of the stone staircase. On one path is a fish vendor's stand, made of little more than rough-hewn lumber held together with a few nails. That was where she would go to buy her fish. Mother would not allow her father-in-law, my grandfather, to eat fish at all, and so when the old folks were away, she would sneak out to get some for the two of us, then cook it over the brazier to eat. When we were done, she would go to the pond and throw the bones in the water so my grandparents would not know what we had eaten.

Probably the reason I remember all this—the warmth of Mother's back against my little two-year-old body, the cold sensation of the metal pot against my ankle, and the colors of the rockfish, black porgy, and the greenlings lined up on the narrow counter of the fish vendor—is that it was soon before Mother went away to work in Nakatsu and Shimonoseki. For me, the warmth of Mother's back was synonymous with the happiness of the mother-son relationship soon to be lost to me.

In the countryside when a mother carries her child, it is customary for her to put on a short coat, like the type worn by a housemaid, and cover the child on her back. I never remember Mother draping one of these coats over me. If she wore a covering like that, it would take time to take me off her back. It seems to me that the fact she never covered me with her coat was an indication she was always ready to take me down, or in other words to dislodge me from my happiness.

My next memory of her back dates from a little later, after she started working in the singles dormitory at the Mitsubishi Mining Company. She had finished some business at Grandmother's house, and she was on her way back to the dormitory, carrying me on her back over her chef's overalls. Not far from the company was the Iwaiya Shop, which sold all sorts of different goods. We had come that far when Mother pointed to a house on top of a precipice across the street from the shop. The house was made of rough lumber sided with cedar bark. It came right up to the edge of the precipice, and in the middle of the wall was a small window that shone gloomily, reflecting the dark sky.

"The boy in that house is a 'two-up' kind of guy. In the ceremony on the emperor's birthday, he got all excited and shouted, 'His Majesty, Banzai!' four times. The military police pulled him aside and threw him in jail." To "two-up," *niyagari* in our dialect, means to get carried away, and a two-up person is someone who is impetuous—usually too impetuous for their own good. The expression probably comes from the world of the *samisen*, where it means to raise the pitch of the second string and play a piece of music in a key signature higher than originally written.

I was not entirely sure what Mother was trying to say, but when I looked up at the small window and the cedar-sided wall above the precipice, I saw a stamp of unhappiness left by some higher force. The true form of that dark force was a frightening entity known as "the emperor"—the commander-in-chief who wore military attire and touched his cap in salute, the same man who was backed by the military police, army, and navy of the entire Japanese empire.

I think that I understood that the boy in that house had been chased from his mother's back by some unforgiving authority. I also sensed that what had made that authority so unforgiving was the war. As the war progressed, times had grown so chaotic that even the jokers we laughed at as two-up kinds of men during peacetime were now being arrested and punished for lèse-majesté. In my terror, I must have gripped Mother's back like a vice.

Another memory of Mother's back dates from when I was around four. She had come back temporarily to Grandmother's house from where she was working in Shimonoseki. The memory takes place on the narrow road along the edge of the fields between the Kawaharas' house and Grandmother's. Mother might have been walking home absorbed in conversation with Kawahara-san. I am not sure about that detail.

In any case, the fava beans were blooming in the fields, and on the left side of the road the water in the pond was sparkling. From Mother's back, I could hear the rustling of the pale green leaves of the beanstalks and the pale purple fava flowers with their dark, almost black, spots. As the breeze moved over them, they seemed to rustle in unison.

"Mut-chan, the war is over."

I am not entirely sure who said this. It might have been Haa-chan, the youngest daughter of the Kubo family who lived just to the right of Grandmother. Perhaps it was Kakko-chan from the Hashimoto family, which lived three doors down from the Kawaharas in front of the company housing. The person who said this must have been nearby, but any memory I had of the owner of the voice has vanished. Because I have forgotten who said this, the voice in my memory is like that of some disembodied spirit, speaking in an exceptionally tender way.

I remember that when I heard this pronouncement, I was immensely relieved. Even though I had been given military toys—a long, silver blade that looked like a slim, shiny fish—and books having to do with tanks and airplanes, I was still utterly terrified of war. It did not help that I had been forced to learn songs like the one that went "I really love army soldiers." Still, even though I was a mere child, I knew enough to be ashamed to say I was frightened of war. If it was true that the war had ended and I did not have to try to escape it any longer, that would mean I had been liberated from the war, fair and square. I would have made it through the war without being chased from the warmth of Mother's back.

Unfortunately, however, the spirit's pronouncement was premature. The enemy planes flew in formation through the sunsets of my youth and caught in the searchlights above the nighttime horizon; they spit out flames and fell to the ground below. It did not have to do with the war directly, but I was eventually taken down from the safety of Mother's back when she abandoned me to go to Tianjin in northern China.

When I speak of the safety of a mother's back, I cannot help but think of my Uncle Ken'ichi. He was one of the many young men during that era who were chased from his mother's back and driven onto the battlefield. Grandmother was no doubt not the most motherly of women. That much is clear from how proud she was that the very same day she gave birth to him she immediately returned to work and emptied a big coal cart with Grandfather. Grandmother's back was well suited to carrying gravel and other hard tasks, but it was probably not the sort of back that would carry a child who had grown much past infancy. Still, even though Grandmother was not the most motherly of women, it still does not change the fact that historical circumstances chased my uncle from the safety of her back.

In every sense, Uncle Ken'ichi seemed to have been born in order to be sacrificed to the war effort. He was born more than a decade after my father, and so the entire process of his personal development coincided with the process of Japan's descent into conflict. In the end, his young flesh and fragile soul were placed as burnt offerings on the altar of war.

He finished the first several years of his grade school education as class president. His grades were good enough that the principal called Grandfather in and asked him to let Ken'ichi go on to middle school, but Grandfather simply shook his head. "As soon as a day laborer's son graduates from school, he's gotta start working to earn some cash." The truth is that my grandparents were not lacking the money to send my uncle to the local middle school if they had just wanted to.

Uncle Ken'ichi just quietly obeyed his parents. When he was quite far along in his studies, he took the test to apply to the National Railways, and he got the highest score of anyone in the area. He was sent to the railway training institute at Moji for half a year before being dispatched to the railway yard at Nōgata. Whenever Mother and I would pass the railway yard on the way home, my uncle, wearing his navy blue uniform, would jump down from the line of cargo cars and wave his white-gloved hand in the air to us. Mother would pick me up in her arms and make me wave back.

Uncle Ken'ichi was tall and had a masculine, attractive face. Such looks were unusual in our family. He was still only seventeen or eighteen, but fate—the same fate that would eventually send him to war and make him breathe his last on the battlefield—gave my uncle's face and body the dignity of an adult. He had been forced from his mother's back into the cruel world, and he had no choice but to become a dignified man all by himself. I cannot see Uncle Ken'ichi as anything other than a full-fledged adult, a man who possessed a certain gloomy dignity in both flesh and soul.

2

When I was a little boy, the back room beside the Buddhist altar in Grandmother's house was always the scary room for me. This room, which was hidden behind sliding *fusuma* doors, had been built onto the house as an addition. Dappled shade moved across the glass doors looking out onto the garden, and the daylight stretched across the new *tatami* mats on the floor. It should have been the brightest room in the entire house, but as I remember it the back room was always the darkest.

That room belonged to Uncle Ken'ichi. He worked in the railway yard, and after he woke up in the morning, he still had to walk more than thirty minutes to get there. That probably did not leave him even enough time to open the wooden sliding doors outside the glass doors and let in the light. After he left for work, neither Grandmother nor Mother would go into his room to open them.

When he worked the night shift, he would stay in the house until evening. He would not open the wooden doors those days, or on the day when he was off duty once a week. Only rarely, on quiet mornings when he and my grandparents had gone to work, Mother would enter the room and slide open the wooden doors as she dusted the room and sang to herself. Still, even then, she would hurry up and slide the doors shut as soon as she could, whether the dusting was completely done or not.

This was unusual for Mother, who was so meticulous about cleaning that it was almost a psychological compulsion. She would sweep and dust three or four times a day, and typically she would leave the glass doors open for a little while to carry out the dust dancing in the air. I wonder if Mother and Grandmother didn't make the decision not to open the wooden sliding doors of his room out of sympathy for him, since so much of his adolescence was shrouded by the dark clouds of fate. The darkness of the back room, where the wooden doors were kept shut even in the middle of the day, was appropriate considering how much darkness was foisted on his youth by outside forces.

In the evening, when he returned home in his railway overalls, he went right into the back room. He used to take judo lessons after work, so as he stomped with his big feet from the front door across the dining area to the back room, I would smell for a few seconds the pungent scent of a young man. This masculine smell would mix with the scent of his navy overalls, which had started to fade from all of their repeated washings. Sometimes I would get peevish and throw a tantrum while Mother was busy folding the laundry in the sitting room. When this happened, the *fusuma* would slide open and Uncle Ken'ichi would stick his closely cropped head through the opening. He would have a fierce look on his face.

"Mutsuo!" This would startle me, and I would stop crying. "Mutsuo, it will be *Les Misérables* for you."

As he emerged from behind the *fusuma*, he had a book in his right hand. It was one of the volumes of the *Collected Works of World Literature* published by Shinchōsha, and on its cover was a color image of a man wearing something like an alpine hat. The drawing of the man, who was carrying something that looked like a big gunnysack on his back, was so large it took up the entire cover of the book. His expression was unclear, hidden by the shadow from the hat, but the darkness inside him oozed from every pore. Grave and overbearing, he seemed ready to step right off the cover. The sound of the words *Les Misérables* also terrified me. When my uncle said them, he broke the words into three incomprehensible units of sound—*Remi, zera, buru*—that sounded like a curse filled with frightening power. I would usually stop my peevish fretting when I heard those words and was shown that petrifying picture.

If I still would not stop, Uncle Ken'ichi would grab my thin wrist and pull me into the darkness of the back room. He would close the *fusuma* behind him, making a sharp slap as it shut. Next, he would push me down between his feet. Next, he would take his judo belt from the nail on the wall or the belt from his uniform. He would then beat me without voicing a single word.

I would also stay quiet. The limply dangling judo belt became firm and tense with my uncle's power, and as I felt it strike the back of my neck, I would say over and over to myself, "He and I are the only ones here." Even though we were victim and assailant, those frightening few moments full of tension were something shared by only the two of us—moments of intoxication accompanied by a certain sort of dizziness. This was how I came to learn about the intimate relationship between aggressor and victim. As I think about it now, I wonder if Uncle Ken'ichi's whippings weren't an outlet for complicated, gloomy feelings about the nation and family system that had stolen all the joy of adolescence from him—systems that sent him off to war and that he was utterly powerless to resist.

Uncle Ken'ichi spent his free time reading and practicing his writing in his dark room. He only came out for dinner, and even then he hardly said a thing. When my grandparents asked him a question, he would think but answer with a simple "Uh-huh" or "Nuh-uh," still carrying the food to his mouth. When dinner was over, he would retreat again to the back room where he would stay awake for a little while longer, not making a sound. I was still awake, too. If Mother was there, then I would be in her futon. If she was not, I would snuggle into Grandmother's covers. For a while, the light in his room would continue to shine through the cracks in the *fusuma*. Finally, I would hear the quiet sound of a switch being flipped, and the light would go out. When he went to sleep, he did not snore or even breathe loudly.

I do not think that I am wrong in saying the one comfort Uncle Ken'ichi had in life was my mother. He was only seven when she came to the house as a seventeen-year-old bride. Grandmother was nearly fifty when he was born, and since she never really treated him like a mother would, I suspect he felt a certain motherly attraction to his sister-in-law, who was ten years his senior. After Grandmother got in the bath, my seven-year-old uncle would pull the lined kimono she had set aside over his head and sit absentmindedly by the dining table watching Mother. She remembered this well and told me about it later.

He was thirteen when my father died. My father was fifteen years older than he was. It only makes sense that after his brother passed away, Uncle Ken'ichi's motherly feelings to his sister-in-law gradually grew in new directions. Even my grandparents began to hope Uncle Ken'ichi and Mother would marry. This was not just out of consideration for his feelings toward Mother. Farming families have a tradition of practicality: when a first-born son dies, it only makes sense to them that his widow would marry the next-born son and he would raise the first-born's children as his own.

My grandparents' hope only fanned the flames of Uncle Ken'ichi's feelings for Mother. In those days, a young man who saw it as his ethical duty to obey his parents would naturally feel emboldened if his parents supported his feelings in any way. Still calling her "Nee-san, Nee-san," he began to invite her out, to places like the cinema and the festival at Taga Shrine.

When Mother and Grandmother quarreled, as they often did, Mother gladly drew Uncle Ken'ichi into it. He always supported her side, saying, "Now, Mother, aren't you wrong?" When it came to the question of marrying him, however, my mother was firmly against it. My uncle, who was a man of very few words, had never courted her directly, and my grandparents had never put a formal proposal before her. Still, she was in a state of readiness, prepared to refuse if they stopped beating around the bush and broached the subject.

In those days, fidelity to one's deceased partner was considered a virtue. Mother remained true to the memory of her husband, at least as far as everyone else could tell. The memory of the happy six years she had spent with my father were likely still fresh in her mind, but perhaps that was not the only thing holding her back. By refusing Ken'ichi, Mother was also refuting the old convention of passing the eldest son's wife to the next-born son. Her refusal might have also had to do with the whiff of Grandmother that seemed to cling to Uncle Ken'ichi—something best symbolized by the story of my young uncle draped in Grandmother's kimono.

Once, Uncle Ken'ichi came down with a case of empyema and had to undergo a serious operation at the local hospital. I remember going to see him afterward. He was recuperating in bed on the second story of a wooden, western-style building. Here and there, the pale blue-green paint had peeled off the walls. His head was resting on an ice-pillow wrapped in a towel, and the whole surface of his face was painfully swollen from his upper lip to both cheeks. A pack of ice also hung from the ceiling and rested on his nose.

Mother worked hard to give him the most attentive care possible. She changed his ice, spoon-fed him rice gruel cooked with egg yolks, and on and on. Because they were now patient and caregiver, Mother was free to set aside her refusal of convention and her antipathy to whatever trace of Grandmother might still cling to him. Her diligence showed how much she enjoyed those leisurely stretches of time caring for him.

"Ken-chan, is there anything else you'd like me to do for you?"

Uncle Ken'ichi still could not speak, and so he responded to her questions by moving his eyes. She asked more questions than necessary, and these came out in a fawning tone as if she were his older sister. I remember her commonplace questions and his responses with his eyes revealed signs of a love they had tried to suppress but could not hold back completely. I also remember it was strangely uncomfortable for me to be there with them.

It would not have been the least bit hard to understand if Mother and Uncle Ken'ichi had become lovers. Even though she was almost thirty, Mother looked like a young maiden with her hair drawn back in a bun and her refusal to wear the white makeup of a middle-aged woman. She and my uncle, who looked so neat with his closely cropped and nicely scented hair, would have made a handsome couple.

3

A draft notice, printed on the infamous red paper that indicated deployment, arrived for Uncle Ken'ichi. I have three memories of his being sent off to war.

The first memory dates from the day before his deployment. Mother and Uncle Ken'ichi went to the photography studio in town in order to have a commemorative picture taken together. By this point, he had quit his job at the railroad and completed his preparations to go. All he had left was a single day, and it was as precious as a jewel. No doubt he wanted to spend some of his final hours with Mother; that way, he could carry some pleasant memories along with him to the front.

It was not necessarily easy to do something memorable, however. Things were rough for everyone in those days; plus there were few places two adults might go in a country coal-mining town to do something they would be sure to remember. In the end, he came up with the idea of having a photo taken together. When Mother heard his suggestion, she had no reason to refuse. If anything, she was probably secretly grateful that he had come up with an idea she would have no reason to rebuff.

Dressed in his finest clothes, a slate-colored sweater with neatly pressed trousers, Uncle Ken'ichi was the first to leave the house. A little later, Mother hurriedly rushed outside. She was also wearing a slate-colored sweater and a dark gray skirt.

"Mommy, where are you going?"

She did not answer me and hurried away. She walked by the row house where the Kawaharas and the Kanekos lived, no doubt trying to catch up with my uncle somewhere between the company housing and the Hashimotos' house. The path went around the pond and appeared again on the other side of the Hashimotos'. For a while I watched her and Uncle Ken'ichi hurrying along like two spring butterflies dancing back and forth in tangled patterns in the air. I watched them for a few moments until they disappeared into the shadow cast by the bank of a hill. Somehow, I doubt I cried as I watched them go.

All I remember about the day Uncle Ken'ichi left was how sultry it was there on the platform of Nōgata Station. With the scent of the crowds gathered there, it was stuffy and unpleasant. Someone had hung up a flag of the Rising Sun. People had written their best wishes for him in black ink on the white part of the flag around the red orb in the center. He was dressed in the uniform of a military recruit, and his work colleagues were throwing him into the air over and over again.

I stood near my grandparents holding Mother's hand. She was dressed in a kimono covered with a pattern of arrow feathers. I watched him and the others absentmindedly. The only time I indicated my pride at being connected to the guest of honor was when someone walking along the platform stopped as if in surprise. First I would look at Uncle Ken'ichi, who was being tossed into the air, then look back suggestively at the bystander to indicate my connection with him.

The time I remember best of all was when we sent off Uncle Ken'ichi from Moji. He was departing for Niigata, where he would get on the airplane that would carry him to the battlefield. We took the Chikuhō line from Nōgata, transferred at Orio, and took the Kagoshima main line to Moji, the station where the line originated. All in all, it took two and a half hours to get there, so in order to see him off at nine-thirty in the morning, we had to leave Nōgata at a little after five o'clock.

That was the first time in my life anyone ever woke me up while it was still dark. Mother and Grandmother probably tried to soothe and humor me the whole way to the station. I still remember with crystal clarity rubbing my sleepy eyes and looking across the platform to see the sun rise in the sky over Mount Mitachi. The black, nighttime sky gave a strong convulsion; then the expanse of the darkness quickly became lighter as if a membrane had been peeled from its surface. There was a second convulsion. The sky grew lighter still. Once again, a third convulsion and more light. In this way, the dawn slowly broke across the sky. That was how my first dawn looked to me.

We got off the train at Moji. There were five of us trailing along: my grandparents, Mother and I, and a young relative named Fukie, who had been briefly discussed as a possible marriage prospect for Uncle Ken'ichi. As we walked, we kept asking the locals how to get to the private house where he was staying. The house was in a residential area named Kogane-machi. After a while, he came out with some of his colleagues. He was wearing a military uniform and rucksack, and at his side were his bayonet and canteen, which hung at a diagonal from his waist.

When Uncle Ken'ichi saw us, he raised his right hand to his military cap and saluted. I suspect this salute was directed more at Mother than anyone else. From there, we walked with him to the gathering place in front of the station where the military vehicles were waiting. We talked the whole way, but what was there really to talk about? I suppose that in a way there was too much to talk about, but we did not broach the important subjects. Instead, we just stuck to unimportant exchanges, such as "Did you sleep all right?" and "Now, be careful." I was shocked by the number of soldiers who appeared one after another from both sides of the road. The soldiers and their families filled the road to the station almost to the point of overflowing.

There was a big crowd in front of the station. They did not appear to be organized at first, but gradually they sorted themselves out. The crowd divided into two distinct groups—the military men and their families—then the military men started to congregate by platoon.

Uncle Ken'ichi said to his parents, "Stay well." To Fukie, he just nodded. Next, he bent down and took my hand between his. "Listen to what your mommy tells you," he said. As he held my hand between his, Mother pulled at my other hand. I wonder if the masculine warmth of Uncle Ken'ichi's large hand didn't travel through my small body to reach her as well. Last of all, he turned to Mother and said, "*Nee-san*, you take care of yourself, too." Mother nodded over and over again as if she did not know what to say. He saluted us again and, grinning so that we could see his big white teeth, he turned around and joined the soldiers. He buried himself in the long line, which meandered along like a great serpent. Slowly the line disappeared into the station.

The next day, Uncle Ken'ichi was transformed into the drops of moisture on the inside of a lidded bowl. Each day, Grandmother would set an extra meal at the table for him as a way of hoping for his safe return.

She would place a lid over his food, and by the end of the meal she would look to see whether or not moisture had condensed inside. She believed this method of fortune telling would help her know his fate.

After we received word he had left for Burma, she started using a button to tell his fortune. She would pass a string through a button and dangle it over his picture. From the swaying of the string, she could tell whether he was safe or not. Apparently, someone in the building and repairs facility taught her this far-fetched method of divination.

One night about a year later, Mother saw Uncle Ken'ichi in a dream. He was wearing his army cap and saluting as on the day of his send-off. He looked as though he wanted to say something, but as after his surgery, he was only able to smile with his eyes. Just as she was starting to call out to him, she woke up.

The next day, she set out to buy some things in town. She had gone no farther than the corner of the Kanekos' house when she came back, her face completely changed. She cried out to Grandmother, "Ken-chan is dead!" For some reason, Grandmother happened to be in the house that day. Although my mother and her mother-in-law were not always on the very best of terms, that day they clasped one another's hands and wept. The reconciliation brought about by the death of their shared loved one continued for some time.

Eventually the box containing Uncle Ken'ichi's ashes arrived. The box was made of unfinished wood wrapped in bleached cotton cloth, and although his remains were supposed to be in it, the box was as light as air. Not believing it to be genuine, Mother and Grandmother opened it together. The army told us he had died of sickness on the battlefield, but inside there was nothing but two or three strands of hair.

Grandmother simply could not bring herself to give up on her only remaining son. One day, she took me to town to visit the home of one of his former colleagues who had been assigned to a neighboring platoon. The house was behind an alley off of one of the more bustling streets, and we opened the latticed door and went inside. There, we found a dark concrete floor flanked on two sides by sitting rooms. The concrete floor led into a courtyard and on the other side of that was another door. When we opened that door, we saw a sixty-year-old woman using the light from the *shōji* to pick up some gauze bandages spread out in an enamel sink. She was using a pair of disposable, wooden chopsticks to lift them to her eyes. I remember the swollen red flesh of her eyes, and the thought of the disagreeably warm touch of the gauze soaked in boric acid was enough to send shivers up my spine.

Grandmother was probably hoping the old lady had received some letters from her son, and since he and Uncle Ken'ichi were once colleagues and were in neighboring platoons, perhaps one of the letters might have mentioned him. The old lady, however, did not have any news about her own son, much less Uncle Ken'ichi. I later heard from Grandmother that the old lady had also received word of the death of her son.

The temporary reconciliation between Mother and Grandmother did not last terribly long. That is only natural. Both of them had completely different feelings for him, so those came to bear on the way that they thought about his death.

One quiet afternoon, I was seated on the veranda in the sun looking at a picture book. The book was about soldiers, and on the last page one of the soldiers who was on the verge of death shouted, "His Majesty, Banzai!" I asked Mother, who was doing some mending nearby, "When soldiers die, do they really shout that?"

"No, what they really shout is, 'Mother . . .' But . . ." Mother paused, stopped her mending, and stuck the needle in her hair. I watched her as she hesitated. "But I doubt Ken-chan said 'Mother' at the end." What did she mean by that? Could Mother have hoped that instead he called out "Nee-san" as he lay dying?

After that, she hardly spoke about my Uncle Ken'ichi. Her silence was probably partly out of consideration for the man who had passed away. In his eyes, my mother had been a virginal maiden; she had been like the sacred mother to him. In her eyes, Uncle Ken'ichi had been holy—a chaste innocent until the very moment of his death.

Because Mother did not talk about him, his memory became an increasingly abstract principle; he became the ideal embodiment of manhood. She reinforced that idea when sometimes in an unguarded moment, Mother would slip and say, "You aren't Uncle Ken-chan's little boy . . ." No,

I was not like him. In my eyes, Uncle Ken'ichi was a divine incarnation of masculine virtue who had come from the Great Beyond and had returned there far too swiftly.

4

When Mother and I moved to Moji soon after I entered school, we found ourselves right in the middle of the war, since the big industrial zone that stretched across northern Kyūshū was a major bombing target for the American air force. We lived a little ways from the port district of Moji in the direction of Kokura. Our house was in a dusty neighborhood along one of the old highways. I soon made several friends. Tamo-chan from the Shiokawa family was small in stature and quick witted. Mit-chan from the Unno family had a big head and big eyes. He would also burst into tears at the drop of a hat, so because of that someone had nicknamed him Onion. There were others, too: Yoshiaki-chan from the Teraura family, Onion's brother Ei-san, and Ei-san's classmate Ishida.

Soaring into the air about two blocks away from our new home was a big, redbrick beer factory that looked like a European castle. Behind it was a rocky ledge, and right below that the sea. When the tide went out, it would leave behind an exposed sandy area right below the ledge. As little boys, we would take off all our clothes there and play around buck naked.

The straits of Shimonoseki stretched before the sandy area like a large river. Enemy planes had dropped a seemingly infinite number of underwater mines there. We would be fooling around at the water's edge, pushing our bodies against the waves when suddenly we would hear a deafening roar. We would look in the direction of the deep water and see a transport vessel that had been ripped in two. This happened once or twice a week. As we watched this vision of death unfolding nearby, we would shade our eyes as if trying to catch a glimpse of something dazzling. The bigger boys would swim toward the scene of death to catch some of the black porgies and young sea bass that the shock of the explosion had sent floating to the surface.

We were living in the middle of a peculiar festival known as war. For us, the explosions of the underwater mines were the fireworks set off in the middle of the festival. When we heard their deafening report, our hearts would begin to pound, and if we were at home, we would run to the seashore at full throttle. The adults were no different. After the explosions, the shore would become full of people who had come to gawk at the strange sight of the fires out at sea. It would sometimes become so crowded that from overhead the seashore would look black from the dark-haired heads of the onlookers. Clearly, the adults were hoping for the fireworks to be as big as possible. If they learned a boat did not suffer much damage, the disappointment in their eyes was obvious, but whenever it came time to protect ourselves from air raids or to knock down the houses of those who had been evacuated, those same adults put on serious expressions that showed they were busily defending the home front.

Once when we were playing at the seashore, one of the mines exploded, and then right away the warning sirens began to go off. All of us scurried up the rock ledge, ran down the road by the sea, and scattered in the directions of our individual homes. It was only after I reached home that I realized I had left my shorts wedged between the rocks below the ledge. If Mother came home, she would no doubt scold me for forgetting them. I flew out of the house, still buck naked. I ran down the street, feeling the midsummer sunburn on the back of my neck. There was not a single soul in the road. I held my breath as I ran. I figured that if I did not breathe, I was just like a dead person and the enemy planes would not be able to find me.

I scampered down the rock ledge. When I located the balled-up shorts stuck between the rocks, all of the tension and strain within me melted, and I simply stood there. Right in front of me was the magnificently indifferent sea, resplendent with the brightness of the midsummer sun. The sea, filled with brightness since ancient times, had usually worked to insulate Japan from war in the past. When I looked out to sea now, however, I saw a boat broken in two by an explosion. The bow had already sunk, and the stern, which was on fire, was on the verge of disappearing under the waves. Apart from the small reverberation of the waves coming into shore, there was no sound. Here, at least, war was both disturbingly quiet and disturbingly bright.

Going from my house in the opposite direction from the beer

factory, there was a place called Dairi Wharf. The Greater Japan Sugar Factory located nearby would fill gunnysacks with sugar and pile them there to send to the soldiers in the South Pacific. On our way to and from school, we children would open holes in the sacks with knives and use canvas sacks to catch the white sugar that spilled out. Holding our school slippers under our arms, we would wet our fingers with saliva and stick them into the sacks, licking the sugar that clung to our fingertips, as we took a different route to school than usual to avoid being seen.

The sirens and air-raid warnings sounded an inordinate number of times, even at night. My eyes were still half-shut with sleep when Mother put on my air-raid hood, cotton army-issued gloves, and *tabi*, then rushed me to the air-raid shelter by the seashore. Even though Moji was bombed heavily, the air raids were concentrated on the main port almost two miles east of us. The bombs also fell across the strait on Shimonoseki and on the steel-producing town of Yahata, which wrapped around the straits and was several miles to our west.

I still vividly remember the sight of Shimonoseki burning as I ran with Mother to the air-raid shelter. The town of Shimonoseki is said to have one of the longest shorelines in Japan, stretching from Hikoshima all the way to Hinoyama in the northeast. All along that shoreline is the town, built on a connected string of low hills. For a moment, there were several fires burning separately, but before I knew it they spread to the sides, forming walls of conflagration. Across the night-black water, I watched the flames rise quickly where the shadows of the hills and the sea came together. They spread in every direction. The fires on the opposite shore were strangely beautiful. It was exactly like watching the flames of hell through a telescope.

The attacks of the B-29 squadrons had become a daily occurrence. Whether we went to school or not, the warning sirens would chase us back, and as we scattered to return to our individual houses, the air-raid siren would go off, chasing us to the shelters.

Sometimes the monsters that flew through the skies would be knocked to earth. One particularly quick boy managed to run to the site where a plane had fallen, and there he found a fragment of bulletproof glass. In class, he pulled it from his pants pocket and ground it into the top of his desk. He showed us that if we put our noses to it, it gave off a mysteriously sweet and pleasant smell. "Aroma glass" became one of our most prized treasures, and any child who managed to get some earned the respect and envy of all the others.

I do not remember when, but an enemy plane once happened to fall in the forested hills of Nagaguro there in Moji. I ran to the site, trailing behind my friends Tamo-chan and Onion. The plane had fallen in an open area of miscanthus grass, which was surrounded by the woods that spread over the base of the small Mount Yahazu. The silver duralumin body of the plane had been blown to smithereens, so it was difficult to ascertain the original shape of the plane. The surrounding woods were cordoned off by nets, and no one was allowed to enter. Stern-faced adults wearing armbands walked about inspecting the fragments, recording notes in their notebooks, and talking in hushed voices. We went home empty-handed in the end. I still remember, however, the mercilessly burned spots here and there in the tall grass.

As the war grew more intense, the morning assemblies and the teachers' lectures grew increasingly nationalistic. All of the students in the school were made to run from school to Tonoue Shrine and back again every morning—about one and a quarter miles round trip. When we got back to class, we were made to repeat, "We will serve our emperor with loyalty, and our parents with filial piety." Our drawings were of enemy planes burning and falling from the sky, and our compositions ended, "I will grow up soon, become a strong soldier, and beat the hateful Americans and British."

When school ended, however, things would change. We went to the second stories of the houses along the seashore. These were all vacant because of the evacuations. There, we would sing a song to the tune of "The Old Man Who Made the Cherry Trees Bloom." The words, however, were not the traditional lyrics:

> The priest at Tonoue Shrine
> Carries the portable shrine and sings
> In this war
> Japan will lose, Japan will lose

On the day when the war did finally end, I was in a narrow alley by Tamo-chan's house flying paper airplanes. He ran up to me and said, "Mut-chan, the war's over." When I heard this, perhaps I thought about the false pronouncement that I had heard on Mother's back.

I will never forget that day, August 15, and how the bright blue of the sea slid into the narrow alley. Tamo-chan continued, "We don't have to go to school anymore!" I felt like dancing. No more war. No more school. We were as free as the ancient primitive people who had neither of those things. We were as free as birds.

But at the end of August, a new semester started, just as before.

Heaven and Hell

1

The following fragment probably comes from the very first song I learned as a little boy:

> A fire lights on the head of the *ketsuguro*
> Splash—it sticks its head in the water and puts it out

A *ketsuguro* is what we would call a grebe in our dialect. It is a kind of waterbird known elsewhere in Japan as *kaitsuburi*. In our dialect, the word *kaitsuburi* is pronounced *keetsuburi*, and people misunderstood this as meaning *ketsu-buri*, which means "ass-shaking." Since the body of the bird was dark all over, this word was further transformed into *ketsu-guro*, meaning "dark assed." These dark, little waterbirds would duck their heads underwater, making a movement that looked just like they were trying to put out a fire on top of their head. That is the behavior the song is describing.

When I was a little boy, I whispered these two lines to myself like some sort of incantation. I was outside, and it was raining. When the rainy season came, I would always stand outside in the mud where the little frogs would hop about, and I would grow wet as the fine raindrops fell on me. From Grandmother's front yard, I would stare with fascination as the *ketsuguro* dove soundlessly into the heavy water of the pond, swollen from the rain.

Who was it who taught me this song? Perhaps it was Grandmother, or perhaps one of the other children in the neighborhood. When I remember this song, however, there is no one around me. I am always alone. What's more, I am always whispering this song to myself, scarcely speaking the words aloud. Perhaps heaven had felt sorry for me, a small child left alone by both his mother and grandmother, and had given me this song as a broken toy to comfort me.

Grandmother was probably the one who taught me the next song I remember:

One *kejo*, two *kejo*
Three *kejo*, four *kejo*
At the base of Shikoma, the bird who eats nothing
In the forests of Harima, in all directions
The *machocho* flowers of the *dedenden* trains
Have they bloomed, haven't they bloomed? Take a guess. . . .

The word *kejo* is probably a counter for places. I am not sure. When Grandmother said "one *kejo*," she took her large hand, which was as rough as a piece of wood, curled her fingers so that her hand became one big tube, and put it on the *tatami*. When she said, "two *kejo*," I made my small hand into a tube and placed it on top of hers. Then, when she said, "three *kejo*," she made her other hand into a tube and added it to the pile, and then at "four *kejo*," I added my other hand. As the song continued, whoever had their hand at the bottom pulled it out and put it on top of the stack. At the end, she would say, "Have they bloomed, haven't they bloomed? Take a guess," and then repeat the line a second time. When I would finally tell her they had bloomed, her hands transformed from tubes into a swarm of bees. She would say, "The bees are stinging, the bees are stinging," and the fingers would begin to attack the soft flesh of my arms, neck, and legs.

I knew that saying the flowers had bloomed would start the attack from Grandmother's fingers, but I never told her, "No, they haven't bloomed." That was because the swarm of bees unleashed by Grandmother's hands had a mysterious kindness about them, and the "stingers" that poked my flesh would caress instead of pierce. In any case, the bee attacks that sprung from Grandmother's fingers only came when we were relaxing after dinner, and they only lasted a moment or two. Most of the rest of the time, I was alone, with nothing else to do except stare amazed at the *ketsuguro* on the pond.

Those were the days when Mother was working as a maid in Nakatsu and Shimonoseki, and so each month she would send a certain portion of her paycheck to her mother-in-law as child support. Most of that money Grandmother squirreled away for herself. Meanwhile, she took me to other people in the neighborhood and left me to stay with them. She only used a small fraction of the money Mother sent to pay the neighbors who took care of me.

The first family she left me with was the Kawaharas next door. I loved Granny Kawahara's story about Ishidōmaru, but for a young boy with a restless soul that made it difficult to stay still, it was boring to spend all day quietly cooped up next to an old lady suffering from palsy.

One time I picked up an old piece of burnt charcoal and I wrote on the wall by the Kawaharas' entryway, "Kawahara Tarō is a dummy, Kawahara Kuni is a dummy" in simple, *katakana* letters. When I was staying with Mother at the Mitsubishi dormitories, one of the young employees taught me how to read and write, so by that time I was able to write *katakana*, *hiragana*, the English alphabet, and a handful of *kanji* characters. I had expected the Kawaharas would praise me, saying, "He's so little, but he can write so well," but instead I was chastised sternly. Granny Kawahara was upset but would have gotten over it; however, her husband refused to keep me after that.

I went to stay with the Kanekos, who lived next door to the Kawaharas. The husband of the Kaneko household, Uncle Kinshirō, was famous for his friendly disposition. When people would come over, he would sit properly with his legs folded under his thighs, and his haunches resting on his feet. He would always put his hands on his round knees, and as his visitors regaled him with their opinions he would nod after each sentence and say over and over, "Indeed, you are quite right."

Behind Kinshirō's back, Grandmother and the others would call him "West, Face West." For instance, they would say about his wife, "Kimi-chan has been facing west with West, Face West for three years now." I remember that once when I was with Grandmother in the fields, she dug out a small, reddish-brown grub from the dirt and showed it to me, saying, "Look, it's Kinshirō-san!" The kind of grub she was holding was popularly known as a West, Face West. The reason was that people believed if you would say, "West, Face West!" to it, its tail would wriggle and the grub would start pointing to the west, nodding like Kinshirō.

Unlike him, his wife, Kimi-chan, whom I called "Auntie," had a huge appetite. In fact, when Mother asked her to come out and help harvest the barley, she would prepare enough food for two people just for her own consumption. To top it off, she would pull toward her the communal tub of rice that everyone was supposed to share, and she would help herself to the contents. Unfortunately, however, there were many children in her family, and she was forced to live in poverty, unable even to have three square meals per day. As a result, when Grandmother took advantage of her and asked her to take care of me, she took me in without a second word.

She had five or six children, all born right after one another with hardly any space in between. After they went to school in the morning, Auntie and I were the only ones left at home. She would play with me for a little bit, but she was lazy and liked to gossip, so it would not be long before she would go out, wanting to shoot the breeze. When she left, she would tie me to the shiny, black pillar in front of the sooty stove in their kitchen. Auntie Kaneko would inevitably forget to close the *fusuma*, and she would go away, leaving the sliding doors slovenly half open. Peering between them, I could see across the open veranda to the deep waters of the pond where the *ketsuguro* were diving over and over into the water.

According to Grandmother, the place where Auntie went most often to idle away her time was the *udon* shop on the other side of the lake, just in front of the Mitsubishi Mining Company. As she stood there on the dirt floor of the restaurant and talked, she would help by passing out bowls of *udon* noodles, and if there was a noodle or two still left in a bowl after a customer finished, she would stand by the sink and slurp them down.

I happen to remember a fragment of a short song about the *udon* shop that goes, "The cauldron in the *udon* shop has nothing but hot water...." The final words *yuu bakkai*, which mean "nothing but hot water" in Kyūshū dialect, are pronounced the same as an expression that means "nothing but talk." In other words, the song has a double meaning: it was a witticism used to make fun of people who talk all the time but do very little work. Still, to me the song called up the image of a large black cauldron sitting atop a pile of flaming charcoal briquettes and full of boiling water. The hot water inside the cauldron made me think of being boiled inside, so it was the first image of hell to enter my young imagination.

According to Mother and Grandmother, the middle-aged cook who worked in the *udon* shop had a cruel streak. Before killing a chicken to use for broth, she would pluck out its feathers, leaving it with bright red skin. Then she let it waddle around the dirt floor of the kitchen as she took hot water in her ladle and poured it directly onto the poor bird. The chicken would cry out in agony and flap its featherless, unsightly wings, which were nothing but raw flesh. Meanwhile, the lady from the *udon* shop would dance around, tickled by the bird's suffering.

One day when she was out buying some more chickens for the shop, she ignored a stoplight by the railroad tracks and tried to cross. A train was coming from the right, belching smoke as it approached. The crossing guard shouted, "Hey, lady, watch out! You'll get run over!" but she did not hear. After the train rushed by, he saw that one of her feet had been severed, and she was trying to drag herself along, her *furoshiki* slung over her shoulder. Right then, however, another train came along, this time from the left. That train cut off her other foot. She was trying to cross, pulling herself along with nothing but her hands, when next a cargo train came along. They say that her corpse was completely dismembered, and the pieces of her body were scattered over twelve square yards.

"The chickens were taking their revenge"—this story was one that the local people repeated for quite some time after the accident. They always seemed to take pleasure in it.

After the cook in the *udon* shop died, Auntie had no place left to go. Before long, the whole Kaneko family moved into town, and Grandmother was left to find another home in which to leave me.

2

Despite the neglectful way Auntie treated me, I am grateful to her children, who were several years older than I. When they returned from school, they taught me the following song:

> Will this make a bean-filled bun?
> Will this make a baby chick?
> *Oppan-pan*

This song was a sort of incantation I would chant when playing in the mud. I would pack mud into a chipped sake cup that I had found in the trash or a broken ladle made out of a shell; then I would turn it upside down and pull away the vessel as I sang this song. The lump of mud that was left behind on the roof tile or fragment of board was always in the shape of a bean-filled bun. It never turned out to be a warm creature with soft golden feathers, but each time I picked up the vessel and emptied its contents, my heart would flutter with excitement, as if a miracle might transpire and I might actually find a golden bird underneath. Later on, I would greatly benefit from the assistance of this incantation. It might be a bit of an exaggeration to say this, but it was thanks to the spiritual power of this spell that I was able to escape several months of hell.

After the Kanekos moved away, it was time for someone else to take care of me, and I was left at the home of a worker in town. I say that it was "in town," but it was really a single building along a concrete wall in back of a factory on the edge of town. It faced north and therefore got little sunlight, so there was a pale electric light on inside even during the daytime.

The main inhabitant of the house was an old woman of around sixty or so. She did not have any children of her own, so she had adopted a man and his wife into her family. All in all, there were three people in the family, but they were unrelated by blood. In addition, they were all afflicted with a mild case of tuberculosis, so what familial relations they had were spoiled by poverty and disease. When the three of them sat down to dinner together, the handful of words that passed between them hardly amounted to a real conversation. Even so, when the lady would dish up the rice—which actually consisted of a larger portion of barley than rice—she would try talking to the others, but the young couple would just sit there, silent as a rock, without saying a thing.

Early in the morning, when it was still slightly dark outside, the young husband, who was emaciated and pale, would tie a bundle containing a packed lunch to his back, then set out to work. When the sun came out, the old lady would also go work as a helper in someone's house. Back at the house, the young daughter-in-law, who had the unhealthy chubbiness that marks the early stages of tuberculosis, sat with her legs flopped to the side as she sewed bits of silk cloth to earn a few extra yen.

Once, this chubby, sickly ghost who spent her days sitting in the poverty-stricken darkness next to the torn *shōji*, became pregnant. She was irritable from sunup to sundown, and every time she would catch a glimpse of me, she would immediately pull out a ruler two *shaku* long and strike me. In order to avoid this great mass of unhappiness masquerading as a young woman, I would play outside all day in the dust-covered street. The road, which was cut off from the rest of the world on both sides by the factory walls, was unpaved, and on days when the sun was out the dirt would grow as dry as a bone. I would urinate on the dry dirt, gather up the soft mud I had created, and then pack it into a teacup. As I turned it over, I would sing,

> Will this make a bean-filled bun?
> Will this make a baby chick?
> *Oppan-pan*

I sang this over and over, dreaming that a miracle would take place.

Middle school students who had been mobilized by the armed forces would also walk down the street. These young men, living in the dark season of war, would walk past, towels hanging from the back of their pants like tough guys. As they walked by, they would make fun of me, the young boy who picked up urine-soaked mud and rolled it into little balls like rice dumplings. I can still remember the whiteness of their teeth, polished clean with the ashes from their fireplaces.

When lunchtime rolled around, the old woman came home. She was the only one who was nice to me, so I would stay beside her as I finished lunch. After she cleaned up the mess from lunch and left again, I would hurriedly rush outside again.

There were times when Grandfather would stop in to see his grandson on his way home from Mitachiyama. I still remember how one time my little legs were straddling the big, dark hole in the toilet when I suddenly heard Grandfather's voice: "Has Mutsuo been doing okay?"

In a voice that was entirely different from when she spoke to me, the daughter-in-law responded kindly, "Why, yes, he's as fit as a fiddle." She then turned in the direction of the bathroom and called out, "Mut-chan, it's your Grandpa!"

I opened the bathroom door with a clatter and flew toward him. Grandfather, who was still standing in the entrance with its dirt floor, went to hug me, then asked the daughter-in-law, "Mind if I borrow Mutsuo for a little bit?"

"No, go right ahead. Take your time."

Grandfather was wearing leggings over his *jikatabi*. I followed him, keeping a certain distance between us. He asked me in great detail about how I was doing, but I only responded by nodding or shaking my head. To read my response, he had to look over his shoulder and take in my expression. He was completely bewildered by my loss of speech in the course of only a single month.

We left the bustling, main road, crossed an overpass that took us over the train tracks, and arrived at Taga Shrine. That evening, the shrine was hosting a night festival, so the grounds inside the shrine walls were filled with vendor stands and tents that would be used for shows. The whole place hustled and bustled with a pleasant energy. Grandfather called me off the path to a slightly more secluded spot between the evergreen bushes, then put in my hand some small coins wrapped in a piece of paper. Grandfather must have known that money was of no use for a child like me. After all, I lived behind a factory in a street without any shops and spent my entire day playing in the mud. Yet even so, Grandfather probably felt he could not leave me empty-handed.

Just as I had suspected, the gift Grandfather had given me was snatched away as soon as I got back. The daughter-in-law did not even bother to stand up as she took it away and shooed me back outside. I did not protest as I went back outside, squatted in the dirt road in front of the house, and began to play with the dirt, hoping that a miracle might occur.

It was there, while living in that dark and depressing house behind the factory, that I first experienced the sensation of being truly alone. I had also been lonely with the Kanekos since there was no one to talk to, but when night fell, it was close enough to Grandmother's house that they would send me home for the night. Once back at Grandmother's, I would let forth a torrent of words as if the dam holding them back had suddenly let go.

This time was different, however. The daughter-in-law's beady little eyes would glint at me even when I tried to talk to the old lady. As a result, I grew so silent that I would only nod or shake my head, even when they asked me a question. In fact, when I played alone outside in the mud in the afternoons, I felt that it was wrong even to whisper my special incantation to myself. I resigned myself to repeating it in my head instead.

I am not sure exactly why, but for some reason I was sent back to Grandmother's house. This time, there was someone to play with me, even though I had become a strange, withdrawn little boy during the time I was away. My playmate was Haa-chan, the youngest girl in the Kubo family, our neighbors to the right. She was fifteen years old and had bright red cheeks. She was so tall that the regular kimonos would not fit, so underneath her yellowed apron, she wore a large-sized, lined *kasuri* kimono.

Her father, whom we knew as Little Uncle, was a real man about town but did not hold down a job. With his curly hair and eyes that opened really wide, he reminded me of the "octopus priest"—one of the main figures we children would draw so often in our graffiti. As we sang the following song, we would draw crude pictures of an octopus with a big, round bald head like that of a priest:

Three chopsticks it had
Three rice balls it had
The rain fell in heavy drops

The snow fell in heavy flakes
Oh, what a frightening octopus priest!

With each line of the song we would draw another part of the octopus.
While singing the first line, we would draw three parallel, horizontal lines
for its forehead. With the second, we would draw three circles: two for the
eyes and one for a mouth. With the third, we would draw several vertical
lines for its legs. With the fourth, we would draw lots of little dots representing the suction cups on its legs, and with the fifth and final line, we
would draw a big round circle around the face to complete the body. By the
time we drew the last line, we had completed the drawing. But I digress.
Little Uncle was a skinny man with a bony and furrowed back with lines as
a round, ribbed fan. Still, when he caught a carp and slung it over his back,
he would cut a grand figure like Kintarō in the children's tale.

As a side note, it was an octopus that was responsible for the death
of Little Uncle's wife. She was eating one when it got stuck in her throat
and killed her. Little Uncle never took a second wife, and instead he raised
his three daughters all by himself.

According to Grandmother, there was a time when a young man
who lived a rather fast and loose life came and stayed for a while in a little
cottage on the Kubos' property. One day, when Little Uncle was gone,
the man gathered his three daughters together and started behaving in
an inappropriate way with them, coming on to them one after the other.
One might have understood if he had molested just the oldest daughter,
but the middle daughter was twelve, and the youngest one, Haa-chan, was
only seven. To make matters worse, the man had syphilis. Before long,
the daughters were covered with scabs, like an old boat encrusted with
barnacles, and for some time they had to walk with their legs spread apart
like crabs.

Little Uncle sold his daughters one by one into houses of prostitution. Perhaps the symptoms of their illnesses subsided on their own, or
perhaps their illness was treated after one of the periodic health inspec-
tions that prostitutes were forced to undergo. Haa-chan was the only one
who was spared this fate. Her body was too big, and she was not especially

gifted in terms of mental capacity, so she was left to live at home and watch over the place.

There were times Haa-chan and I would spread a mat on the floor in front of the Kubos' place, and we would play house. I remember one time she took a male flower and a female flower from a squash plant, tore off the petals, and rubbed the exposed stamens and pistils against one another. Her voice suddenly grew quiet, and her small eyes sparkled strangely as she said, "Look, they're having sex."

When I was out in the sunshine in front of the Kubos' house, there would be times when I would focus on a dark house there in the middle of the other houses. A series of misfortunes had taken place there. First, the husband spit up blood and died. Next, the wife had a stillborn baby, and she died soon afterward from complications, leaving only the old woman in the family behind. I later learned that the old woman came to Grandmother's house and asked if she could adopt me so that I could carry on her family name, but Grandmother—who was really more like a mother to me at that time—refused to give me up to that family, which was as good as ruined. Indeed, there was so little left in that household that one could hardly even say there was a family there. One day, the old woman was found keeled over, dead as a doornail on the soiled *tatami* mats inside the dark house. I learned this later, about the time I turned ten.

3

Half a year after Mother left for China, I was left at my Aunt Tsuyano's house. She lived rather far from Grandmother in Nōgata. One would take the Chikuhō line for about two hours, then change at Chikuzen Harada onto the Kagoshima main line, then travel for about two more hours before reaching the town Hainuzuka. The name of this town is written with three characters meaning "Feathered Dog Mound"—a strange name that hints at some strange composite creature like the legendary sphinx. From there, one would take a bus for more than thirty minutes to Fukushima in Yame-gun. It was there, in that little community that smelled of miso paste, that Aunt Tsuyano had married into a new family.

I say she married into a new family, but her husband Ii-shan was Grandfather's nephew, so even after she married, her name remained Takahashi Tsuyano just as before. By that time, my older sister Miyuki had been sent into this family for adoption, due largely to my aunt's insistence. When that happened, my sister's surname did not change; she went from being a Takahashi to becoming a Takahashi.

Partially because of the way the situation with my sister was handled, Aunt Tsuyano and Mother were not especially close. In Aunt Tsuyano's eyes, my mother probably looked like a loose woman, considering that after my father's death she had gone to work in Nakatsu, Shimonoseki, and then eventually China. Perhaps there was also some jealousy and resentment toward Mother since she traveled about with relative freedom. After all, Aunt Tsuyano had little choice but to spend all day long cooped up in the house.

Aunt Tsuyano seemed to have turned the resentment she felt for Mother against me. When one opened the dark latticed door to her house, there was a small area with a dirt floor. Beyond that was another small area, about the size of two *tatami* mats, and crowded behind that was a staircase. They lived in two rooms at the top of that steep staircase; one was four and a half mats wide, and the other six mats. In other words, it was an almost impossibly small place for four people to live. When I was five, I was forced to go up and down those steps over and over again to bring up water. Terrified of my chubby, pale aunt who sat next to the long hibachi on two cushions in the bigger of the two rooms, I would go into the backyard and use what little strength I had to pump the water. It was also my responsibility to bring up the old washbowl we used as a chamber pot. We usually kept it where we washed our hands, but at night we put it by our bedding. The washbowl-turned-chamber-pot was well worn, and the enamel on its surface was chipped here and there. It was also my job in the morning to go throw away the lukewarm urine that had been deposited in it.

Aunt Tsuyano told me to call her "Mother." She told me she was my real mother and tried to convince me that my mother in China was really my aunt. When she realized that I would not concede to this lie, she made me call her my "Fukushima mother" and Mother, my "China mother." She invented a song and made me sing it:

> China mother
> Raggedy mother
> That's right!

I was afraid of being hit, so I would repeat her song, blubbering and on the verge of tears. She would continue:

> Fukushima mother
> Good mother
> That's right!

As I repeated this song like some pathetic mynah bird, I would long for my raggedy mother in China. My Fukushima mother was not a good mother in any sense of the word.

The thing I remember most about her was that she was constantly punishing me. She would tell me I had taken too long in bringing up the water from the pump, and she would scold me. She would tell me I had spilled water on the staircase, and she would scold me again. At every meal, she would tell me I wasn't holding my chopsticks properly; then she would grab my ear, pull me away from my food, and throw me down onto the *tatami*. Sometimes my aunt and her husband would pour drinks for one another on their dinner trays. On those occasions, my sister Miyuki and I would be made to sit at a separate little dinner table. Those times, I would never be scolded or reproached, no matter how clumsily I held my chopsticks; however, those lucky occasions were few and far between.

Aunt Tsuyano's husband, Ii-shan, was a field officer, and he often had to travel to a place called Ōshima. Whenever he went, he would inevitably be gone for four or five days. In Ōshima there was a woman who was referred to as "Auntie in Ōshima." She was his lover, and she would take care of him when he was away. On those evenings when he did not come home, my aunt's punishments were even worse than usual.

If pain goes beyond a certain level, one no longer pays any more attention to the fine gradations of suffering. What was more frightening to me than the actual punishments Aunt Tsuyano inflicted, however, was the sight of her right in front of me as she threw herself into her punishments, thus making them even more intense. Her pale, chubby, small face never turned scarlet, not even when she was really mad. Instead, I could tell exactly how upset she was from the color of her eyes, which would grow more and more bloodshot by the second as she fixed her unflinching gaze on me. When I look back on it now, I realize that what I experienced there was a sort of hell, but it was not just hell for me: my aunt was in hell as well. I was able to sense her misery even in the midst of my fear.

One day, Aunt Tsuyano opened the pantry and found that a bean cake she had placed on a small tray had gone missing. I was summoned right away from the backyard where I was playing with my sister Miyuki, and I was given the third degree. I say "given the third degree," but in reality, she would not allow me to answer back. The only responses to her questions came in the form of her own violence. By the time I was about to stop breathing altogether from fear and pain, my aunt remembered that earlier that morning she had cut the bean cake in two and given the two halves to me and my sister to share.

"Oh, that's right. Mommy gave it to you. Oh, oh, how unfortunate. Oh well, oh well." With these words, she suddenly started stroking me.

Miyuki just looked on intently when Aunt Tsuyano was being violent with me. She had been adopted into Aunt Tsuyano's family when she was two, so she had become her daughter through and through. She probably thought of me as an interloper who had elbowed his way into the family, when before she had been able to monopolize whatever maternal affection there was to be had. I remembered that at the memorial service for my father, Grandmother had told the women at Dannaji Temple that the girl who thought she was my cousin was really my older sister. Apparently, she did not even remember that we were brother and sister. Still, I could not tell her such a thing, even if she had tried to rip it out of me.

The staircase I had to go up and down to fetch water was a frightening place for another reason as well. Aunt Tsuyano usually made my sister and me take naps after lunch. Afterward, I would be walking around the gloominess, caught somewhere between the waking world and the world of dreams, when I would fall down the stairs. This must have happened at least ten times. No doubt I had to go urinate. I was probably wobbly as I got to my feet, but there is some part of me that suspects that someone helped me fall by giving me a little push from behind. It is a frightening thought, but I am sure that at least some of those times I fell, there was a malicious hand that nudged me down the stairs.

Facing the pump in the backyard was Granny Ushijima's back-door. She was Grandmother's younger sister, and she used to be known as the "old lady from the miso shop" because she had married into a family that ran a miso shop in a neighborhood of Nōgata called Chiko. By the time that she was fifty, she had done her hair up in the *shimada* hairstyle and gotten married four times. I remember asking her once, "Granny, why did you get married four times?" She answered, "Marry four times, and you're a wife." In her sentence, thick with dialect— *yonkai iku ken, yome-san tai*—there was a pun: *yo* is the first syllable of both the words *yon* (four) and *yome-san* (wife). But the marriage to the miso maker did not last long. He died almost right away, and she married for the fifth time, becoming Granny Ushijima. Continuing her joke, she'd explain that she had become a *gome-san*—changing the first syllable of the word *yome* (wife) to *go* (five).

Her husband, Grandpa Ushijima, had immigrated to California, but when the Pacific War began, he was repatriated to Japan, thus setting foot on Japanese soil for the first time in fifty years. Every morning, when my sister and I went to tell him good morning, he would have his arthritic feet wrapped in a hand towel and propped up on a wicker chair. Meanwhile, he used a spoon to scoop a boiled egg out of the shell to eat it. Whenever he saw us, his eyes would grow narrow, and he would say, "Oh, what good children, good children . . ." Then he would have his wife give us a stick of candy.

There was a time when Granny Ushijima worked with Mother at the Mitsubishi dormitories, and partly because of that she was quite close to her and therefore very nice to me. However, there was also a certain sense in which she was even meaner to me than my aunt. When I was little, she taught me a song:

Beneath your belly button, inside the triangle
The hard lump itches, it itches
Shall I scratch it with my big cock?

I went around singing this lewd song, barely managing to pronounce the words; after all, I was little and had no idea what the words meant. This would send her and Aunt Tsuyano rolling on the *tatami* in convulsions of laughter.

Aunt Tsuyano had once been adopted by Granny Ushijima, but she had left to go home to Grandmother's house, so the relationship between the two was never the same after that. Because of all that had transpired between them, the only time there was any sort of unity between them was when they were making a fool out of me. When a guest would come to visit the two of them, their favorite thing in the world was to have me sing "Beneath Your Belly Button." In fact, the times I sang were the only times my aunt was nice to me, so that made me throw all the more energy into my performances.

The few months I spent at my aunt's house represented the worst of my era of fear. Still, there are a few beautiful memories that remain from those months and that are just as hard to forget as the unpleasant memories. There was the sight of the Yabe River, so clear and blue that it almost hurt my eyes. I had seen the river while riding sidesaddle on the back of Ii-shan's bicycle as we made our way to Hebaru, the little town from which he and Grandfather had hailed. Also, there were the fish that glittered like rainbows. I remember seeing them in Grandmother's town of Tagata one time when my aunt took me there.

But the most unforgettable thing of all was the time I went with my sister Miyuki on a Buddhist pilgrimage. In the Chikuhō district, a bunch of old ladies and young girls gathered early in the year, when the peach blossoms were coming to an end and the rape blossoms were just beginning to fill the fields with yellow. The women then passed through the yellow fields, going from temple to temple. This was a special time for the temples, and the priests would hang out purple banners and greet the pilgrims with tea and little snacks.

Miyuki and I also tagged along in the procession of pilgrims, the tra-

Cover of the 1970 Japanese edition of *Twelve Views from the Distance*,
showing a montage of my mother and me superimposed over the port of Moji.
The photograph in the foreground was taken immediately before my mother
suddenly departed for China. Photomontage by Yokoo Tadanori.

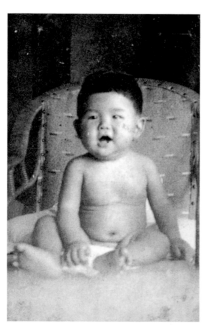

Me as an infant

My older sister
Miyuki and I

My parents, Hisako and Shirō, with my older
sister Hiromi before her death from meningitis

My mother, Hisako, and I

My father, Shirō

Uncle Ken'ichi (*center*) with his comrades-in-arms
wearing the uniforms of the Japanese imperial army

Uncle Ken'ichi as a young man in a school uniform

Uncle Ken'ichi in a military uniform

Uncle Ken'ichi (*right*) with a schoolmate

My father, Shirō (*second from left*), dressed in a military outfit

My mother, Hisako, dressed in a kimono

ditional pilgrims' bags hanging around our necks and rosaries grasped in our right hands. I still remember the pale red and green candies that a priest gave us in the garden of a little temple where the earliest cherry blossoms had just started to bloom. I took the candies and put them in the bag hanging around my neck. And then there were the broad beans stewed in soy sauce and sugar that I ate at a temple that we reached by crossing a little wooden bridge. The beans were piled on a small plate. I will never forget the light feeling of freedom their simple color and taste gave me. As I ate them, a sleepy sky opened up overhead, filled with the songs of larks hidden from view. The yellow of the rape blossoms, the purple of the banners, the songs of the skylarks, the reverberations of the bells, the tastes of the candy and the sweet stewed beans, the smothering aroma of the lotuses as the snakes wound their way through them—despite the distance of the years, all the impressions that streamed in through my five senses still remain deep within me, as vivid as they appeared to me that day.

Despite the distance of time, my memories of the aunt who terrified me so much also remain intensely vivid. In fact, even today she still resembles the same woman from the distant past. Miyuki ran away from her, just as Aunt Tsuyano had run away from her adoptive mother, Granny Ushijima, long before. Aunt Tsuyano and Ii-shan got a divorce, but the man she took as her next partner, who was twelve years younger than she was, also left her. Left alone, she adopted a crippled little girl as her daughter, and to this day she still lives in the same tiny, second-story rooms where she lived all those years ago.

4

A half-year later, I was taken back to Grandmother's home. It was there that one morning I was taken to Shimonoseki to meet my mother who had just returned from China. It was with her return to Japan that my era of fear came to a close. Soon after I entered elementary school, Mother and I moved to Moji. There, in school, I found a far greater repertoire of children's songs than I had ever heard at school in Nōgata. For instance, the other boys and girls would sing this song when playing *Jan-ken*, or Rock, Paper, Scissors:

Jan-ken, Maa-chan, Shii-chan
The monkey bit them all

The names in the first line were just names that did not refer to anyone in particular. In just about every school, there would be someone who went by those nicknames. If both players had chosen the same thing and the winner had still not been decided, they would continue the song:

Jan-ken, the lieutenant general
Even after losing, the monkey bit him

Perhaps the words *lieutenant general* had entered our vocabulary because of the war, but the song really didn't make much sense. Then there was another silly little song that children would sing when we were playing Hide the Wooden Clogs:

Hide, hide the wooden clogs
A small mouse underneath a bridge
Took some sandals in his teeth, *chu, chu, chu*
Chu, chu, who ate the *manju?*
No one ate it, I was the one who did

As we sang the song, we would point to one person, then move to the next with the rhythm of the song. The person we were pointing to at the end of the song would be the one who was the *demon*—the word that we use in Japanese to mean the person who was "it." The demon would then have to close his or her eyes, and everyone else would take their clog or their shoe—just one of them, not both—and hide it somewhere, perhaps on the ground, in the trash can, or on the roof. When the demon started looking for them, everyone else would jump up and down wildly and make fun of the poor victim as they sang, "Poking around upwards, poking around down." Whoever's clog the demon found first would become the next demon, and the game would start all over again.

At recess, there was a game called Do It, Do It, Blind Man that everybody would play. The person who was the blind man would squat down and close his or her eyes. Everyone else would then gather around and clasp their hands to form a ring:

> Do it, do it, blind man
> Drink a cup of tea

They would sing this as they spun around. Still bending his head down, the blind man would say, "Not yet, not yet." Then everyone would chant as if to reproach him:

> Not yet, you say
> But who is that behind you?

The blind man would take a wild stab at it and guess, "Yot-chan" or "Hiroko-chan." If he was wrong, then the rest of the group would take no time in calling out, "That is a big, big mistake, mistake," and they would continue to spin around.

And then there was a game called Little Priest, in the Middle, in the Middle. Once again, the person who was the little priest would crouch down, and everyone would form a ring that spun around him and sing:

> Little priest, in the middle, in the middle
> Why's it you're so short?
> Since you're so small, try standing up

The little priest would stand up, and the ring of others would squat down. Then the little priest would go around the circle, tapping each of the others' heads as he sang:

> On one plate, two plates, three plates
> I put it down
> How warm! How sad! Bud-dha-made-of-me-tal

The little priest would tap one person on the head with each of these last syllables. The last line *Atsu ya, kanashi ya, ka, na, bo, to, ke* was basically meaningless, but it was easy and fun to remember because of the repetition of the sounds.

There was a similar game called Little Boy from China. One boy would be the little boy from China; everyone else would sing to him; then he would respond. The exchange went like this:

> *Little boy from China, let's go play*
> Right now, I'm eating my meal
> *Whatcha having with your rice?*
> Pickled plums, pickled radish
> *Give me a little*
> Wait your turn

Sometimes, when the little boy from China was asked "Whatcha having with your rice?" he would shout, "A snake!" Everyone would then let out a scream and run away.

As I joined in the circles, spun around, and sang these songs, I could not help but notice that all these songs and games with the circles involved a certain social pattern in which one person is often in the position of a reviled outcast—the demon. The round of Paper, Scissors, Rock, which started all of our games, served as the ritual that divided the demon from everyone else. I now realize that as I was passed back and forth from one person's house to another, I had become the demon—alone, outcast, and reviled by everyone.

Of all the songs that we children sang, the most frightening was one called Heaven and Hell:

> Heaven and Hell, to Enma-san you go
> This child is a bad child, to the mountain of needles
> Fly, fly away

When we would sing this song, everyone would stand in two lines facing one another. Everyone would push the child they referred to as "this child" back and forth between the right and the left lines, moving him down the line until he was finally spit out at the very end of the rows. Would the fearful child, spit out onto the mountain of needles, ever choose to become the demon again?

As I think about it now, I cannot help but feel as though the adults around me were playing a game of Heaven and Hell with me, passing me from one set of adult hands to another. If I managed somehow not to transform into a demon myself, it was no doubt thanks to those illusory glimpses of heaven delivered to me in the little fragments of song I heard as I made my rounds through hell, where I was trembling, despairing, and so alone.

The Various Types of Sea

1

I was four years old when I first encountered the word *sea*. That was after Mother ran away to China to be with her lover, telling me only that she would be away for a short time as she did her shopping. It was three months after her disappearance that a big package arrived from China and Grandmother finally leveled with me.

"Mommy went to China."

"Where is China?" I asked.

It was in her response that I heard the unfamiliar word *sea* for the first time. "It's on the other side of the sea, really far away."

When a word first presents itself to a young soul, it always appears suddenly like this. As it struck my eardrums for the first time, the sound of the word *sea* conjured up the image of some dark, expressionless, enormous thing before me. This expressionless thing stood as a barrier between Mother and me, separating the two of us. If so, then perhaps my mother's love affair, which I was only vaguely aware of, was also wrapped up in whatever this unfamiliar word *sea* might mean.

Just as all children do when presented with such situations, I quickly tried to fill in the substance of this new concept that had presented itself to me. "What does *sea* mean?"

Grandmother thought for a moment, then said, "It's like the pond, but it's so big you can't see the other side."

With this, I imagined the sea as being like the pond in front of her house—the very same pond that would rise nearly all the way to the road during the rainy season but would grow so shallow at the peak of summer that the fish would come to the surface and gasp for air. I imagined the sea to be like the pond with frogs crying out from afternoon until evening, making sounds like those of cows. I thought of the sound of the *yosshoi* birds, which would travel each night across the pond from the thickets on the opposite side. I imagined the sea to be like the pond where the black-and-white dragonflies would dip their tails to put out the fires inside, or like the pond into which I would wade barefoot with Mother and Grandmother to collect snails and water chestnuts. The images of all these things and more converged in the single word *sea*—so many images it probably would have taken me two hands to count them all.

Grandmother's description of the sea was, needless to say, not very accurate. Still, I don't mean to blame her. She had probably only ever seen the sea a few times in her life. One of those times would have been soon after her family had been reduced to poverty in western Yame-gun in Fukuoka, when she moved with her sickly husband and young children to Nōgata. She traveled by train, and I imagined she must have caught a glimpse of the sea through the dirty windows and smoke pouring out of the engine. When she went with her son and wife to Yahata after that, she may have had other occasions to catch a glimpse of the sea, but I imagine that was about the extent of her experience with it. For both Grandmother and Grandfather, life meant work, so seashell hunting on the beach, swimming in the sea, and other things like that had no connection to their existence whatsoever.

The first time I ever saw the sea was a year after her disappearance when my relative Non-chan took me to Shimonoseki to meet Mother upon her return to Japan. As we rushed from the new station to the hotel where she was waiting, I caught glimpses of the sea each time we came to the end of a block—a strip of blue laid like the tile of a mosaic between the houses and warehouses. The blue was so deep it seemed to roar with color.

"Mut-chan, the sea!"

As Non-chan said this, I nodded in agreement. Indeed, this serene

thing between the rows of buildings—this thing that roared with blue—
was no doubt the very same sea that had kept me apart from Mother.

When I saw my mother for the first time in a year, she was seated
in front of a bay window on the third floor of a hotel. Behind her, the
sea filled the window. She was wearing a dark blue, Chinese-style dress
decorated with a clover pattern, and she leaned against a wicker chair. As
she did so, I noticed small, mysterious vibrating things on the calves of her
lightly crossed, white legs. When I pressed my cheek against the glass of
the bay window and looked at the sea brimming and shaking in sunlight
directly below, I realized the things dancing on Mother's exposed calves
were tiny fragments of the sea.

Looking down on the water, I saw that it was entirely different from
the blue sea I had seen at the ends of the blocks outside. The water was
a dark, deep, almost stagnant green. I looked back at Mother, who was
holding a cigarette in her left hand. On her ring finger was a ring that
sparkled with a piece of jade the same color as the sea below.

Perhaps it was because the green of the jade was so deep, but the
fingers of my mother looked pale, and she looked plumper than before.
Each time she lifted the cigarette to her mouth, I could see green veins
running from the palm of her hand down her forearm, tracing a beautiful
line that seemed to rise to the surface of her skin.

During the time the sea had separated us from one another, some
sort of change had taken place within her—something that could not be
detected with the naked eye. During the year she was living in her lover's
house in China with his wife and children, she had become pregnant with
his child and disposed of it with the help of an abortion doctor. Of course, it
was impossible that anyone would have told me this, considering that I was
so young. Still, the senses of a child are acutely attuned to minute changes,
and somehow I sensed that Mother was not the same person she used to
be. In other words, the nurturing umbilical cord that used to connect the
two of us—the cord that carried not just nutrients but also connected us in
an open, mutually receptive relationship—had been severed, and what had
separated us was the sea.

When Mother came home to Grandmother's, she started to look
for an apartment to rent near Shimonoseki. She probably wanted to live

in that area because it would be convenient for when her lover Ōgushi-san traveled on the ferry from Pusan, Korea, to Shimonoseki. I held Mother's hand as we walked through the hilly streets of Shimonoseki, then took the train to the neighborhood of Yatabu, which was filled with many lotus ponds. As we walked, I found myself unable to talk to her in the same carefree way that I had before. Whenever I found myself slipping back into our old ways and talking about trivial things, the blue sea would appear on the far side of the slopes or through the forest of pine trees. No matter how tightly I held her hand, the sea would sneak in between us. We were no longer a single unit of mother-and-child. Instead, were two separate entities, *mother* and *child*, linked only by a tenuous conjunction.

One time when I went to Grandmother's house, I felt sick to my stomach, as if I was going to have a bout of diarrhea. The sky was leaden that day. I suffered my discomfort silently as we walked the morning slopes of Shimonoseki and the country roads of Yatabu. It was on the way home, when we were seated on the second floor of the ferry from Shimonoseki to Moji, that I suddenly found that I could not hold back any longer. The sea was rocking gently beneath my bottom. The swaying of the sea underneath the ferry took all the tension from my body. It was gentle enough to lull my backside into a gentle slackness, and before I knew it, I had leaked into my khaki-colored shorts.

When we got off the ferry at Moji, we went into the bathroom at the dock, and Mother cleaned me up, mumbling unhappily to herself the whole time. On the train home, I felt as if I were dreaming. After the diarrhea, I felt listless and languid, and I could still feel the gentle rocking of the sea underneath my bottom, even though I knew there were steel wheels rolling beneath my seat. There were rails under them, and nothing but sand and gravel under them. Nowhere was there any water to be found . . .

But the sea continued to rock beneath me, even after we reached Grandmother's house. It was underneath the veranda where I sometimes walked and looked at picture books. It was under the path I took when I put on Mother's clogs and went down to the general store to buy *ramune*. Even now, more than twenty years later, that sea continues to rock beneath the futon where I sleep and dream.

2

The summer after I first started attending school, Mother and I moved from Nōgata to Moji. For the previous half-year, Mother and I had been living apart from Grandmother, nearly a mile away in the neighborhood of Kamenko, where we rented a three-mat room from an old lady who was nearly ninety. Our humble furniture was fastened onto a horse-drawn cart, which set out for Moji a little before five a.m., before it was even light out. I still remember the driver had a cloth tied around his head and knotted underneath his chin.

It was probably around ten o'clock before we left the old lady's house and got on the road. The lonely old lady who sold cheap confections to the children would be all alone again, unable to collect rent for the room. She had not wanted us to move because of the loss of income, and as a display of her feelings, she had hid her stooped body resolutely inside the *shōji* and refused to see us off. The same female relative, Non-chan, who had taken me to Shimonoseki to meet Mother, was with us again. This time, she helped us carry some of our things.

We arrived at the new house around two-thirty in the afternoon, and Mother and Non-chan began sweeping. The house was in the neighborhood of Dairi, which butted up against Kokura on the west. It was located along an old highway that ran from the seashore along the slopes of the hills. Two blocks west of where we lived was a red-brick beer factory that soared into the sky. The clatter of the horse-drawn carts that delivered the beer shook the front hall and the front windows twenty-four hours a day, and the *tatami* in the house, which had been vacant for half a year, was completely covered with dirt and dust from the road out front. The horse-drawn carriage we had sent ahead of us from Nōgata in the dark arrived at the new house after nightfall. By that time, Mother and Non-chan had just managed to finish cleaning the place.

I woke up early the next morning and went out to the seashore. On the left side of the new house was an alley probably about three yards wide. The alley dead-ended into the workshop of a carpenter who specialized in boat building, and just beyond his house was the sea.

That was the first time in my life I had seen the sea so close up.

The morning sea was at full tide. The wooden, joined floor outside the boat builder's workshop had been eaten away by the salty wind coming off the sea. The tide had swollen as if it were trying to subsume the floor, but the sea did not lap at it with waves. Instead, its movement was much more gradual. The water simply rose, crept toward the wood, and then subsided, creeping back again.

The color of the sea there was entirely different from what I had seen through the rows of houses in Shimonoseki or from the third-floor bay window of the hotel where I had my long-awaited reunion with Mother. The sea there was neither blue nor green. It was as transparent as celluloid; however, a sea that is transparent is also easy to soil—the transparency of the sea allowed me to see just how dirty the water was. There was no way a young boy like me could have known the words, but I think I could have also said that the transparency of the sea made it *everyday* and *banal*.

This banal sea with its transparency was harder to fathom than the sea that had been so blue that it had seemed to roar at me. Likewise, it was harder to understand than the sea that wanted to suck me in with its green. This transparent sea was far more common, more unceremonious, and more cunning, and for those reasons the more I looked at it, the more unearthly and eerie it seemed to be. The word *umi*, which means "sea" in Japanese, is a homonym for the word that means "birth." Not coincidentally, it seemed to me that the blue sea, the green sea, and the transparent celluloid sea all seemed to be singing a song of birth and death. This singing transparent sea, however, seemed to have a corrosive power missing from the other types of sea. For instance, as I stood with my feet at the water's edge, the water crept casually between my toes, as if trying to gently subsume my soft skin.

Creeping forward, creeping back . . . As it repeated these same simple actions over and over, the sea gradually withdrew to the depths, returning to its center of gravity far from shore. It would leave behind things in the wake of the retreating water: wet, green seaweed that looked vivid and fresh, gulf weed covered with sand, bits of straw, and driftwood. In other words, every time a wave came into shore, it would leave behind the wreckage of the sea's song of birth and death. This wreckage would lie

on the sandy shore, forming a silhouette of the wave's highest point until
the next wave reached even higher and washed it away.

When afternoon rolled around, I took a metal pail and went down
to the seashore. About fifty yards to the east of the boat builder's workshop was the ice factory where the man renting us our new house worked.
I had taken special notice of the place because I had seen a bunch of
pointed rocks gathered together there on the sand.

There were creatures living at the base of the rocks by the water's
edge. I had learned that when I had gone to Kiyama with Mother on the
Fudō pilgrimage and played by the edge of the waterfall. I climbed down
a little precipice to the sandy part of the shore and used all my strength to
move one of the rocks. Just as I had thought, in the indentation where the
rock had been, the retreating sea left a little puddle of salt water. A bunch
of small creatures that had been spit up from the dark bowels of the sea
were wriggling in the hole. The sea is an enormous body of water, but it
is also a source of unending birth. Even though I tried to cup my hands
together as quickly as possible, I still was unable to catch the little sleeper
gobies and other fish. Before long, the only things I had caught in my pail
were little crabs too young to have much power in their pincers yet.

I went to the water's edge and scooped up some fresh seawater for
the strange, little sea monsters with their eight legs and two sets of pincers. I then put in some seaweed, thinking it would be handy for them
to hide underneath. Despite my careful attention, however, by the next
morning, the seawater in the pail had turned lukewarm, and the small
creatures were upside down, showing their white undersides and horizontal stripes. Every last crab was dead.

The bluntness of their deaths was clearly something different from
the death the sea was singing about. The death in its song was fundamen-
tally linked to birth, so in it there was a gentle promise that death was not
all there was. The death of being cut off from the sea, however, had nothing whatsoever to do with birth. It was just death, plain and simple. Even
though I did not have the words for it, that is what I felt as I carried the
corpses of those little creatures in the pail to the water's edge and poured
them back into the shallow water.

When the tide was out, people would come and dig fishing bait out of the sand. On the fifteenth day of each lunar cycle, when the sun and moon would cooperate to create an especially dramatic tide, the narrow strip of sandy beach was especially crowded with people who had come to dig bait. It was easy to find *kebu*, or lugworms, which looked like reddish millipedes. You would find them just by turning over small rocks or scratching at the sand with a piece of driftwood. These were used only for fishing at the water's edge, but for deep-sea fishing the fishermen would use a *honmushi* worm, which was as thick as a finger. To find those, one had to dig deep at the water's edge and scoop out the water over and over. We children were the ones who searched for the *kebu*, while the adult fishermen would dig for the *honmushi*.

I continued to collect the little crabs that lived on the rocks at the edge of the water. No doubt people thought me ridiculous when I turned my back on the people looking for bait and put my useless little crabs into an unsightly metal pail originally intended for use in the bath. Children carrying empty cans for *kebu* would come over, take a look, and make a face that seemed to say, "What the heck?" And with that, they would walk away.

Naga-chan was one of the children who came to look. Unlike the other children, however, he did not walk away. Instead, he asked, "You're not a sea person, are you?"

"Nope."

"Where'd you come from?"

"Nōgata."

"Where's Nōgata? Is this your first time at the sea?"

"Yep."

Right then, a hoarse voice called from the direction of the boat builder's workshop, "Nagato, we're going!"

Naga-chan yelled back, "I'm coming," then turned to me and asked, "You ever seen someone throw a net?"

"Nope."

"Wanna come take a look? Grandpa goes all the way to the pier by the beer factory to throw his."

Naga-chan had already started walking in the direction of the boat builder's workshop. I followed him, carrying the metal pail at my side. Looking over his shoulder at me, Naga-chan seemed to wonder what on earth I wanted with all those crabs. A moment later, he spoke up: "You should throw them away." He took the pail from my hands and dumped it on the dry path where we were walking. No doubt the poor little creatures would be trampled by people's feet and crushed to death. Even if they weren't, they might be left upside down to die there, unable to get back to the water's edge. I bent down to flip them over one after another, but Naga-chan encouraged me to forget them. "That kind of crab's no good for anything."

Naga-chan's grandfather must have been around seventy. The top of his head was bald and bronzed by the sun, but the whiskers on his chin were white and thick like some wizened Buddhist teacher. He was wearing a dark gray pair of *jinbei*, and in both hands he carried his nets and some baskets for fish. He was slightly stooped as he walked along, his legs spread apart stiffly, but he was robust and brisk enough that Naga-chan and I sometimes would have to break into a short run to keep up.

We passed through two redbrick storehouses on the grounds of the beer factory and came to a rocky part of the shore. There were two piers, one in the shape of the letter *I* and the other in the shape of the letter *T*, and stretching the ten yards or so between them was the sea. Naga-chan's grandfather walked quickly out onto the *T*-shaped pier, and Naga-chan followed.

There was a space between each of the boards on the pier, and looking down I could catch glimpses of the sea rocking underneath. I could also see laver and seaweed rocking with the sea, jellyfish floating toward the surface, and fish darting quickly to and fro. As I gazed down, I felt as if the stripes of sea were themselves part of the pier and the pier itself was nothing but the gaps in between. I was terrified that I would be pulled through the gaps by my ankles and fall feet first into the sea.

When we finally reached the farthest point of the pier, Naga-chan's grandfather dropped the net in the water to get it wet, then pulled it back up again. Next, he lined up one by one the little weights he used as sinkers. Once he had done this, he collected them again in his right hand, and holding the body of the net in his left hand, he looked back and forth across the water's surface.

All of a sudden, the net flew out wide into the air, then fell slowly through space. It hit the surface, sending a delicate splash up a couple of inches or so, before sinking quickly into the invisible depths of the water below. The only thing left in the old man's hand was the rope attached to the net.

Moments later, the old man began using both hands, which were as tough as *shibugami*, to haul the net back in. As he pulled the net up, the water ran out of it, falling back onto the surface of the sea below. Once the net was on top of the pier, I could see many different sorts of steel-blue and rainbow-colored fish inside, flapping vigorously. Naga-chan ran the basket for the fish to his grandfather. His grandfather pulled the fish out of the net one by one and threw them into the basket while teaching me their names: sea bass, conger eel, flounder, rock trout, mullet . . .

Naga-chan was also known for his skill at catching crabs. When I say this, I should point out the kind of crabs he caught were not *isogani*, the useless little crabs that I had been catching. He caught *zugani*, the hairy crabs that lived in the rock formations in the rock precipices above the sea, and *beragani*, which had points on both sides of their bodies. To catch them, he would take an old bamboo basket that was no longer needed in the kitchen, stick four metal skewers into it at different points, and then put fish heads on each of the skewers. Next, he tied little broken pieces of brick or small stones around the outside of the basket to serve as weights. That done, he would go to the top of the rock precipice and move the basket up and down in the water. When the basket would grow heavy all of a sudden, he would know that there was a crab in it, and he would quickly pull the basket back up.

Speaking of sea creatures, two doors down on the right from my house was the home of Matsushita-san. He was a fisherman by day, but he also served as head of the local neighborhood group set up during the war by the government to help take care of the population. Of the boats stored at the boat builder's workshop, his was the one that stood out the most. His was the first one in the entire neighborhood to be equipped with a semi-diesel engine, and he was terribly proud of that fact.

In the evenings, we would receive word when Matsushita-san's boat came back. Mother and I would go out to the seashore, and the boat would float up to the edge of the water, pulled by a wire attached to the stern. We would walk, still wearing our wooden clogs, to the place where the sea met the shore and look over the side of the boat. At the bottom of his boat was a seawater tank with different compartments that held different kinds of fish. There would be a group of sea bream and beak fish, of rock trout and gunards, of blowfish, of tiny sharks and lizardfish, and so on. All of these fish would be swimming about vigorously.

Matsushita-san's father—Grandpa Matsushita—had only one eye and wore a false eye in the place of the other. He would reach into the tanks and grab the fish, dividing them and putting each kind into a different basket. Matsushita-san would carry the full baskets to a concrete platform where he would empty them out again. Mother and I would point to the fish flopping around on the concrete to indicate which ones we wanted, saying, "That one, that one, and that one." The fish would then be put onto a scale to determine their cost. I never got tired of squatting down to look at the rich colors the sea had spit from its dark belly onto the platform before me. Once Mother had paid the bill and taken her kettle full of fish, she would tell me to get a move on. It was only then that I would finally stand up to go home.

3

There was a girl who would walk, stooped over, along the edge of the water. As I put the little crabs from the seashore into my metal pail—a game that still continued to entertain me—I looked with curiosity at what she picked up from the shallow water.

The girl tended to walk most often when the sun was setting across the straits over Hikoshima, the southwestern part of Shimonoseki, and the sunset was dyeing the sea pink all the way from the deepest water to the water's edge. Sometimes the things she picked up in her white fingers would catch the flame of the sunset and emit a beautiful sparkle of light.

At some point, we started to have brief conversations. Her name was Hiroko-chan, and she lived in the house right in front of mine. She never went out in the street in front to play, and that is why I had not known where she lived.

What she was picking up on the seashore were shards of glass. The sky-blue shards of glass were from the bottles of the carbonated, citrusy drink known in Japan as "cider." The bluish-green shards were from bottles of Ramune, another popular carbonated drink. The brown ones were from beer bottles. The thin, translucent ones were from medicine bottles. The cloudy white and pale pink ones were from bottles of makeup or face cream. There were even times that she would occasionally find bright red or purple shards that had come from bottles she could not identify.

Hiroko-chan would break these shards into even smaller pieces on a rock, then select only the pieces that had the most beautiful shapes. She would then wet the pieces at the water's edge and hold them up to the sunset to show me. The shards of glass would glitter beautifully in the last light of the setting sun. The sunset would outline her luxurious hair, soft, pale-blue cardigan, and skirt, and she would look like a flame—a vision out of a dream.

"It's like a jewel, don't you think?" She smiled as she asked this question. But the shards in her hands were not the only jewels there. Clad in a cardigan with feathers around the neck—clothing incredibly rare during the time of war—Hiroko-chan's soft and gentle figure itself struck me as a rare and precious jewel.

"But when it dries out, it'll turn into just a regular old piece of glass."

One time Hiroko-chan showed me the jewel box in which she carefully kept her treasures. It was a small, empty box of paulownia wood lined with dark green velvet, and inside she had carefully lined up her jewels— diamonds, rubies, sapphires, emeralds, and opals. They had dried out completely and lost their shine, but they still emitted a faint scent of the seashore, commemorating the fact they had once been soaked in seawater.

Her father was an elementary school principal, so she had lots of books at her house. Of the books she showed me, there were two that left an especially deep impression. One story went like this. One evening when the weather was nice, the main character looked out in the distance and saw a house with golden windows. When he walked all the way over to take a closer look, he saw that the windows were made of regular glass. The reason they had looked like gold was that they had caught the light of the setting sun. The reason I liked this story was that it reminded me of Hiroko-chan with her jewels.

The other story was Andersen's "Little Mermaid." Hiroko-chan was unable to swim, just like the mermaid who was no longer able to swim after climbing onto land. Although she could not swim, the mermaid unmistakably belonged to the water. Likewise, Hiroko-chan was a daughter of the sea through and through. And it was precisely for that reason that she was able to pull up such magnificent treasures from the belly of the sea.

The fingers with which she picked up the shards of glass from the edge of the water were white, but the lines at the joints were a pale pink, and her fingernails were like agate, the rosy pink of dawn. Her hands were delicate and moist overall, and the vessels just beneath their surface were as beautiful as blades of grass. When I was out of sight, I furtively spread out my fingers and took a look at my own hands. Mine were darker in complexion, the skin strangely dry and the fingernails distorted. I took some hand cream from the stand where Mother did her makeup, and I tried slathering it on my hands. Still, my hands did not become as moist and attractive as Hiroko-chan's. With this, I was forced to recognize that humanity was divided into two groups: those who had beautiful hands and those who had unsightly, even distorted hands.

One day, the two of us were crouched on the seashore showing one another what we had found that day when five or six boys from the neighborhood passed by. The boys looked at us and said in a deliberately loud voice, "They say Takahashi and Inoue get into the bath together . . ." Inoue was Hiroko-chan's surname.

The two of us would sometimes meet down on the seashore, but of course we had never taken a bath together or done anything that intimate. Still, even though their slander was completely false, I felt embarrassed about what the mean boys had said. At the same time, I have to admit there was some small part of me that took a strange pleasure in it as well. To hide this, I picked up some seaweed that had washed up to the water's edge, then threw it down for dramatic effect.

Hiroko-chan had a younger brother Kin-chan, who seemed to suffer from some sort of neurosis. One day, he ran right out of the alley and was hit by a truck. He let out a little whelp like a puppy and died straight away. For quite a while, Hiroko-chan did not venture out of the house.

One evening, I picked up a stray kitten and took it to her front door. There was one pane of glass missing in her door, and so I dropped the kitten inside, thinking it would help keep her company after her loss. The next evening, I saw Hiroko-chan down on the seashore for the first time in ages. She asked me, "My dad said some boy threw a kitten in the door. Was it you, Mut-chan?" Terrified that she would see right through me, I denied it vociferously.

I began to engage in a kind of primitive fortune-telling to tell my future with her. For instance, if there was a log at the edge of the road, I would think to myself, "If I can walk the whole way down on top of the log without falling off, then I'm going to marry her. If I fall off, then we can't get married." With that, I would start walking carefully across the length of the log. If I did fall off, I would start over again, saying the same thing. I did this over and over again until after numerous tries, I finally made it all the way across and heaved a big sigh of relief.

Another thing I would do was throw my wooden clog in the direction of the sunset. That was a game other children would use to predict whether it would rain or be clear, but when I did it, I changed the game so that the answer would have to do with whether I would marry Hiroko-chan or not. There was nothing I wouldn't use as a means of trying to tell my future with her. I would keep trying over and over until I inevitably got the answer I wanted, but afterward I would always realize how absurd my methods of divination were, and I would become uneasy about whether or not I could trust the results.

Hiroko-chan and I were placed in the same class in the fifth grade of elementary school, but whenever I ran into her, I would blush bright red and become completely tongue-tied. Even in class when the teacher called on me, I would become discombobulated and confused if I thought Hiroko-chan was listening.

At the end of our fifth-grade year, we had the school race. When I had run six miles and come almost all the way back to the school gate, Hiroko-chan surprised me by jumping out of an alley and shouting, "Takahashi-san, hang in there!" She did not say, "Mut-chan," her childhood name for me. She had used my surname, "Takahashi-san," with the suffix indicating polite respect. I could not help but feel that she had used this adult form of address to maintain propriety in the eyes of the public, but hiding behind her formality were her personal feelings for me. This thought spurred me on as I squeezed out my last ounce of energy and dashed for the finish line. Even so, I took seventy-sixth place overall.

4

At some point, a lady by the name of Korenaga-san moved into the other apartment in our building, so that she resided just on the other side of our wall. She had big eyes that would dart around in every direction, and at the end of her sentences she would say, *Nee?* ("Isn't that so?"), in a way that made her sound like someone from Tokyo. She worked for the same ice manufacturing plant where our landlord worked, but rumor had it that she was the mistress of the plant manager.

Mother and Matsushita-san would complain, "That woman's his 'cat,' so she probably tricked him into giving her the room rent free!" When they used the word *cat*, Mother and Matsushita-san were probably referring to the ways that Korenaga-san flashed her eyes and spoke in a cooing, seductive voice—what is commonly known in Japanese as a *nekonadegoe* or a "cat-petting voice."

However, when the war came to an end, her husband came home from where he was stationed in Taiwan, and like the other women in the ice factory, she immediately quit her job. In no time at all, Korenaga-san also left to start working at the Yahata Steel Manufacturing plant. He was a contractor in charge of finding labor. When the end of the month would approach, he would walk around the neighborhood borrowing seals from various people. Everyone would lend them to him with a smile, but once he was gone, Mother would spread rumors about Korenaga-san's "phantom population." He had created a roster of laborers who did not actually exist, and he was cheating the company by taking the payment destined for those phantom workers. Those were the difficult and trying years of the immediate postwar period, but the Korenagas did not seem to suffer too much, probably thanks to those phantom workers of his.

I am grateful to Korenaga-san for helping me finally get accustomed to the sea. He was a big man, and he swooped me up effortlessly as I ran about at the water's edge. He held me under his arm and carried me out until the water came up to my navel. Still holding me under his arm, he put me facedown on the surface of the water and said, "Look, move your hands. Kick with your legs!" Moments later, he said, "All right? I'm going to let you go now," and sure enough, he did.

I got frightened, and I quickly put my feet down to stand up. As I tried to get my balance, a small wave knocked into me, sending salt water into my ears and nose. Some of the water flowed from my mouth into my stomach. He grabbed me again, and the whole process started over again. I tried so hard not to get any salt water in my mouth that the second time ended up even worse than the first.

"Just let all the energy go out of you and try floating there like a blob." It was not possible for me to let all the energy out of my body, and I did not know how to just float like a blob. I was desperate to find an unguarded moment and escape from the grasp of his long arms.

I kept trying; then one day, all of a sudden, I found that I was able to float in the water. I was behind the ice plant in a stretch of water with no one else, and without the help of anyone at all, I found I could do it. I had faithfully followed the advice of Korenaga-san and just let all the energy go out of me and simply floated there. Overjoyed, I kept trying it over and over, letting the energy go out of me and letting my body float on the water. After getting that down, it was nothing to lift my head and move my limbs. A year later, I had improved to the point that I could swim out to a boat in deep water.

The sea had been strewn with mines during the war, and every once in a while one would explode. One moment, a ship would break in half and begin spitting forth fire. The next, the clear sea would swallow it right before our eyes, still maintaining its calm countenance the whole time. The sea would continue to reflect the summer sky so intensely that it looked as if it had merged into the sky itself. The sea that gave birth to everything also brought death.

About a third of a mile beyond the beer factory was a shore in a neighborhood called Matsubara, and there the seashore was especially endowed with seaweed and shellfish; however, swimming was forbidden there. One day, a person who was fishing in the deep water off of

Matsubara dove into the water from his boat. He was swimming toward the shore when suddenly he let up a loud scream. The boat rowed over to him, cutting its way through the bloodstained water. Three or four sharks swam away. The man was rescued, but his leg had been ripped off at the thigh, and moments later he died from the loss of blood. As soon as we heard this news, we ran to the scene of the accident. No one was there any longer, but on the sandy beach, there were dark spots of congealed blood.

Nishikawa-san lived on the left side of Matsushita-san, on the other side of a narrow alleyway. Although they were related to each other by marriage, he and Matsushita-san were not really friends. "It's just that Nishikawa guy is such a difficult man," Mother explained. We, the children, called him "Nishikawa, the *pon-pon* man." That was because he owned a thirty-ton boat with an engine that made a *pon-pon* sound as it spit out bursts of steam. Nishikawa, the *pon-pon* man, was certainly a difficult man, but he was not bad at heart.

One day early in the afternoon, I was swimming when a voice called out to me from the deep water. "Hey, you've swum this far? I'm going to Hikoshima, so if you want, I can take you along." The voice belonged to the *pon-pon* man. I swam toward his boat using the overhand, crawl, and the breaststroke—cycling through every stroke I could think of. He leaned over the end of his boat and lent me a hand as I climbed in.

The deck was filled with sunlight, and the sea breeze blew across it, exhilarating me. The self-satisfied knowledge that I had swum all the way out to a boat in the deep water thrilled me all the more. He unwrapped a rice ball from a bamboo husk and put it into my hands. As the other boats passed by, he would point to them and explain, "That one's a steam launch. That one's a trading vessel."

It was after three o'clock when the boat reached the inlet at Hikoshima. We were tired so we took a little nap in a shaded part of the deck. When I woke, the sun had already descended quite a bit, and most of the area around the boat was in the shade. The *pon-pon* man pointed to the hill that was still bathed in light and said, "You want to swim over there? That's Shimonoseki, so if you get that far, you can brag and say you swam all the way to Shimonoseki."

The place where we were was a little inlet along a landfill that had been created between Shimonoseki and Hikoshima, which were originally two separate places. Shimonoseki was really only about one hundred yards or so away. I slid feet first from the side of the boat into the water, and I quietly started swimming.

I was swimming along doing a frog kick when, with only about thirty yards left to the shore of Shimonoseki, I felt my leg buckle. It refused to go back to its original position. I realized that this was what people were talking about when they talked about cramps in their legs. I wondered if I was going to die. The sea surrounding me grew cold and heavy. I looked across at the coast of Shimonoseki. The rays of the evening sun illuminating the roofs of the warehouses at the edge of town and the green slopes of the hills by the seashore were dazzling. I turned slowly and looked at the *pon-pon* man's boat. The boat was completely covered in shadow, and no one was on deck.

Having no other choice, I treaded water for a little while. Before long, I realized that the leg that had been constricted by the cramp a moment ago was now able to move more freely. I turned away from Shimonoseki and made my way slowly back toward the boat.

The *pon-pon* man came up from below deck. He looked at me and smiled, "Did you make it all the way to Shimonoseki?"

"Nope," I answered.

"What was the matter? You scared?"

I just smiled, without saying anything. I shut that brush with death away inside me, but it was the first time that I truly felt with my own flesh the entirety of the awesome power of the sea—its ability not just to give birth but to bring death as well.

Princes and Paupers

1

To a young soul, there is nothing more frightening than stories about kidnapping. Children always suspect there are kidnappers lurking outdoors, and those kidnappers are inevitably lying in wait for them.

The first kidnapper to come after me was the *yosshoi* bird. At night when I was fretting about, unable to sleep, Mother would whisper quietly into my ear, "You'd better be quiet. The *yosshoi* bird will come." I would hold my breath, and Mother would begin telling me the story of the *yosshoi* bird and the *kakkō* bird.

There once was a naughty little boy who would not stop crying. His mother threatened him by telling him that a *yosshoi* bird would get him, but he still would not stop. To teach the little boy a lesson, she put him outside. He continued crying for a little while, but then she realized she did not hear him any longer. Perhaps, she thought, he had grown tired of crying. Thinking the boy had suffered enough, she opened the door, but there was no one outside. The *yosshoi* bird had come and snatched the boy away.

Shocked by his disappearance, she pulled on one of her black leggings, but before she could pull on the other, she was already out the door looking for him. The little boy's name was Kakkō. She ran about, yelling, "Kakkō! Kakkō!" and at some point in her search, she turned into the type of cuckoo known in Japanese as a *kakkō* bird.

"And that is the reason the *kakkō* bird has one white leg and one black leg." That was the punch line, which ended the story.

As I lay in my futon listening, I conjured up a vision in my mind's eye. The *yosshoi* bird is a huge, frightening, monstrous bird with a color so dark that I could not even make out its silhouette in the darkness; instead, it just seems to melt away into pitch blackness. The only thing I can make out is the beating of its wings against the darkness. And Kakkō, the little boy that the bird had seized by the pajama collar and hauled into the air, is me.

As we fly through the air, I turn from the flashing eyes of the monstrous bird carrying me through the air, and I look over my shoulder. Behind me, Mother, still wearing her flannel nightclothes, has turned into a bird and is flying in my direction. Her beak is opening and closing. She is trying to tell me something, but there is too much distance between us for me to hear. She keeps chasing me, but the distance between us never decreases.

Suddenly Mother would say, "Listen, the *yosshoi* bird is singing."

Even when the wooden shutters were closed, sure enough, if I pricked up my ears, I could pick out the faint cry of the *yosshoi* bird singing in the thicket on the far side of the pond. I imagined looking across the surface of the water, which was no doubt shining in the moonlight.

The next stories about kidnappers that my family used to threaten me had to do with the circus. In the countryside a little ways from Nōgata, there is a Shintō shrine called Tada Shrine dedicated to the two deities Izanami and Izanagi. On the day of their annual festival, the streets leading to the shrine would be lined with tents and stands containing different sideshow acts. There would be a haunted house, a snake lady, a human tank, and some sort of strange girl known by the enigmatic name *kirin batenren*, but among all the brightly colored signs and the sounds of the little bands playing music by the gates to the sideshows, the thing that stood out the most was the tent housing the circus troupe and their animals.

I never once set foot inside the tent, but there were moments when I would hear a band playing noisily, and the curtain, which was embroidered with landscapes of India or the South Pacific, would lift a little, giving me a glimpse inside. If I stood on tiptoes, I could see young boys and girls riding horses. Their bodies were stiff inside their rayon jackets and spangled clothes, and their flat noses were made up with powder.

Mother would grab my hand and say, "Those little boys and girls didn't listen to their parents, so they were kidnapped and sold to the circus."

Still, their lot in life didn't look so bad to me. The occasional glimpses inside the tent reminded me of a glittering vision one might see inside a secret box of jewels, and even though the clothing worn by the little boys and girls might be cheap, it made them look like the princes and princesses I had heard so much about in stories. If they weren't princes and princesses, then why were they able to wear such gorgeous decorations on their clothing? If they weren't royalty, why were they able to coat their noses in white powder? After all, white powder was a sign of aristocracy. If it was true that all those boys and girls had been kidnapped and had tragic pasts, their tragedy was just all the more proof that they were specially chosen people.

Like all young people, I was scared by the stories about kidnapping, but there was some part of me that secretly wished that a kidnapper would come and take me away. What would the kidnapper look like? Maybe he would look like my father who died 105 days after I was born, or maybe he would look like my Uncle Ken'ichi, who had died on the Burmese battlefield.

I daydreamed over and over about the big, white-gloved hands of a kidnapper snatching me away. I would think these thoughts even when I was with Mother out in the sunshine or when I was snuggled with Grandmother in the futon, but I would also think them when I was lonely from being farmed out to one family after another. The kidnapper's big hand would lead me to some place out in the distance, to a place where there were people—some cheerful, terribly lively gathering missing from my own life.

In the end, however, the first real-life kidnapper who came to get me was the lady from the Shinshōji Temple. I believe it was after the memorial service on the fourth anniversary of my father's death when we were at the temple, drinking some tea. An older lady who worked at the temple said to Grandmother, "Aren't you going to put your grandson in kindergarten?"

Grandmother shook her hand as a sign that she was not. "That would take a bunch of money."

"Why'd you think so? He'll learn things, and you won't have to look after him during the day. It'll be cheaper than paying someone else to look after him."

The last part was what made Grandmother change her mind. Mother was home from China by that point, but she was on a long trip with her lover Ōgushi-san from Osaka to Kyoto, then Kyoto to Tokyo. If it would only take a portion of the money that Mother had sent for my care, then what more could she ask?

A few days later, I heard the voice of a young woman at the door. "Mut-chan, time to go to kindergarten."

Grandmother had put on my best clothes for the kindergarten entrance ceremony, and she had wrapped a *bentō* box in cloth and put it in my hand. I was all ready to go, but as soon as I heard the voice, I suddenly became scared and ran into the back room.

"Isn't Mut-chan here?" asked the voice.

Grandmother's voice responded, "Sensei, he was looking forward to you coming till just a moment ago, but then he heard your voice and ran away. This is his first time, so I guess he's a little shy."

The young woman said, "Is that so?" She seemed to understand. Once again, she called out, "Mut-chan, time to go to kindergarten!"

The next time, the two of them intoned the words together. Their voices overlapped but not perfectly. "Mut-chan, time to go to kindergarten."

Grandmother came into the back room and tried coaxing and wheedling me to go, but in the end she lost her patience and hit me. She pulled me toward the door by the ear, but each time she dragged me by a pillar, I grabbed it and held on for dear life. Even so, it did not take long to drag me out to the teacher whose voice I had just heard. There were other students waiting there with her.

The lady I had heard was the daughter of the lady from Shinshōji Temple who had originally suggested I go to kindergarten. Her name was Kitamura-Sensei, and she was in charge of the kindergarten—a position that ran in the family. Kitamura-Sensei wore her hair down in a way that suited her well, and without any makeup she looked to me like what I would call a "big girl." She had the kind of cheerful, clear voice that one can only find among young women.

"All right everyone, let's go!"

Shorts and canvas shoes, skirts and shoes, loose work pants with sandals—each of the children was dressed in his or her own way. They followed happily after Kitamura-Sensei, talking among themselves. I was wearing a woolen shirt with my shorts, and over that a padded, sleeveless kimono jacket decorated with the pattern of a rabbit, while on my feet were wooden clogs. I followed the others at a little distance, still sobbing.

The other children were going to kindergarten for the first time as well, but why were they all having so much fun? Why were they all so carefree? With the teacher at their head, the happy line of students looked as grand as an army of child soldiers quickly marching off into some new, unfamiliar territory. As I trudged along reluctantly behind the group of happy students, I must have looked like a captive their scouts had taken hostage.

2

The kindergarten was in a hilly area about one and a quarter miles from Grandmother's house. To get there, one would have to walk along the edge of the pond by our house, then continue on the path until it disappeared at the edge of the hills. Once down the slopes on the other side, the path would dead-end into another path running along the railroad tracks. As I climbed the stone steps from the path to the temple where the kindergarten was held, I could look down and get a clear view of the back of Nōgata station and the intricate tangle of railroad tracks, which looked like some kind of anatomical chart. During recess, I would often stand alone on the stone steps and watch the trains, which looked like toys as they came and went.

I had difficulty adjusting to my new environment. At the beginning of the week, the head of the kindergarten, who was also the head of the temple, came and talked to us. Before he came, we children would wipe down the floors with a dry rag until it shone with a black luster, and we would sit there, legs folded properly beneath us, as we listened to him talk. He was as fat as Budai, the ancient Chinese priest who loved children, and he smiled just as much. He would tell us stories that were very easy to follow, punctuating them with rhetorical questions for emphasis, like "Isn't that so?" or "Don't you think so, too?" The other children would all say, "Yes!" in unison. I would open my mouth in the shape of the word *yes*, but I never actually said it. When he heard the other children say "Yes," he would nod with satisfaction and move on.

I remember one thing he taught us, a song he wrote called "A Day in the Life of a Good Child." I just remember the beginning, which goes like this:

Wake up early, wash my face
Pray to Lord Buddha, eat my rice . . .

This was followed by a list of humdrum things one would find in a day in the life of a good little boy or girl—saying good-bye when leaving, going to kindergarten, listening carefully to the teachers, going home and announcing "I'm home," changing into play clothes, having fun playing outside, going home when the sun sets, washing one's hands, eating dinner, taking a good bath, changing into pajamas, and saying "Daddy, Mommy, good night" . . .

Like the song, every day at kindergarten was a repetition of the same humdrum routine. In the morning, we would have story time, singing, and playtime. Playtime would start with the song "Ball Your Hands and Open Them," then "The Apple Talking to Itself." After we ate our packed lunches, we would have rest time, then craft time during which we would fold origami or cut shapes out of paper. This would be followed by drawing, writing practice, and other similar things. During the summer, there would be naptime, which we spent on the spacious *tatami*-covered floor of the main hall of the temple. After waking up in the cool breeze, each of the children would receive some little snack from the teachers.

I had a terrible time getting used to everything—story time, singing, playtime, crafts, drawing, and even the writing practice. Whenever I was beaten down by unhappiness—after all, even my mother and grandmother had abandoned me, and I was being passed along from one house to another—I escaped by burying my face in my folded knees and retreating into my own little world. That world was the one place where I could behave exactly as I wanted, but kindergarten was trying to wrestle that place away from me in the name of the "group." I tried to protect this treasured space of my own by withdrawing from the others and spending as much time as I could alone.

Kitamura-Sensei was with us when we walked to kindergarten; however, when I went home at the end of the day, I walked home alone. I remember one day when I was walking home—a clear day in autumn, I believe. I was walking along the edge of a muddy little river that went along the railroad tracks when suddenly I found two big children blocking the road in front of me. The sleeves of their clothes, which were narrow and clung to their forearms, were dirty. Without saying a word, they threw me into the river. I didn't cry as I crawled out. Barefoot and dirty, I walked back home at my usual quick pace. The other children, as well as the women who were coming back from their shopping, looked at me suspiciously.

When Grandmother saw me, she hit me, without even asking what had happened. Terrified, I stammered, "Some kids I'd never seen before pushed me into the river."

"It's 'cause you were acting absentminded again." She seemed to think I brought this on myself by not paying enough attention and thus failing to avoid trouble when it came my way. She slapped me across the cheek again. As she dragged me to the bath and poured water over my head, I told myself this wouldn't have happened if I hadn't been forced to go to kindergarten.

The reason Grandmother was so angry was that I had lost my padded kimono jacket and wooden clogs in the river. It was beyond her imagination to realize that it took just about everything a five-year-old boy had to manage to get back to the riverbank without drowning, especially when he had just been thrown into the water by bullies he had never even seen before. She could not afford to have such luxurious thoughts. She put me in a faded serge robe and led me to the riverbank. When we found the padded jacket floating in the muddy river, Grandmother's mood finally improved. She borrowed a pole from one of the neighboring houses and fished the jacket out of the water. We only found one of the wooden clogs. Perhaps the other had gotten stuck in the mud.

By winter, I still had not yet really made friends at kindergarten. There was one day when the sky was heavy and overcast—a day when a smudgy, dirty cold seemed to gather in the air. I had been feeling a gripping pain in my stomach since morning, but there was no way that I could use my stomachache as a reason not to go. Grandmother was paying good money and "keeping" me at kindergarten so that she would not have to take care of me herself. She was paying for it so I had to go no matter what. Grandmother was a day laborer, and that was the way she thought. Cradling my aching stomach in my arms, I followed the children behind Kitamura-Sensei, taking the very last position in the row. Pulling up the rear behind the Kitamura Youth Exploratory Expedition, I must have looked more like their unfortunate captive than ever before.

While everyone else was singing, I was able to get by simply by opening my mouth. While everyone else was drawing, I was able to get by with a few scribbles. And while everyone else was singing, "Ball your hands, Open your hands, Clap your hands, Ball your hands, Open your hands again, Clap your hands, Make a frog with those hands," I was somehow able to get by, imitating the motions of a frog.

When it was lunchtime, I turned my back on everyone as usual and opened my lunch. Next to the barley and rice, she had placed a blob of sweet bean paste made from half-crushed beans, and on the surface of the bean paste was a dead locust the color of grass. It was Grandmother's turn to do the preparations for the Buddhist sermon to be held in our neighborhood, so she had made the bean paste for the gathering but decided to give me a little bit of it as well. The locust had probably hopped inside when Grandmother was cooking the beans down, opened the lid, and was stirring the pot. I closed the lid of my *bentō* box immediately, but the strangely sweet-looking purple of the bean paste and the vivid green of the locust made my stomach, which had been feeling unsettled since morning, feel decisively worse.

After lunch, all the other kids played tag, hopscotch, and the game How Many Fingers Am I Holding behind My Back? in the yard before the main building of the temple. I leaned against the dark trunk of an oak tree and gazed absentmindedly at the children who seemed to be having so much fun. The cold that had started out the morning still had not given

way to the warmth of afternoon. If anything, the cold seemed to have gotten worse. Because the leaden chill had continued unbroken since morning, the dirtiness I had sensed earlier in the cold seemed to have grown
that much worse.

As I watched the other children move about, I felt something rum-
bling in my lower abdomen. By the time I sensed this, it was already too late.
I had already soiled the woolen green pants Grandmother had made me
wear that morning. "I've blown it. . . ." No sooner had this thought passed
through my head than all the nervous energy I had expended in my attempts
to make it through the day suddenly dissipated. The nervousness that had
melted continued to flow from my lower abdomen to my buttocks, and my
bottom, which was leaning against the tree trunk, grew unpleasantly warm.
The accelerating slackness brought with it a sort of ecstasy.

The movement of my bowels, which had started before I was even
prepared, eventually came to an end. As I recovered from the state of
relaxation that had come with the release, I felt the warm, foreign object
between my buttocks and the wool pants begin to lose its warmth. As it
cooled, this foreign object became clearly just that—a foreign object—
forcing me to think about what I had just done. There was not much time
left before craft time. I grew even paler and quieter as I worried about how
my embarrassing act would soon be exposed to everyone.

The bell rang from the window of the teacher's room. The boy who
had been the demon in the game of tag transformed back into a regular kindergartener, and as he walked by he was the one who noticed the
strange smell. He strolled around me and the tree once, then looked at me
closely. I returned his look with desperate intensity in my eyes. Unable to
stand my intense glance, he averted his eyes and shouted, "He pooped his
pants!"

The children let up a shout and gathered around me. Tears welled
up in my eyes, obscuring my vision. One of the teachers came running
over and led me back to the toilet, washing me in the bath behind the
temple kitchen. I do not think it was Kitamura-Sensei, because if it were,
my embarrassment would have been a hundred times worse.

"Look, you're all clean now. If your tummy hurt, why didn't you say
something?" The whole time she had been washing me, I had been worry-

ing about how I would act when I walked back into the classroom where everybody was, but as I stood up, I realized that the bathroom window was open and everyone was on the other side peeking in.

I shook my fist at them and threatened them, raising a howl—not even a real word. Although I had said things previously in their presence, I couldn't help but feel that was the first real sound I had made since entering kindergarten. The group had humiliated me, and in response to that humiliation, I had no choice but to raise my voice to threaten them. . . . That is the lesson I had learned in the extremes of my embarrassment.

3

One clear day in April of the following year, I set out with Mother, who was wearing a kimono of dark red crepe and carrying a purple parasol decorated with a picture. We left the house of the old woman who sold cheap confections and was renting a room to us. We had moved just a short time before, and she was taking me for the first time to the school that was about a mile from our old house.

Students had to undergo something like an oral test upon entering school, so the two classrooms next to the school nurse's office were being used for interviews. As with kindergarten, I did not stop crying from the moment that I entered the school gates, even though the gates were surrounded by cherry trees in full bloom. My tears came from already understanding that the kidnapper known as "school" was far more merciless and far more despotic than kindergarten had ever been. The reason I knew that was that the kidnapper known as kindergarten had come for me in the form of the lady who worked at Shinshōji, but this time the kidnapper was lying in wait for me inside the school gates. It had been ordered that children were to be brought inside, and we had to obey. If Mother or Grandmother had stood up to the kindergarten kidnapper when it had come for me and refused to let me be taken away, they probably could have gotten away with it, but this time, there was no refusing. The kidnapper this time was the official structure of society itself—all children had to go to school. This time, my personal, private space would surely be wrenched away from me for good.

The rooms where the oral tests were being held had been divided into several sections with curtains. When it was my turn, I entered one of the sections, accompanied by Mother. We were made to sit in front of a table. On the opposite side of the table was a female teacher. Sitting around the table were two other female teachers.

The teacher on the opposite side of the table made a slight bow to Mother. I was still in tears, so the other teachers around the table tried to make me feel better by saying, "Mut-chan's been to kindergarten, so he knows everything, doesn't he?" Somehow these kidnappers had done their research on me. My sobs grew all the worse.

The teacher on the other side of the table took out some cards with different colors on them. "What's this?"

"That's red."

"That's right. What about this?"

"Blue."

"And this?"

"Purple." I continued to cry, even as I answered the questions.

Next, she brought out cards with pictures on them, and I named them as she held them up. "A lamp . . . Electricity . . . A car . . ."

In the countryside where I am from, people often mix up *r* sounds and *d* sounds. This was probably a test to see if I could distinguish between the two sets of sounds. The word for "lamp" is *ranpu,* "electricity" is *denki,* and "car" is *jidōsha.* Even though I was crying, I still pronounced all the words correctly.

They had me say all of the numbers from one to one hundred in my weepy voice, asked me to write my name "Takahashi Mutsuo" in *katakana,* and then they finally let me go. I say "let me go," but my reprieve only lasted a short time. The following day, the kidnappers called me back, and this time, there was no refusing. And with that, my era of youthful freedom was taken away from me once and for all.

A few days after school started, I was on the playground during the recess between our first and second classes when accidentally I knocked over a little sapling that been planted next to the slide. It was a Himalayan cedar. The boys in my grade immediately gathered around me and started chanting, "We're gonna tell the teacher," then "Takahashi knocked it over," then once again, "We're gonna tell the teacher."

I screamed and started running toward home, toward where I knew I could find Mother. As soon I left the school gates, a variety of aromas assailed my nostrils all at once: the scent of young leaves, the flowers of the broad beans, the rice seedlings in the nursery, the dirt road, the light, and the wind. Those were the scents of my childhood happiness. I had left school and found the beloved scents that school had forbidden me to experience anymore. As these familiar and nostalgic scents caressed my cheeks, ears, neck, and knees, I realized perhaps it was possible to escape, and the unexpectedly simple method of knocking over a sapling seemed to have been the way to do it. I felt surprisingly light and buoyant with the thought.

Mother was out in the sunny part of the garden, wearing a cooking apron, and the sleeves of her kimono were tied up. She was stretching clothes on tenterhooks to remove the wrinkles. When I saw her, the tears welled up in my eyes once again. I threw my arms around her midsection, which was covered with the apron, and I buried my face against her body.

"I knocked over the school tree and I'm gonna get yelled at. I'm not going to school anymore!"

I had thought Mother would say to me, "So you're not going back to school anymore, are you?" But she didn't.

"Mommy will go to school and apologize to the principal for you."

She undid the ties holding up the sleeves of her kimono. She took off her apron, and putting it on the edge of the veranda, she led me back to school.

There was only one thing left that I could hope for—that the principal would refuse Mother's apology and say, "No, no. That little boy's bad. We can't let him go to school here." If that were to happen, Mother couldn't force me to go to school.

When we reached the gate that I had entered not so long ago with tears rolling down my face, I stopped and took another good look behind me at the light-filled world of freedom. I inhaled the scent of freedom deep into my lungs. If the principal refused me, then the free world would still be there to take me in. I would be a free little boy forever. If the principal did take me back, however, then the world of freedom would recede from me forever. If I was being cut off from the free world, then it was the school gate that formed the boundary of my new circumscribed world. That was why, at that very moment, it was so important for me to take in the colors of freedom through my eyes and to breathe in the scents of freedom through my nostrils.

We walked into the principal's office and Mother greeted him. I peered at him from behind Mother. When I stood behind her, I felt as though I was still a little bit closer to the free world.

"It's been a while." The principal was a small man with a shaved head, and he was wearing the khaki citizens' clothes so common during the war. He stood up and walked toward us. "You're . . . Kōno-san, aren't you?"

"Yes, Kōno Hisako. You're right, it has been ages. . . ."

As the principal looked through his silver wire-rimmed glasses at the student he had taught more than a decade ago, his eyes grew narrower and narrower. "Yes, sure enough, you are Hisako-san. So, you mean, this little boy is yours . . . ?"

"Yes, this is my son. Today he did something bad. He knocked down a tree you were growing, so he came running back home. . . ."

"A tree?"

I looked hard at the principal. With one word from him, my fate would be decided. For a moment, his face took on a stern expression, and that gave me hope. But his expression quickly turned into a smile, and he said, "No need to worry. No problem, no problem. It's good for little boys to be rambunctious." He rubbed the top of my head.

Mother went with me to the classroom to get my backpack. That day, I was allowed to go home early. Mother took my hand and led me out the school gate, but as she did so, I could not help but notice that the scents, colors, and sounds had changed from earlier in the day. Everything had faded.

The methods of kidnappers are extremely ingenious. No matter how much I thrashed about, I still could not escape the net that had closed around me.

4

That does not mean, however, that I did not learn anything while caught in the kidnapper's net. The time I spent caught in the net gave me a valuable course in human relations.

There was a boy by the name of Kōno in the same class with me at my new school. This little boy, a distant relative on Mother's side, was an honor student. I remember being struck by his bright round eyes, his fleshy red cheeks, and the healthy-looking thighs that stuck out of his khaki shorts.

Kōno was popular, and everyone wanted to be friends with him. A crowd of followers would trail along behind him wherever he went. This did not make him arrogant, nor did it seem to bother him. He seemed in great spirits, perhaps even triumphant, and this attitude reminded me of the kind of innate elegance one might expect from a prince. If a prince were to get caught in the hands of a kidnapper, then surely he would work his way free while remaining calm and collected like that.

During recess, I stood at a distance from Kōno's retinue. I remember their pointing at me and saying in voices loud enough to overhear, "Takahashi lives alone with his mother in a place so small all they've got is three *tatami* mats." Kōno's house, however, was a huge estate built on a rock foundation and surrounded by a boxwood hedge. His retinue burst out laughing, but Kōno himself never looked at me with distain. On the other hand, I suppose that he never reproached his followers either. His bright, easygoing eyes would just gaze at the rustling trees in the distance or the birds flying through the sky.

The retinue interpreted Kōno's lack of responsiveness as tacit complicity and grew increasingly nasty. "Takahashi's got no dad; he's just got a mom." Kōno's father was the principal of another nearby elementary school, and everyone knew his mother for her beauty. Everyone burst out laughing again.

I wanted to approach this alluring prince, but the cruelty of the other boys surrounding him always kept me away. I had to move farther away from Kōno and his hangers-on in order to protect my dignity. If I did ever get the chance to talk to him, I didn't want to talk from the vantage point of a subject paying homage to his lord; I wanted to talk to him as an equal.

It was quite hot one day after class. The earliest cicadas had already started buzzing in the courtyard, and I could hear them through the hallway windows. I was in the hallway washing up with a rag when I saw Kōno walking down the hallway in my direction. He was alone, something quite rare for him. All the students were supposed to chip in and clean the school, but he never did. Instead, someone else would do his work for him. He seemed to accept that calmly and proudly, without ever thanking the person who did the work on his behalf.

There we were, the two of us alone in the hallway. I realized this valuable opportunity could slip away in the blink of an eye, and my heart began to pound. Looking in the mirrors hanging in the hallways, I could tell my face was getting redder and redder by the moment.

I wanted to start speaking then and there, but instead I wrung out a cleaning rag in the black, filthy bucket of water and started sloppily wiping the floor while moving in his direction. As I wiped the floor, the sweat began to bead up on the back of my neck. Right then, his crowd of followers loudly walked up and gathered around him. The ring of followers were pointing to me and saying things. Someone called me a "weirdo," so I quickly fled into one of the classrooms.

In the afternoons, Kōno was always surrounded by his followers, but in the evenings, after he finished his preparations and other studies, he might spend time with his older sister who was in third grade, or he might even be alone. The Kōnos lived about a block away from the house of the middle-aged lady where we were then living. There was a road that went alongside their big house with its stone foundations and boxwood hedge, and the road led to a large field of barley behind them. Right at the line between the Kōnos' property and the barley field, there stood a handful of Nezumimochi trees covered with kadsura vines. When Kōno finished his studies, he would usually pass through the trees and go down to the road.

Thinking I would recoup the chance to get close to him that I had lost at school, I decided I would lie in wait for him under the trees. From where I stood between the trees, I could see the window frame of the room where he studied, but when the window was shut, I could not tell if there was anyone inside or not. Perhaps he might have gone into town with his older sister and beautiful mother. The colors of the sunset faded over the outlines of the mountains beyond the field of barley, and the pale blue darkness of twilight began to descend over the bundles scattered throughout the field.

Suddenly, I heard a rustling sound. Kōno had unexpectedly come out of the room where he was studying. I panicked, dashed into the neighboring barley field, and crouched down, pretending like I was picking up fallen ears of barley.

I remember he was wearing white shorts. When he walked out from between the trees, he noticed me. I was so keenly aware of his presence that I could barely think of anything else, but still I pretended to be oblivious. He turned to me as if he were about to say something.

Right then, there was a rustling in the trees, and Bon-chan, one of his retinue, started to walk toward him. As he walked, he yelled out, "Hey, Takahashi, whatcha doin'?"

I kept my face downward, trying to maintain my dignity. Without looking at him, I answered as nonchalantly as I could. "Picking up ears of barley."

"Barley, eh? That's right. Your folks don't have any fields of your own." He spat out these final words cruelly.

The entire field belonged to the Kōno family. I stood up and left their land without looking back. And with that, I lost any chance I might ever have for the prince, surrounded by the castle walls of his boxwood hedge, ever to call out to me again.

When the second semester began, I started attending a new elementary school in the port of Moji. There were princes in that school as well. There was a boy named Yano in the next classroom over. He had a fair-skinned, long face with thick eyebrows and lips so red that they seemed to be wet all the time. He was also the star of the Arts and Sciences Club. There was a girl named Kawaguchi who was in the same class and who would wait on him hand and foot. In fact, at the Arts and Sciences Club and other places, she would put his socks on for him, even when people were watching.

"When I grow up, I'm gonna marry Kawaguchi." Yano didn't hesitate to say audacious things like this out loud. Our other schoolmates might say things about his boldness behind his back, but they never made fun of him or complained to his face about these unchildlike declarations. The word *marry* had very graphic implications to us, but when it came from Yano's mouth, it carried a certain solemnity about it. Yano never spoke to me even once.

By the time I was in first grade of elementary school, I already understood that humanity is divided into two groups, princes and pau-pers, and that the only way for the paupers to reach the little slice of heaven afforded people in their position was to climb up a ladder to whatever lay above. The rules made by the kidnappers—in other words, the rules of kindergarten and school—were made for the sake of the princes. I was reminded over and over again how incredibly difficult it is for paupers to maintain their place on their own ladders, there among the rules of the world of school. I hated the rules of the kidnappers, and I hated school, but I had already been captured, and there was no way to free myself of their rules ever again.

The Shore of Sexuality

1

From the dawning, distant shore of my young sexuality, I hear the strains of a certain song:

> *Gikkon battan*
> Shall I put on the *obi*?
> Whom shall I put the *obi* on?
> Shall I put the *obi* on Mut-chan?
> *Gikkon battan* . . .

This song is what one calls an *ayashiuta*, a "humoring song"—a song that we would sing to entertain a small child—and it was accompanied by a particular game. An adult would lie on their back, bend their knees up, then have a young child straddle them. The adult would stick out their hands and take those of the child, and then by distributing the child's weight over all four limbs, the adult would raise the child up and down while singing the song. *Gikkon battan* is onomatopoeic in Japanese for the sound of a loom shifting back and forth, and as the adult says this, he would lift the child up then lower him once again.

Who was it that performed this role for me during the dawn of my earliest youth, singing this song to me? Was it Mother? For most of my early days, she was far away. Grandmother or Grandfather? Both of them worked from morning to night and hardly had any free time at all to humor me with games like this. My uncle? Such games hardly fit the image of my pale-faced uncle, who during his late teenage years seemed at least five years older than he actually was. He was too taciturn for such things.

So who was it that might have played these games with me? I cannot remember. All I know is that now, two pale legs rise from the far shore of oblivion, wrapped in layer upon layer of mist, and I am poised on them as they rise up and down like a children's carousel. On my face is an expression as if I am about to burst into tears at any moment. Visible in this expression is both anxiety and a sense of intoxication.

I can safely say that was my first experience with the intoxication of sexuality—or to put it more precisely, that was my first sexual experience, and in it I experienced both anxiety and a sense of intoxication, rolled up into one. When Mother embraced me and carried her on her back—those feelings did not have to do with sexuality. Perhaps that is because mother and child, who relate to one another through the acts of embracing and carrying, are linked through the invisible tube of the umbilical cord. At best, mother and child are little more than two elastic, adaptable masses of different sizes. I believe it was when I was taken away from Mother's breast and placed on the legs of the man I cannot remember that I had my first experience with sexuality. I say this because it was in this childhood game I first experienced the sensation of rubbing against the flesh of another in the particular way one associates with sex.

One characteristic of sex seems to be rhythm, and I cannot help but wonder if the true nature of that rhythm isn't actually wrapped up in anxiety. Rhythm involves repeated rising and falling, and both rising and falling are types of flight that take one beyond the boundaries of one's ordinary state. No sooner was I hurled toward the unbounded emptiness of the sky than I was pulled back; no sooner was I tossed into a bottomless fall into hell than I was pulled back once again. . . . In the anxiety that took hold of me with each repetition of this cycle, I took another step on that faintest of staircases and learned a little more about the sensations of sex. This knowledge was transmitted to me not intellectually but through the more intimate sense of touch—through the flesh of my hips straddling the man's adult legs and the smooth skin of my inner thighs.

The connection between anxiety and sexuality are even clearer in another children's game called You Can See Tokyo. The adult would cover the child's ears with both hands and raise the child high above his own head. This would be the part of the game we called Up High, Up High. When an adult was doing Up High, Up High, he was trying to show the child how big the world is. Since Tokyo was so far away from where we lived in the rural countryside of southern Japan, it became a symbol to us of something terribly far away. If the child could "see Tokyo" when the adult lifted him into the air, it meant he could see far into the distance.

I wonder if this game wasn't also a vehicle to allow adults to give children their first taste of sexuality. The game involved a dizzying cycle of rising and falling. With the adult's hands firmly clamped on either side of my head, I would be elevated to an anxiety-filled zenith, and my feet would dangle in the air. Next, I would be cast into a hell by a force as strong as anything I could imagine, and at the terrifying nadir of this fall, I would finally find my feet on the ground once again. Later, after I learned about that thing called sex, I couldn't help but remember the game You Can See Tokyo.

The person who played that game with me was Inatomo-shan, one of the young inhabitants of the Mitsubishi dormitory whom Mother watched over for a while. Inatomo-shan was tall and had the distinctively feverish cheeks of a young man suffering from the early stages of tuberculosis—cheeks that feel like a fire in the moments just before it dies out. When he would get drunk, he would often grab me and say, "Hey little guy, I want you to grow up soon so we can go out and buy dancing girls in Susaki." Maybe comments like this were the reason the game You Can See Tokyo felt so sexual to me. In the end, this large young man went home and died of illness.

What was it that I saw as a little boy playing this game, held so high in the air? Inamoto-shan would lift me haphazardly and repeat the question, "Can you see Tokyo? Can you see Tokyo?" If I did not reply "I can," then he would prolong my state of anxiety until I would grow flustered and cry out in a shrill voice, "Yes, I can! I can see it!" I yelled partly to get out of my predicament, but at the same time I did experience the illusion that I could see something shimmering for a moment on the farthest edge of the space where I was held dangling.

Was what I saw shimmering in the distance really Tokyo or just the world that Tokyo represented to me? I suspect that in that distant vision I was becoming aware of the existential relationship between my young soul and the vast, outside world that seemed to lie so far beyond the self. I suppose that you could simply say that something "moved" me, but I think it is more accurate to say that in my excitement I was experiencing sexual feelings.

The sexual feelings that connect the individual and the outer world are suspended in insecure, empty space: they are an insecure bridge, suspended in the air, like two legs moving up and down, *gikkon battan*. For me, the pillars supporting the bridge came in the form of the rising and falling thighs of that unknown person who played the game with me and sang me the song, and in the form of the tall, thin body of Inatomo-shan. The bridge of my earliest consciousness, supported by those rising and falling thighs and Inatomo-shan's body, is now wrapped in the multilayered mists of oblivion, extending toward the distant shore of my dawning sexuality.

Speaking of shores, the shore of the pond in front of Grandmother's house was another important place in my developing awareness of sexuality. A sluice was located there at the edge of the dike, and the adults used it to regulate the height of the water in the fields. Two doors down from Grandmother on the right side was the home of Granny Tejima, the faith healer, who had a well surrounded by stone statues of bodhisattvas. Walking along the edge of the pond from there, one would come to the irrigation sluice that consisted of little more than a dam and a sliding door, which allowed the water to flow through when opened. Behind the sluice was a deep reservoir filled with water that would flow through the open sluice into the rice paddies below. The long, narrow reservoir, which was about nine feet deep and made of concrete, was filled with water. For long stretches of the year, it was necessary to divert water to the rice paddies so that the rice would grow, and so the reservoir by the sluice was quite deep. As a result, it had water in it most of the year—not only during the rainy season when the water rose to the base of the *sasa*-covered hills around the embankment, but also during the midsummer heat when the pond grew shallow under the blazing sky, revealing the bladderwort and carp at the bottom.

The sluice was all the more frightening to me because the mechanism that opened and closed it was always under water. When I wouldn't stop crying, Grandmother threatened me by saying, "I'll throw you in the water by the sluice." Moreover, one of her most common warnings was, "Now, don't go down there and play on the edge of the water by the sluice."

Because the edge of the water was off-limits to me, I was all the more attracted to it. The prohibition that excited me so much and drew me near the water's edge might have had to do with a story Grandmother told me about a young boy who got sucked into the sluice. As the story goes, the boy did not listen to his parents' warnings. One day when he was playing all alone at the edge of the water, he was pulled into the sluice. The neighbors split up and looked everywhere for the boy. They found his clothes abandoned in the grass near the edge of the water, but they never located his body, not even in the fields below.

Beyond the sluice was a thick clump of reeds, and in the middle of that was a platform of rough boards that stuck out into the reeds about three feet. I remember there were often Korean ladies there on the bridge, pounding their clothes in the water to wash them clean. The area between the sluice and the end of the platform was always wrapped in mist, which rose from the water among the reeds. The air there seemed to shimmer with the heat.

Although the mist and heat devils almost always enveloped the platform, I have one memory in which it was fully illuminated. The memory dates from early afternoon, probably in late July. The water, which had swelled to a high point during the rainy season, was finally showing signs of subsiding, and more than seventy percent of the sluice was exposed to the light. Small waves lapped at the land, and clumps of bladderwort, blackened water chestnuts, and snail shells lay scattered where the water met the soil. There, a group of buck naked children had gathered at the water's edge and were making a loud fuss as they jumped into the shallow water.

One of the children grew frantic as he twisted his body and tried to peel off a leech stuck to his anklebone. One boy was painting his feet, stomach, and the small protuberance below his waistline with wet mud. They were splashing in the water and chasing one another.

The dazzling figure at the center of the group was a boy named Sentarō. His house was located along the road that ran between the

Korean ladies' wooden platform and the nearby hills. This young orphan lived alone with an old lady in a small, crude, windowless shack surrounded by the dark, gloomy green of a bunch of elderberry trees. He must have been around fourteen or fifteen years old, but he had grown so tall he could hardly fit into the tiny house. Of all the children, Sentarō was the only one who was not naked. He had wrapped a black piece of cloth around his waist to hide himself, but poking from the side of his covering, however, was a protuberance of flesh, far more developed than one might expect from a boy of his age. He was letting the other smaller children play with it in their hands. In the middle of the soft grass that peeked out from underneath the cloth, his flesh formed a small tower that swelled and revealed a vividly pink tip, touched with a drop of shining moisture.

The children surrounded him like a fence, but I was able to catch a glimpse of his strangely erect flesh between their bodies. As I did, I felt my throat go dry, and my heart began to pound at a much faster rate. Then all of a sudden, Sentarō's eyes, which had been closed and tilted toward the sun, turned to me and smiled.

"Mut-chan, wanna come over and try holding it?"

Even before these words were completely out of his mouth, I took off running, my clothes tucked under my arm. I clambered over Granny Tejima's stone wall, dashed in front of the Kubos' house, and ran into my grandparents' empty house. Both of them were at work, and no one was there. I locked the door from the inside.

Entering the main part of the house, I went through the eating area and walked by the Buddhist altar. Once I reached the veranda, I threw my legs out and sat on the wooden floor. The veranda looked out in the direction of the water where the boys were. The light passing through the glass doors, which were frosted in a pattern the shape of ferns, had made the room quite hot. Even though I had just run away, as I thought about Sentarō's erect flesh, the protuberance between my own thighs grew angry and hard, and I took it in my own hands.

I have the vague suspicion that the real reason Grandmother forbade me to go play by the sluice lay in that strange, direct form of pleasure, so different from that I had experienced in the games *Gikkon battan* and You Can See Tokyo.

2

When we moved in the second semester of my first year of school, the port of Moji presented me with an entirely different environment from the one I was used to. I had developed a certain bad habit two years before, but my new environment had prepared hitherto unknown sexual experiences for me, which I discovered after we moved.

A new place demands a ritual of rebirth and tribute from anyone who wants to become part of their new surroundings. As a symbol of my own rebirth, I changed the pronoun that I had been using to refer to myself—*uchi*—to the first-person pronoun *washi*. There are multiple pronouns that mean "I" in Japanese, and the one I had used until then in the countryside of Nōgata, I realized, sounded childish and slightly feminine. The pronoun *washi*, in contrast, was what all the boys in Moji used to refer to themselves. This change of pronouns may not have seemed like much to the outside world, but to me it was a sign that my spirit, which had so far seen little more than the clammy darkness within me, had suddenly started to soar like a great, masculine eagle toward the piercing light of the sun. Perhaps it is no coincidence that the word *washi* was also a homonym for the word meaning "eagle."

The gift one gives as tribute to one's new environment must also show signs of manliness. I had decided to give the gift of the bawdy songs I had picked up in Nōgata. Perhaps I chose this gift because I knew that bawdy songs were a sign of impudence. Plus, when men sing lewd songs to one another, they lay their hearts bare, erasing any distance between them. As I walked home from school along the glittering railroad tracks, I sang some of my dirty lyrics to my new friends Onion, Tamo-chan, and Yoshiaki-chan:

> Warships like twats
> Cannons like cocks
> Trumpets like assholes . . .

In the original Japanese, the first line was *memeko gunkan*, but as I offered them the gift of this song from Nōgata, I was sure to modify the lewd word *memeko* to *omeko*, the way the word was said in the dialect of Moji. My song was greeted by loud cheers and applause, and the four of us went home singing this song in a chorus at the top of our lungs. Rumors about our behavior quickly spread. Onion and Tamo-chan told people, "Mut-chan is a real pervert." Being a "real pervert" was in our eyes a synonym for being a real man.

I was immediately invited to join the Student Neighborhood Association for the students at the Citizens' School. Minami Hon-machi, the seaside neighborhood in which I lived, belonged to the first section of the third division of the association. When we went to school, we would congregate by the division to which we belonged, and we would line up under the banner that read "1 of 3."

The leader of the first section of the third division was Sei-yan, who was in the second class of higher school. For that reason, the meetings of the Student Neighborhood Association took place in the second story of Sei-yan's house. When everyone arrived, Sei-yan, who was pockmarked and had deeply set eyes, would say, "I call the September meeting of the Student Neighborhood Association to order." All the members would then drop their pants and remove their underwear so they were completely naked from the waist down. Next, they would huddle together like a mass of live bait from the tackle shop and indulge in licentious activities. I, however, did not drop my pants. Instead, I stepped away from all of them and went to the partially open window to look at the persimmon tree in the courtyard outside.

I am not trying to say that I never engaged in similar behavior. I would often engage in similar licentious games with Yoshiaki-chan. He lived near my new house, in the alley between the Matsushitas' house, which was two doors down, and the Nishikawas' house, where the middle-aged man with the big belly lived.

Sometimes when I had a fever and was lying in bed, Yoshiaki-chan would come over to play. I remember one time when he crawled inside my futon and put his cheek, which was as cold as porcelain, against my feverish cheek and said, "Um, Ei-san did something weird to me."

"What'd he do?"

"Something weird, kind of like this . . . and this." As he said this, he rustled around under the covers. With his eyes gleaming like a cat's in the pale darkness under the comforter, he fumbled around with the erection protruding between his legs.

I said, "I can't really figure out what you're talking about if you do it all by yourself. How about I pretend to be you, and you be Ei-san?"

Now that we had adopted our roles, I felt his hand enter the front of my pajamas and start rubbing my erection. I flushed bright red and said in a meek voice, "And then? Then what'd he do?"

"Then he made me do something weird."

Now it was my turn, in the role of Yoshiaki-chan, to rub him, who was still playing the role of Ei-san. Mother did not pay attention to our childish games, even though we frequently adopted new identities and acted out these sexual dramas.

Now when I think about it, I realize that Yoshiaki-chan might have been a secret agent working on behalf of Ei-san. Ei-san was the third son of Unno-san, the head of the neighborhood association for adults, and he was Onion's older brother. Both Ei-san and Onion belonged to the first section of the third division of the Student Neighborhood Association, but because their father was head of the adult neighborhood association, Ei-san did not attend the meetings. Ei-san dreamed of chairing a sexual seminar independent of Sei-yan's school of sexuality.

Eventually, Yoshiaki-chan stopped coming over, perhaps because he had finished investigating whether or not I would be an appropriate candidate for Ei-san's sexual seminar. I am not sure, but in any case a boy named Ishida soon took Yoshiaki-chan's place. In front of the house of the big-bellied man was a neighbor by the name of Shigematsu-san, and Ishida lived in the back of the alley by his house. His father was a postal worker, but a few generations back his ancestors had belonged to the samurai class.

Ishida was two years older than I, and so his frequent visits pleased Mother, who assumed he would be a good role model for me. Unlike when Yoshiaki-chan came over, Ishida and I would not perform dramas in which we adopted new identities; instead, we would just jump right into the sexual games.

After engaging in these activities for a while and thus passing through the first stage of induction, Ishida took me to see Ei-san. He said, "Ei-san, this guy has really become a full-fledged pervert."

Ei-san was a shrewd-looking third grader with a relatively dark complexion. He nodded, "I see, I see," then turned to me and said brusquely, "Come over tonight."

I nodded in agreement and followed Ishida outside. On the way home, Ishida and I were both quiet. He did not say a word and just kept on going while I went inside.

That evening after dinner, I visited the Unno home. The adults in the family each greeted me individually. The mother smiled and said, "Well, we're glad you could come over and play." She had dusted her broad face liberally with white powder, but it was possible to tell she had once been beautiful. She wore a slightly soiled kimono over her tall frame. Their father, who was short, had a red face, and smelled of alcohol, joked, "It's the Buu-yan of the Takahashi household. Welcome!" The second son of the Unno family, Ei-san's older brother, was quite pudgy and everybody knew him as "Buu-yan," which meant something like "Mr. Fatso" in local slang. Then he lined me up with the other boy and said, "Buu-yan from the Unno family, Buu-yan from the Takahashi family." Since my head was so big, I suppose, I might have looked fat.

They let me—Buu-yan from the Takahashi family—go into the room beside the living room. There were no lamps in the room. I sat cross-legged on the *tatami* mats, which were illuminated only by a thin sliver of light that leaked through the *fusuma*. As I did so, the *fusuma* on the dark side of the room slid open, and Ei-san then Onion came in.

Ei-san said in a hushed voice, "Take off your pants and underwear." Both of them were wearing nothing below the waist.

As we rolled around on the *tatami* mats, half naked, wearing only our shirts and rubbing against one another's bodies, I was still acutely aware of the crack of light leaking in through the *fusuma*. Sometimes I would see a person's shadow pass back and forth across it, and I would hear the rustling of the family outside. Ei-san and Onion, however, did not seem to pay any attention to their family at all.

All of a sudden, the *fusuma* on the light side of the room slid open, and someone came in. I reflexively stiffened and shut my eyes. When I dared to open my eyes a moment later, all I saw were a pair of feet walking across the *tatami*. The feet walked across the room, opened the *fusuma* on the dark side of the room, and disappeared. A few moments later, the same set of feet approached the *fusuma* on the dark side of the room. The door slid open, and this time, they walked across the room toward the light.

I was so stiff and nervous that I do not know whether the set of feet belonged to the mother, the father, or one of the elder brothers, Buu-yan or Ken-chan. Whoever it was, they must have seen our indecent behavior, but they did not stop to reprimand us. At the same time, Ei-san or Onion did not seem to mind the intruder at all. I found the whole thing very strange.

We started rubbing against one another almost every night in the dark room of the Unnos' house, and in the process, I started to think nothing of the footsteps that would walk by as we were playing our hushed games. Sometimes the feet belonged to the mother, sometimes to the father, sometimes to Buu-yan or Ken-chan, but no one ever stopped to reproach us.

One day I was playing in the road when Onion came up and whispered in my ear, "Someone's at our house right now. My brother says to come over."

I obeyed. We walked along the earthen-floored passage that led from the front entrance to the kitchen. Then we went into the backyard. Onion opened the door of the chicken coop and went inside. I asked him, "You want me to go in there?"

"Just shut up and come in."

I bent over and went into the coop, which smelled of half-eaten spoiled food and manure. In the back, Ei-san and Ishida were holding on to a Leghorn.

"You guys grab one, too."

Onion was able to capture one quickly. I just loitered about, so Ei-san stuck the chicken he was holding into my hands and grabbed another.

When we carried the chickens into the light outside, Ei-san declared, "Now we're going to do it with the chickens." Ei-san explained how the strange ritual would unfold. "First you put your index finger in the chicken's behind, then pull it out. You wipe the shit on your finger on a piece of paper. Next you stick in your dick."

Just as he had said, Ei-san buried his finger in the chicken's back-side, then pulled it out, and wiped it on some paper. Then he took his erect penis, pointed as a penknife, from the front of his pants and buried it in the backside of the chicken.

Ishida, Onion, and I went down the line in order and repeated Ei-san's actions. The sensation of the warm flesh of the chicken's orifice around my hardened penis was tremendously strange.

"Are you in, everyone? If you are, let's go out in front."

With Ei-san in the lead, the four of us made a procession and walked out into the brilliant light in front of the house, each carrying a Leghorn in a strange position below our waists.

A woman who was passing by looked at us and asked suspiciously, "What on earth are you doing?"

"Just playing."

We climbed to the second story of an empty house along the sea-shore and, some of us facing right, some of us facing left, we threw the chickens into the air. We sang every licentious song we knew and played until evening came.

3

When the war forced the people living along the seashore to evacuate, their houses had been left vacant. The houses had neither windows nor doors left. Inside one, there were two rooms with a bare floor of rough planking, which had been stripped of all *tatami* matting. There was noth-ing in between to divide the rooms, and so there was a clear view of the bare staircase at the back of the wall. Upstairs, there were two more rooms that had been stripped to the bare boards. Here and there were places where the boards had given way under people's weight, revealing a hole that went all the way down to the floorboards of the first story.

The second-story windows had no glass, so they were little more than gaping openings for the breeze to blow through. Beyond the win-dow-shaped openings was a stretch of sea, which was so bright it seemed to pierce our eyes. Beyond that, we could see the green trees growing on Hikoshima in Shimonoseki. In a certain place on the floorboards, there was a stretch of sand that had been brought from the seashore. The sand had been blackened by fire. The bad boys would light fires on the sand and roast chestnuts and potatoes. There were still high baseboards standing, so people on the street below could not see what secret mischief we children were up to in this palace of miracles.

There was a lot of graffiti on the baseboards in front of the charred sticks the boys had used to roast the chestnuts and potatoes. Some of the graffiti consisted of the kind of direct, crude phrases you might expect to find, but there were also more abstract bits of graffiti that were like codes: something about a sea urchin with the top split open or the "sun" that belongs to the natives of Papua New Guinea. The word that means "sun" in Japanese is written with two characters that mean "fat" and "yang," as in the male principle of the yin-yang duality. These sexual double meanings were not immediately obvious but were intriguing to us children nonetheless.

I couldn't help but notice that in the middle of the graffiti were the words "I want to fuck Kayoko." Kayoko was Ei-san's sister, and she was older than he was by three years. There was no way that Ei-san and Onion could not have known what was written there, but they never tried to cover it up or rub it out with a burnt piece of charcoal. It is not impossible that one of them was the one who wrote it on the wall. In their house, men were men, and women were nothing more than women. They didn't think of their sister as any different from any other woman. Brother-sister bonds didn't mean a thing.

Kayoko was able to let the foul and abusive language fly just as well as they could. I did not necessarily like her, but when I read the graffiti, I started thinking of her as a sexual being for the first time. Like Ei-san, she had a dark complexion and firm features. She would part her hair in what we called a "seven-three" cut—seventy percent of her hair on one side, thirty on the other—and she would hold it in place with pins, which made her look like an adult. The hair along the nape of her neck was cut straight across. Although she was fastidious about her appearance in some ways, there was also something slovenly about her. Sometimes it was possible to catch a glimpse of that side of her, for instance, in the sun-burned legs she tried to hide. I began to think I wanted "to fuck Kayoko," too. This was because of the spell the graffiti had cast over me. It was through the spell of language that I began to see Kayoko for the first time and to desire her.

I went home and immediately after entering the front door I wrote on the white wall, "Hisako got fucked." Hisako was, of course, my mother's name. Mother scolded me terribly, but for some reason she did not physically lay her hands on me. Maybe she thought that I was writing about her and her lover Ōgushi-san.

Perhaps Mother's scolding exorcised the devil from me. I forgot all about Kayoko. The one whom I had really liked was Inoue Hiroko-chan, who lived in front of us. One time, I took her to the shed behind our kitchen. There were no windows, so it was dark inside. The concrete floor felt cool on our feet. It smelled like morning in a deserted graveyard. Using a piece of graphite, I wrote a message in *katakana* letters on the floor, putting the letters in the reverse order, from back to front: *ta-i-tsu-ri-bu-ne-ni-ko-me-o-ta-bi-na-shi*. Blushing bright red, I told her to read it from back to front. When read the proper direction, it said, *shi-na-bi-ta o-me-ko ni ne-bu-ri-tsu-i-ta*, meaning "I licked her withered twat." When I think about it now, I realize that this was an expression of my love that somehow got twisted upside down.

If Hiroko was my imaginary lover at home, my imaginary lover at school was a girl named Kume-san. I sat next to her in both first and second grade. Her bobbed hair was full of luster; her eyes were bright and perky, and her bottom lip protruded slightly. Overall, she was about the same height as I was. There were times that only the two of us would stay in the classroom with the teacher after class ended and everyone went home. That was because Kume-san was a so-called athlete in penmanship, and I was an athlete in drawing. Everyone would tease us, calling the two of us and the teacher "Woman, man, and half a man." I think that they were half jealous. In any case, I was rather pleased with the situation.

One day after class, it was raining outside. I was drawing a poster about fire prevention. I lifted my red crayon from the picture of the burning match I had just drawn and looked at Kume-san beside me. "I've gotta go pee." The teacher was nowhere to be seen.

"Then go," she answered. She did not raise her head. She was writing the words *Fire Prevention* and was pouring all of her attention into the long vertical stroke on the next-to-last character.

"But it's raining out. It's no fun going outside to the outhouse."

"Then just pee out the window." She lifted her brush from the two dots she had just written and smiled at me naughtily.

"You mean get up on the window and let it go outside?"

"Just get up and go. Nothing to it."

"You won't tell the teacher?"

"Promise. Come on. Do it quick."

Spurred on by Kume-san, I opened the window and clambered up onto the windowsill. At first, my stream of urine cut upward across the rain, but then it fell to the ground in a graceful arc, forming lots of bubbles in a puddle of rainwater.

I got down from the window. Kume-san smiled as if to say, "See, no big deal, was it?" Because we shared this naughty secret, I felt that I had become intimate with her, almost as if I had "fucked her."

During the winter of fourth grade, I went back to visit Grandmother in Nōgata. My Aunt Tsuyano from Fukushima and my older sister Miyuki had recently started staying there. My aunt had just broken up with her husband Isamu, who was known to cheat on her, and she had brought back her new man, a burly fellow named Takagi-san who was twelve years younger than she.

My aunt and her partner slept in the area with the Buddhist altar where my grandparents usually slept, and my grandparents slept in the four-and-a-half-mat-wide eating area. My older sister was told to sleep in the back room that had formerly belonged to Uncle Ken'ichi. At the time, she was in sixth grade, and so everyone was aware she was right on the verge of puberty. That night, my family made me sleep with my sister.

It was difficult to sleep that night. Lying down in the next room was the strange newlywed couple whose ages were twelve years apart. My sister and I would frequently prick up our ears, but we could not hear a thing other than the pendulum of the clock ticking in the dining area. The fact that we could not hear anything just stimulated our imaginations all the more. Neither of us really made the first move, but somehow we ended up embracing one another. One of us got on top, the other on the bottom, and our bodies tangled tightly together.

No doubt my sister thought I was an apprentice brought into the family to work. I had only chanced upon the information that Miyuki was my sister recently, at the ceremony of the anniversary of my father's death when I happened to overhear Grandmother talking to the head nun from the temple. Until that point, I had thought that she was just my cousin, and even after that, we had not talked to one another about the real relationship between us. As we embraced and our bodies entangled, I kept thinking to myself, I am doing something terrible to my own sister!

It was when she said "Ouch!" that I finally stopped my despicable behavior. I had failed to act with my sister the same way the Unno brothers did with theirs.

4

Mother remarried in the spring when I was in sixth grade. To be precise, I suppose it would be fair to say this was, in practicality, her third husband, but she had never officially tied the knot with her second "husband," Ōgushi-san, so according to the law, this was only the second time she was married.

One summer day, Mother and I went with my new stepsister, Hiroko, and my new stepbrother, Tetsuo, to see my stepfather's parents in the countryside. He had come from a small town called Shiraishi. To get there from Moji, we had to ride the Nippō line for about an hour, get off at Yukuhashi, and take a bus for another twenty minutes. The town was located not far from the Suonada coast.

On the way from the Yukuhashi station to the bus stop, Mother stopped in a fancy goods store in order to buy some tissues, but for some reason she took a long time coming back out. As I licked at my ice candy with my stepsister and stepbrother, the only thing I could imagine was that she was asking inside the store about how to get to Shiraishi.

The road between the bus stop in Shiraishi and my stepfather's family's home was sizzling hot. The soybean plants at the side of the road were gasping under their covering of dust, and at his family home there was a dog crouching and sticking out its tongue in the blazing hot doorway. Beyond the soybean trees—in the dialect of northern Kyūshū we call a soybean plant that has started to bear soybeans a "tree"—there was an expanse of rice paddies. From beyond that came the smell of the ocean. Mother walked briskly five paces in front of us down the hot road.

Our destination was a little ways from the road in the middle of a number of rice paddies. We hastily greeted my new uncle and aunt, then went inside, which was so cool it seemed like another world to me. They had pushed open all the doors. There was nothing from the front to the back of the house to block the flow of air.

My aunt gave me a cold glass of barley tea. As I drank it, Mother called from the back where she was changing. "Mut-chan, come here for a second."

I borrowed a big pair of wooden clogs from the house and went outside from the kitchen to where she was. She was walking, apparently looking for a place in the backyard where the two of us could be alone. Finally, she stopped and squatted down on her heels in front of a shed. From there, we would have a hard time being overheard. Not knowing what else to do, I squatted down on my heels, too. I remember that the wind stopped there between the buildings, and the sweat began to bead up on my forehead once again. The cicadas screeched loudly.

After a moment of silence, Mother finally broached the subject as if resigned to her fate. "Mut-chan, you probably noticed, but today Mommy made a mistake and soiled her kimono. . . ."

I got the gist of what she was trying to say. Once I did, the mystery behind her strange behavior on the road that day became crystal clear. Her monthly visitor had arrived all of a sudden in the train, and she had accidentally soiled her kimono. She had gone to buy the tissue paper in front of Yukuhashi station and had used their restroom to take emergency measures. That was also the reason she walked in front of us after we got off the bus at Shiraishi.

Still, it would be a misrepresentation to say that I had known before that moment what had happened. It was only once she broached the subject that it began to dawn on me what had transpired. I looked at her, ready to protest that I hadn't realized a thing, but her face, which was turned toward the ground, was so imposing that I did not say a word. A moment later, she started speaking so I lost whatever chance I might have had to protest.

She explained to me that flowers have pistils and stamens, and that there were males and females among butterflies, too. Of course, none of that was any surprise to me. I knew what subject she was trying to discuss with these preludes, and it tickled me to hear her say these things. However, when she stopped beating around the bush, the information she delivered was completely new to me.

She picked up a stick and used it to draw a picture on the ground that showed the fundamental differences between the female body and the male body. That is when I learned that there is a dark, warm spot inside the female body called the uterus, and that every twenty-some days an alarming accident called ovulation takes place inside the darkness. I learned that if just a single one of the hundred thousand plus sperm released by the man managed to encounter that accident, the encounter would produce the seed of life.

The stick in Mother's hand moved rapidly back and forth. Those were not the shameless movements of the stick that scratched obscene graffiti into the vacant house on the seashore of Moji. Those were not the movements of the piece of graphite that scratched out nasty words on the concrete floor of the shed out back at home. Mother's stick was unflinching. She was teaching me about humanity—about the world. Perhaps she was aware from the beginning what parts of the story I had known and what I had not yet understood. Perhaps she felt that she had to teach me and decided that particular moment was a good opportunity.

"You got it? If you do, you can go now," she said. With these words, she was telling me to leave the shore of infantile sexuality to cross a dark and ancient flow to the shore of humanity. She was, in other words, telling me to join the world.

I began walking quietly back to the main house where my stepsister and stepbrother, my aunt, and my uncle were waiting indoors. The lights had already been turned on to illuminate the early evening.

Skies of Blood

1

There are many different types of skies that hang over the memories of my childhood. There are the May skies, clear as water, visible through the clusters of fresh, veined leaves of the persimmon tree over the corrugated iron fence off to the side of Grandmother's house. There are the skies of the rainy season that drooped heavily from the heavens and, before long, would drop gloomy ropes of rain that bound them tightly to the muddy earth below. There are the skies that would come at the end of summer and would be full of clouds, almost as if someone had blown the seeds of countless dandelions across the surface of a pond. There are the autumn skies that would draw in the red dragonflies, which would rise from the colored tassels of the cornfields and fly off until becoming nothing but tiny specks in the distance. And then there are the heavy winter skies that were usually the unpleasant color of lead but that would sometimes reveal a miraculous streak of blue as the gloomy snow clouds would split. There were many skies: the sky of morning, the sky of early afternoon, the evening sky filled with the kinds of stars described in fairy tales . . .

But the skies that serve as the most appropriate backdrop for my childhood are the ones emblazoned with the setting sun. The pond in front of Grandmother's house is at the center of one of the scenes of the setting sun that lingers in my memories: the edge of the pond forms a curve, and beyond that in the distance to the right is the outline of the hill known as Yamantani. It was right at the hill's pale-red border that the sunsets would begin. (On the far side of Yamantani, obscured from

view, was a place called Uchintani. When I was a little boy and I would
see the edge of Yamantani turn red, I felt sure the homes and fields in
Uchintani must be on fire.) In my memory, I am standing outside Grandmother's house and watching as the sunset grows more intense, gradually extending across the sky on the far side of the pond. Extending from
Yamantani, the blazing sun sets fire to the forest where the *yosshoi* bird
lives and to the roof of the Kantake Steel Plant on the opposite side of the
pond. As the sounds of metal rise from inside the steel plant, the flames
of the sunset igniting the roof send sparks into the air. These sparks dance
over the pond, then eventually fall into the water. As I stood there transfixed in front of Grandmother's house, intently watching the fire spreading across the sky and water, what was I thinking? Most likely, I was
thinking of Mother so far away.

There is another scene I remember. It is similar to the one I just
described, but instead of the pond it features the straits of Shimonoseki.
Similarly, the outlines of Yamantani have been replaced by the outlines of
the mountains of Yahata, and the thing on the opposite shore is no longer
the Kantake Steel Plant but the outlines of Hikoshima. The sunset has
spread over the hills of Yahata, but where the hills give out near Wakamatsu, the blazing sky creeps over the sea toward Hikoshima. The color
hovers over the calm sea, shattering into fragments that twinkle on the tips
of the waves. Once again, what was I thinking as I stood there on the sand,
transfixed as I peered out from between the boats pulled ashore alongside
the boat builder's cabin? Wasn't Mother foremost in my thoughts?

The colors of the sunset—how can I describe them? The sunsets
would start with orange, then move through a spectrum of colors—ver-
million, red, scarlet, then purple—until they were swallowed up in the
dark indigo of the night sky. As the colors went through these transformations, they reminded me of many shades of blood. Like blood—that is
how I thought of them.

For children, sunsets are first and foremost lively celebrations of
fun. Children run about beneath the blazing skies of sunset, chasing bats,
kicking bits of gravel, and singing songs. It is as if the joyously flowing
blood filling the veins of the sky excites the blood in the veins of the children below, filling them with vigor.

However, the joyous blood of celebration can also be terrifying and cruel as well. Children's bodies and minds are open to the banquet of pleasures, but they are also exposed and vulnerable. That is what I mean when I say that sunsets are the most fitting skies for my childhood memories, and that the sunsets over the memories of my youth are skies of blood.

As a little boy, whenever I saw the blood swelling and congealing on the surface of the sky, I would think of Mother. This did not only happen during her absence when I was living with Grandmother or was being passed from one household to another. Even after she returned, I continued to think about her as I watched the sunset. She was often away, and every time she left, I was exposed to the violence of my Grandmother, my aunt, and other adults. That would only make me miss my kind and gentle mother all the more. When she returned, however, I never again found the kindness I had been waiting for. Instead, what confronted me was another kind of aggression. The violence she displayed toward me was something that ran deep in her veins and that even she could not control once it had been awakened. When I encountered violence in my own mother, it only made me yearn all the more for what I believed motherhood should be—eternal kindness.

One scene I remember took place beneath a sky completely covered with blood. In my mind's eye, I see the straw-thatched roof of Grandmother's house, the path wrapping around the pond, the gate at the railway crossing at the end of the path, the railroad tracks extending into the distance, the sluggish river flowing along the far side of the tracks, the large-flowered evening primroses growing alongside the muddy river, and beyond that, the dirty glass windows lining the streets of the town. As Mother and I walk through this landscape, we are bathed in blood from the sunset above.

As she holds my hand, she leads me into town so that she could buy some medicine for the ailment we call "blood paths" in Japanese—a nervous affliction that appears in women, sometimes taking the form of dizziness or even hysteria. Early in the spring, when the buds were appearing on the trees, Mother would inevitably begin to suffer from this ailment. I imagined that the blood that runs throughout the earth would begin to move through the invisible arteries under the ground, and it would flow into the slumbering roots of the trees, erupting like boils in the form of the leaves above. Meanwhile, the same flow of blood would stir the blood in the blue veins beneath her skin and push through each and every hair on her body. At such times, Mother's violence toward me would grow crueler, and ever more unjustified.

There is a word in Japanese, *chishio*, that is written with the characters meaning "blood" and "tide" and that is used to refer to someone's hot-bloodedness or proclivity to fits of temper. If it is true that the movement of the heavenly bodies really does affect the flow of blood, creating something like tides within the body, I imagine the times she was pleasant and calm were when Mother's blood paths were at low tide. During those moments, I am sure she reproached herself for her senseless outbursts of temper. Perhaps that was the reason she took me, her young victim, by the hand and led me into town to buy some medicine to calm her suffering.

The place where Mother bought her medicine was a shop that belonged to her uncle Kōno Bansaku. It was located in a row of nice-looking buildings constructed in an old-fashioned style. The shop was not a regular pharmacy. It only sold a few things: paper, certain goods imported from China, and a peculiarly effective kind of medicine called Dragon Shrine Powder made from a recipe that had been handed down in the family for generations. The medicine came in packages printed with a dark-brown picture of Urashima Tarō riding the back of a large turtle. Inside were ten, twenty, or thirty little gauze pouches of medicine—the number of pouches depended on how much you paid. When I would bring the little pouches to my nose, I would smell the herbs and bark that been had ground into powder, and the comforting aroma filled me with a wave of vague, nostalgic longing.

What was Bansaku's store like? He had enough money and standing in the community to later run as a candidate for city council, so I imagine that the store must have been rather large and had various kinds of imported goods. I only remember a few details, however: the figure of Bansaku himself sitting at the counter by the front door, and the great big *shōji* door behind him.

Standing in front of the low, latticed screen that separated her and Bansaku, Mother spoke to him in polite language that indicated a degree of ceremony that came across as rather cold. "I think perhaps I'll take some of that Dragon Shrine Powder of yours."

"How much do you want?"

"Twenty days' worth, so two packs please. How much does that come to?"

"One pack's eighty sen, so that'll be one yen, sixty sen."

Mother took out her wallet and handed the change to Bansaku.

He counted it and nodded, "One-sixty exactly."

Although they were uncle and niece, they never called one another Uncle or Niece, as you might have expected. Come to think of it, I don't remember him ever saying anything at all to me, even though I was often there with Mother, holding on to her hand. All I do remember is his thin body, bronzed bald head, and expressionless eyes hidden behind rimless eyeglasses.

Mother told me later that this unusual degree of formality had its roots in some old, bad blood within the Kōno family. Even though the Kōno family had once been so upstanding that they had provided the leadership for the village, by the time Bansaku and his sisters—my grandmother Shikano and my two other great-aunts Tomo and Saki—were in their late teens, the family had fallen into complete disarray. The only one that their mother, Kuni, showed any affection for was Saki. Shikano, the oldest daughter, and Tomo, the second daughter, rebelled against their mother and ganged up on their younger sister Saki. Bansaku took Saki's side, however. Still, that does not mean that Saki and Bansaku were especially obedient to their mother, Kuni.

Kuni would spread a straw mat in the garden and put soybeans on it to dry in the sun. Shikano, however, would pull the mat into the shade. Kuni would pull it back into the sun, and Shikano would pull it back into the shade again. She would repeat this absurd, naughty behavior over and over, but neither mother nor daughter would ever say a word, even as the other three children watched from the shade.

Before long, Bansaku abandoned the old house and married into a wealthy family in town, and Shikano, who was more stout-hearted than the others, was left as the oldest child in the household. Although they lived less than two and a half miles away from each other, they never spoke again, and Bansaku didn't even bother to put in an appearance at Shikano's funeral.

The two had not always been on such bad terms. Mother once told me that they had been rather close for a while. Shikano was quite good-looking, so much so that people compared her to Ono no Komachi, a famous beauty from classical Japan, and called her the Komachi of Rokkō. Bansaku was also an elegant, handsome man—a rare commodity in that town. They said that when the two of them, nineteen and sixteen years of age, respectively, climbed up onto the embankments of the Inunaki River, dressed in their *meisen kurume-kasuri* fabrics and talking to one another, they looked like two youngsters in love. Perhaps I am reading too much into things, but part of me wonders if the two of them didn't have an incestuous relationship. If they didn't, then it's hard for me to imagine what might have transpired between them to cause them—a brother and sister who had loved each other so much—to suddenly develop a hatred so deep that it lasted until the end of their lives.

I also cannot help but wonder if it wasn't the frustrations of forbidden love that caused Shikano to live such a colorful, amorous life. After all, she had had seven husbands, plus who knows how many other men in between. It is not impossible that Bansaku experienced similar frustrations but expressed them in a different form, and that was the reason he dedicated himself to accumulating wealth in such a cold-hearted, calculating fashion. Come to think of it, after Bansaku and Shikano became estranged, he fell in love with the youngest daughter, Saki, who looked like Shikano, only somewhat less attractive.

Although her bloodlines stagnated in those dark, country houses, Mother did not become wanton or parsimonious. She never forgot the day her own mother was violated by some strange man in a woodshed while she was still strapped to her mother's back. As a result, my mother came to hate lasciviousness, especially in women. She also hated stinginess. She did not spare any goodwill toward Bansaku, a man so stingy that he had driven his only son to suicide. My mother still had strong feelings, and sometimes she would lose control of the passion that coursed through her veins, and she would grow violent and rain her wrath down on me.

There were many things about Mother's situation that were different from those of other people, but in those days, it was not unusual for adults occasionally to grow violent toward their kids. It sounds strange to say this, but when adults behave violently toward children, they always seem much sadder than the children they mistreat. Children do not fail to notice that, even as they tremble in fear. Nor do they fail to notice that a certain part of the sadness that creeps into the violent expressions of these angry adults stems from the bloody sunsets that color the earth and sky like a set of eyes, red and swollen from weeping.

2

The place most connected with my memories of Mother's brutality is the home we shared in Moji. In my memories of that dark house, located by an old highway running along the seashore and into the hills, there are many places I associate with her anger. There are the sliding glass windows that would shake all day long as the horse-drawn carriages passed by outside. There is the rather light, four-and-a-half-mat room just inside the glass windows where my cherrywood study table was located. There is the dark four-and-a-half-mat room even farther in, next to where we ate our meals. There is the closet that hid the Buddhist altar. There is the chilly, wooden-floored area where she placed cans of rolled barley and rice, surrounded by piles of sweet potatoes. There is the area by the front door, with its one pane of glass broken out and replaced with paper. There is the narrow corridor that ran from the front door to the place where she did the cooking. There is the stove, the toilet in the courtyard, the bathtub and the broken door to the place underneath where we stoked the logs, the storage area that smelled like a grave. . . . My memories of all these places are darkened by her angry eruptions of blood.

I speak about Mother's violence, but intertwined in it there was also an element of kindness. In that dusty, continuously shaking dark house, she was like the goddess Kishimo who ate a hundred children to fill her voracious stomach. What was different about her and the legend of Kishimo was that I was both the child she loved as well as one of the children she devoured. Actually, perhaps there is no difference between loving and devouring. All mothers love their sons, yet at the same time they are like Kishimo, devouring children—the kindness of a mother is actually part and parcel of what makes her so ferocious. These two things are impossible to separate. They are like a single object that changes its hue, like the wings of a beetle that alters its tint depending on the light that hits it. When people tell the legend of Kishimo, they are usually telling a story of the Buddha's compassion, but I think the true message hidden within the tale is that motherhood has a dual nature.

For instance, I remember the time we were sitting on either side of the hibachi in the lighter of the two four-and-a-half-mat rooms. Mother was doing her sewing with a shiny needle on one side, and I was reading a book on the other. She suddenly threw down her sewing, grabbed me by the back of the collar, and pulled me down onto the *tatami* mat. In that moment, I was tossed suddenly from our heavenly world into the blood-colored depths of hell. Later, when I found myself alone with her, I felt nothing but hopeless fear.

When Mother's outbursts of unjustified hostility rained down on me, I did not cry out or protest. If I raised my voice, Korenaga-san, the lady who lived in the apartment on the other side of the dark room, would come over and get involved. Only a single door separated her apartment from ours. That is why Mother would say, "How disgraceful! If you're gonna cry, cry without making any noise!" Driven into the corner of the room, I would cry quietly to myself as I looked at Mother, who stood over me like a statue of Kishimo.

Of course, Mother's anger was not always completely unprovoked. I would sometimes do things to invite it. I had developed a rather warped personality as a result of being passed back and forth between my Grandmother, aunts, and all the other strangers as they played their game of Heaven and Hell. Part of me wanted to recoil from the world. I read people's expressions, acted devious, and didn't necessarily care about very much. I imagine Mother found it hard to put up with my behavior, knowing that in some way it was her own absence that had helped to create it. Still, explanations do not mean very much; they do not actually change things that are right before your eyes.

One time, when I was in first grade, I got sixty percent on a dictation test. Mother flew into a rage, took a hard wooden abacus, and whacked me over the head with it over and over. The abacus broke. The beads flew all over the room, and blood started pouring from my head, which was still soft with youth. Another time, I lifted the lid on the pot above the cupboard where we kept the tea utensils and ate one of the taro roots she had soaked in sake and *mirin*. Mother grabbed me under her arm, marched me out to the seashore, and threw me, clothes and all, into the early winter waves at the water's edge. I was soaked to the bone, but she would not let me back into the house for some time. As a result, I developed a high fever. She was not just punishing me because she loved me and wanted me to do better. There was a rage that would boil up in her blood and that she herself had difficulty understanding and keeping under control. My behavior merely provided triggers that provoked that rage.

I do not think there was anything noble or righteous about her anger—she was not dishing out tough love or punishing me for my own sake. Still, there were moments that as she pulled me around and I wept silently, she would also break into tears. The only thing I can think of that might have caused her to cry like that was some strain of kindness and tenderness intertwined with her rage. At a certain point, her violence started to bring me the same peace of mind as sharing the dinner table with her, exchanging a smile, or receiving some bit of kindness. If some dark blood was driving her to hostility, then the same forces were also driving me to tears. The two of us were a pair. In a sense, we had joined our hands in the blood of violence, and together we had walked out together into the limelight. It was as if we were on a kabuki stage and this was our own moment to shine, and so we made our way along the raised, bloody platform from the back of the theater to the stage at the front.

Just as her violence had an underside of kindness to it, her violence was also a special, secret sacrament that belonged to us and us alone. That was the reason Mother was so unforgiving toward other children who hurt me. One time, I came home crying with a bump on my head. The ones who had given it to me were Shun-chan and Takash-shan, two boys from the Etō family who lived next door on our right-hand side. Mother flushed with rage, flew out of the house, and hunted down the rogues. They ran for a block and barged into Unno-san's house. Mother followed them right in.

No one was at home in the Unno residence. They had just left their door unlocked. Shun-chan and Takash-shan ran from the front door down the earthen pathway that led all the way to the courtyard, and they dashed inside the chicken coop. No doubt they thought she wouldn't follow them there, but in she went. She grabbed the two of them by their collars and picked them off the ground like a cat carrying its kittens. She marched them right back to their own house and gave them a good thrashing right in front of their own mother.

Although I was usually on good terms with my classmate Onion, there were many times when he would try to act big and start teasing me in front of his three brothers. If Mother heard me crying, she would burst outside, grab the arm of the boy who was teasing me, and give it a good twist. When she grabbed Onion, he would immediately start howling; after all, he was a crybaby to begin with, and that was the reason he had been given his nickname. His cries would then make his mother rush outside. Still twisting his arm, Mother would hand him off to his mother in the middle of the street.

In a shrill voice, Onion's mother asked Mother, "You know what everyone says about you?"

"No."

"I'll tell you. Everyone laughs at you . . . a mom who gets in the middle of her kid's fights."

"Go ahead and laugh if you want. I don't come out if I don't have to."

"Must really care 'bout your kid," she said sarcastically.

"Unlike you guys who just keep pumping out kids one after another."

"If he's so damn precious, maybe you'd better lock him up in a money box."

"Sounds good. Quick, go get your money box for me!"

People gathered round to watch them argue. The horse-drawn beer carts stopped, and the postal carrier stopped his bicycle. No doubt they were all looking suspiciously at my mother. The same mother who treated her own child as badly as if he were a stepson had now gone half-mad trying to protect her little boy.

I ran into the house, and scarcely daring to breathe I peeked through the cracks in the door by the veranda. From there, I watched as she and Onion's mother continued to argue.

3

Mother and I were probably a rather extreme example, but other children also learn about the world through the violence of adults. They learn that violence creates, destroys, then remakes the world. They also learn that kindness is really just another name for violence. Children who have learned that then try to put it into practice themselves, but there, once again, they take on certain roles. Strong children end up the aggressors, and weak children end up their victims.

As with adults, violence among children has no real reason. If anything, children innately know that violence is meaningless; however, in those days, we children were living in the greatest possible season of violence—war. Camped out in the courtyard of the Citizens' School were a bunch of soldiers waiting to be shipped off to the battlefield. The punishments they would inflict on each other taught us just how meaningless violence could be. One time when the air-raid sirens were going off, and the students were lined up in groups to hurry out of the school, one of the soldiers kicked me into the mud. The other children would imitate this sort of behavior. Once when I was playing in the road, one of my playmates advertently hauled off and slugged me.

Why was I the victim of violence so often? Because I was weak—that and no other reason. I think people usually assume that those with authority punish others because they are bad, but that is not true. People get punished simply because they are weak. To those with power, weakness is an enemy that cannot be tolerated.

The world of the child is structured according to an order determined by relations of power. Not even our crafty institutions of education, which kidnap children and take them away, fail to make use of that order. The student associations that existed in every neighborhood were no exception. Minami Hon-machi, the area in which I lived on the western shore of Moji, belonged to the first of three student groups. When we would go to school, someone would hold up the "1 of 3" flag, and we would form two lines that marched to school. The leader of our group was Kiyo-yan who lived in the third house on the right in the little alleyway visible from the front of our house. The group did not have a second-incommand, but Okino Tet-chan, the boy who lived on the right side as you walked toward the sea down the alley two blocks down from our house, certainly acted like he was. In order to appease Tet-chan's rival, Unno Ei-san, Kiyo-yan had decided that every morning, the two rows would start their march to school from the front door of the Unnos' house.

Our march to school looked like it was properly organized, but that was only a veneer. In his heart, Ei-san rebelled against the hierarchy that placed Kiyo-yan at the summit as leader. Kiyo-yan's hierarchy was a gymnasium of violence, and at the same time a seminar in sexuality. Kiyo-yan would frequently call together groups of students, sometimes to dole out punishment and sometimes for masturbatory games. These two things happened in roughly equal proportions. Ei-san did not participate directly in those meetings. He dreamed of his own school of violence and sexuality where he could be superintendent.

I was a newcomer to the group, and so Kiyo-yan's faction and Ei-san's faction both scrambled to get me to join. That was before Mother and Unno-san had their showy fight in the street, and Mother was still rather close to the members of the Unno household. As a result, at some point, I seemed to end up with the Unno faction, which was presided over by Ei-san. Kiyo-yan's faction consisted of Kiyo-yan, Tet-chan, Kiyo-yan's little brother who was nicknamed Hippo, Tamo-chan from the Shiokawa family, and the Kitahara brothers. Together, they formed a pretty tough crowd. In contrast to them, Ei-san's faction consisted only of Ei-san, Ei-san's little brother Onion, and Ishida—not a very high-spirited bunch overall. Even so, they had developed a series of hand signals that they would flash to each other like the flags used to communicate between ships at sea.

Stick up the thumb of your right hand, and that was the sign meaning "Come here." Stick up the pinky finger of your left hand, and that was the sign meaning "Run away." Stick up the pinky fingers of your left and right hands together, and that was the sign meaning "Let's masturbate." Make a circle with the thumb and index finger of your right hand, and that was the sign meaning "Give me a little snack." In those days, Ōgushi-san, Mother's lover in China, was sending us tins and boxes of cookies, chocolates, and other goodies, so I had access to all sorts of snacks. Probably one reason both factions scrambled to get me to join involved those imported goodies. I literally reeked of them—their scent still adhered to the fine, foreign clothing he had sent me in the same boxes.

The punishments would be attended by several spectators, who were always the first to see the results. Because Ei-san's faction had only a few members, they naturally engaged in more sexuality than violence; however, the two pillars supporting the group were sex—or what one might also call "erotic power"—and aggression. These two pillars complemented one another; one involved self-indulgence and the other self-chastisement. If one of those two pillars was missing, the foundations of the group would become unstable. One of the reasons Ei-san's faction had begun to bore me was that it was lacking in violence and thus seemed to have lost one of the reasons for its existence.

Once, Tet-chan from the Okino family sent for me. I had just gotten out of class. I had bowed in the front of the little building that housed the picture of the emperor and the Imperial Rescript on Education and then walked out of the school gates. Right then, a shadow came flying up to me from behind and said, "Wait by the *tonderu*." Surprised, I turned around to see Tet-chan's retreating figure as he dashed back into the school yard.

The word *tonderu* was our way of saying the foreign word "tunnel." We would call the part of the tunnel that the car would enter the *ton*, which sounds like the character that means "go away," and we would call the part of the tunnel the car comes out of the *deru*, which means "come out." The *tonderu* we were referring to was five hundred yards to the right from where the road from school dead-ended at the railroad tracks. It was an underpass that ran beneath the railway tracks that led to Minami Hon-machi. The *tonderu* was a shoddy structure that had been built during the war, so naturally the water would pool at the bottom of the underpass. You could go in the *ton*, but you could not go out the *deru* on the other side.

Just because he had told me to meet him there did not mean that I had any obligation to obey. Still, I decided to wait for him at the edge of the pool of water, which had collected beneath the underpass. I squatted in the shade at the base of the concrete wall. From there, he would be able to see me as he approached from the top of the downward-sloping road.

As I squatted there, I couldn't help feeling as if he were a great angel of violence that had taken on the form of a little boy, and I was waiting for him to make a visitation.

Tet-chan appeared at the top of the road. He was in third grade, and that day he was wearing a slightly soiled black uniform dusted with white flecks. His school cap was pulled down, far over his eyes. He had strewn his visibly dirty book bag, made of a rough hempen material, over his shoulder with a cord, and a long, thin towel trailed from where he had tucked it in his back pocket like a tough guy. He was only two years older than I, but still he looked uncomfortably big to me. As I squatted at the base of the slope, he approached me from above. Of course, the fact that he was looming over me helped determine our roles, but more than anything it was the difference in our sizes that determined what our relationship would be and what roles we would play. In other words, it was clear from the start that Tet-chan would be the assailant and I would be his victim.

As he stood in front of me, his eyes commanded me to stand, and then without a word he suddenly hit me. A sudden metallic shock ran from my nose into my brain. I felt a flood of sunset, an inundation of bloody sky. When I finally picked myself off the ground, Tet-chan was nowhere to be seen, and my nose was bleeding profusely. That was when I realized that the dream-like vision of the sunset that had so captured my imagination was full of the same blood now pouring out of my own nostrils.

One time, I was unexpectedly kidnapped by Tet-chan's faction. The place they gathered was at Tamo-chan's shed, located in the same row of buildings as Tet-chan's house. Tamo-chan's mother was a hairdresser, so in addition to the usual things you might find in a shed—small hoes, scythes, and baskets—there was also a whetstone for sharpening knives, a sunken fireplace, and even a circular whetstone that you could turn with a pedal. Tet-chan and the others would brag about how they were ready to fight since they had sharpened their blades and railroad spikes on the hearthstones and the whetstone. They wrapped their weapons in cloth, then hid them in their clothes.

"We don't mess around with Eigorō, Onion, or those guys. The only ones we fight are guys from other groups or the guys over in Kanda-machi." When Tet-chan said this to me, I accepted his statement without arguing. Ei-san's group had no violent tendencies; in fact, they were so powerless that they hardly merited the attention of Tet-chan's glittering blade and spikes. What he said made sense. Their shiny weapons were much better suited for the likes of the bad boys in the second of the three neighborhood associations, or the rogues of Kanda-machi.

Behind the whetstone and the sickles, in the cool, straw-filled darkness of the shed, I joined Tet-chan and the others in their masturbatory games. Meanwhile, the dazzling light of the overgrown garden flooded through the opening in the wall. By the time I started playing those games with them, I had already left Ei-san's faction for good.

At school, there was another hierarchy, and at the top of it was a boy named Tajima, who had a round face and thick, downward-sloping eyebrows. He had lost his father, and so he lived with his mother and younger brother in their uncle's house behind the Yoshitani Pharmacy. Ever since first grade when he had managed to make a third-grader cry, the children at school had treated him as a special luminary.

When I was in fourth grade, I was in the same class with him: Fourth Grade, Class One. I was included among his minions, and we would form our own palace of miracles in the corners of the school storehouse, the floors of the auditorium, and the attic above the classrooms. There, in those places, we would do treasonous things like passing around cigarettes or plotting to steal tomatoes off someone's vines. Each time it began to look as though our hideout might be discovered, we would send out a scout to locate potential spots for our next hideout. Our school was big, about four thousand square yards, so it seemed as vast as an entire country to us. Its size meant there were plenty of places for us to hide ourselves away.

Whenever we left an old hideout behind, Tajima would always call Shibamura, a small boy who everyone thought of as a joker. Right away, he would squat down in front of Tajima. Shibamura was always ready to take a poop, no matter when or where. As he squeezed it out, the rest of us would watch, composed expressions on our faces. That was our ritual. Shibamura was essential for this ritual because he was ready to defecate at the drop of a hat.

We would also eat our lunches in our hideout. When we had *bentō* boxes, we would take out all the things our mothers had put in with the rice and lay them on the lids of the boxes. Next, we would respectfully hold out the lids with the food to our leader. He would use his chopsticks to pick out what he wanted from the large number of offerings, then return the remaining food. It was only after everyone had done this that the donors would start their own lunch. It was rare that Tajima would reach out to take the food on the lid of my *bentō* box. The reason was that I always brought poor people's food, such as soybean husks cooked in broth or round slices of *daikon* simmered until they had become tender. Every time I held out my offerings, I would feel doubly embarrassed: first by what Tajima might think, and second by the opinions of all the others.

One day, there was something special in my lunch: a fried fish that had been softened somewhat and cooked in a fried egg. Should I offer it to Tajima or hold it back? I wavered. If I stuck it out and he didn't take it, I would be humiliated once again. But what would happen if I didn't stick it out . . . ? As I deliberated, I used my chopsticks to break apart the fish Mother had made with such care, and almost before I knew it, I was carrying it to my mouth.

All at once, I found everyone's gaze focused on the point where my chopsticks met my mouth. Hurriedly, I blurted out an excuse: "I've been sick, guys, so my mom said I need lots of nutrients."

Tajima spat, "I don't wanna eat anything his mom made anyway."

No one else said a word. A certain coolness came over the lunch crowd that day, and lunchtime seemed to drag on for ages.

I am not sure how many days later it was, but after our physical education class ended, everybody ran over to the sandbox. I happened to be standing relatively close to the sandbox, so I was the first one in. A moment after I jumped in, someone pushed me over. Tajima had been the second one to get there, and he had knocked me off my feet.

I am not sure where the sudden urge to fight back came from, but as I got to my feet, I started pummeling Tajima's back with my tiny fists. That is not to say that I was not frightened of him. My fear was obvious from my loud sobbing as I swung both fists at him.

Tajima was completely taken aback. One of his completely power-less followers was hitting him, the strong leader. The little weakling was crying as he hit him over and over. Like a colossus surprised by an unexpected shower of rain, he acted utterly puzzled as my feeble fists rained down on him.

The teacher in charge, Tomosada-Sensei, came over. He immediately said, "Tajima, you were at fault."

The colossus who had been just standing there completely confused suddenly let out a loud wail. He ran back inside the classroom, crying uncontrollably. Later, when we returned to the classroom, he was nowhere to be seen. Tomosada-Sensei, all the other students, and I found a message scrawled across the chalkboard:

Tomosada-Sensei,
    You always say I'm the one to blame, no matter what happens. That hurts my feelings. I'm going to get changed to another class.
                             Tajima

Starting the next day, Tajima kept an eye on me. In his view, his followers were like a big bunch of samurai retainers. The hierarchy was determined by where they ended up with each swordfight. I, however, had proved that I was neither his subordinate nor his foe. In his mind, he had assigned me a position that was neither of those two roles. If anything, he seemed to think of me as a sort of sorcerer. With a single magic wand, I—the powerless little boy—had cast a curse over him and his followers, plus his enemies as well. "Hee-hee-hee-hee, watch out! I'm about to cast a terrible spell over all of you!" As I waved my wand and spoke these words, the great swordsmen scattered in every direction like baby spiders.

I saw school as having taken me away from the solitary pleasures I had known before, and the violence of the other schoolchildren had managed to eat away at what little of my privacy remained. However, because I had made a display of resistance against their aggression, I was able to earn back a fraction of the happiness that I had lost. That left me in a rather strange state, but it was still something.

I was a sorcerer—one single point in a vacuum. All of the others feared that vacuum and scattered in all directions, running for air where they could breathe comfortably again.

4

When Mother remarried, it was to a man who was in charge of track maintenance and divisions at the Moji railroad, and so the two of us moved, but only a half-year later the two of them got a divorce. At the beginning of the following summer, I was in middle school. The following memory dates from about that time, on the day of the festival at the port of Moji. Mother and I had gone with my former stepfather to have some fun at Mekari Shrine, which is dedicated to the deity Watatsumi-no-ōkami and is located at the edge of Moji.

Mother and my former stepfather got divorced because his children and I did not get along. They didn't split up because of a fight; if anything, he and Mother still seemed quite fond of one another. He would still come over to our new house once or twice a week. Sometimes, he would even take us to the port or across the straits to Shimonoseki.

That day, my former stepfather saw us back to our apartment, then went back to his home. Mother and I decided to have dinner right away. We were seated on either side of our low table when we heard the refrains of a song coming through the thin wooden wall by the front entrance. The song itself seemed to reek of alcohol:

Oh, feudal lord with the eyebrows
When you take your mistress
And go see the cherry blossoms
People everywhere
Will be talking . . .

When people sing this song, they take their thumb and point first to their eyebrows, then to their eyes, nose, cheeks, and mouth. It was a rather vulgar song, the sort that you might sing to poke fun at someone. It was clear that the man who was singing it was making fun of my former stepfather who was still coming to see Mother even after their divorce.

Mother was holding a glass dish in her left hand, and in her right the chopsticks transporting the *sōmen* noodles to her mouth had paused in midair. Her temples twitched. With a clatter, she put her chopsticks down on the tea table, then pulled herself up to her full height as if to confront the singer.

"Hey, you, Gutter Turtle, just try singing that again!"

The man she was calling Gutter Turtle was Kameji, a day laborer who lived next to us in our cheaply constructed building. *Kame*, the first character of his name meant "turtle," and he drank quite a lot. His apartment was separated from ours by just a thin wall of rough boards so we could hear him even in the privacy of our own home.

Kameji's family was made up of him, his wife, Tomiko, and their son, Tetsuji, who was about to turn two. All three of them lived in a minuscule three-mat room, and they hardly had a stick of furniture to their name. During the day, Kameji was almost too quiet, and when we ran into him in the morning he would trudge off silently, holding at waist level the *bentō* box containing his lunch. When he received his wages, he drank most of them away, and when he was drinking, he would kick his wife and hit his infant son. In the aftermath, he might turn against us.

He shouted, "What? You don't like being called a mistress? I don't care. I'll say it as many times as I want." He wobbled over on his wooden clogs to where Mother was standing in the hallway. He was only wearing a loose pair of underpants.

Mother was furious. "'Mistress, mistress!' How dare you? When was I ever a mistress?"

"Mistress! Mistress! You are a mistress, aren't cha? I'll say it again and again. Mistress. Mistress. Misss-trrr-esss!"

By this point, Kameji had stuck out his chin at her in provocation, and there were only about three inches separating his face from Mother's. His breath reeked of strong liquor. Mother gave him two hard slaps with her open hand, one on each side of his face.

This time it was Kameji's turn to fly off the handle. "You fuckin' whore!" Without removing his wooden clogs, he stormed into our room after her. He grabbed her hair and dragged her down onto the floor, which was nothing but hard boards with a single woven straw mat spread over them.

"Let me go! Let me go!" she screamed, but her voice seemed to be choked by the bubbles of hatred and anger rising in her blood.

Mother's bloody screams made every last drop of blood in my own body boil in sympathy. I could feel every branching vessel and artery in my body burn with the flames of sunset. I grabbed the glass dishes on top of the tea table and threw them at Kameji one after another.

There were noodles dangling from his head, water dripping from his body, and blood gushing from his neck. Furious, he let go of Mother and lunged for me. Still in my bare feet, I dashed through the dirt-floor area by the door of the house and flew into the sunset outside.

I ran between our neighbors, Shirae-san and Yamane-san, dashed past Horimoto-san and Kimoto-san, then between Ishimaru-san and Eguchi-san. I looked over my shoulder and saw that although Kameji was still barefoot, he was now wielding an ax and was close on my heels chasing me.

The road filled with people, and whole groups of neighbors peered out of their windows to watch the drunken man behave like a bloody demon. The sunset seemed to bathe everything in a tragic shade of red—the windows, the faces of the people looking out at us, the dirt road down which both Kameji and I were running in our bare feet, and even the air itself.

From out in the distance, I could hear our neighbor Tomiko screaming in a shrill voice, "Run for your liiiiiife, Mut-chan!" Some part of me couldn't help but realize that there, in the middle of that beautiful sunset, which illuminated both heaven and earth, Kameji and I were engaged in a race to the death. The ax was hanging right over me. I was only seconds away from having my head split open.

Suddenly, like a miracle, the Hirotas' field appeared before me. There was a path right down the middle. I rushed down it as fast as I could go.

A few moments later, I turned to look and saw that Kameji had stopped near the entrance to the path. The ax was dangling limply from his hand. His face, which was already half obscured by twilight, looked strangely sad.

The landlord, Shirae-san, came to get me, and he gave me shelter in the front of his house. Later that night, Mother came to collect me. Below her eye, all the way down her cheek was a big, purple bruise. We tiptoed into the house, trying not to make any noise. From the other side of the wooden wall, we could hear the sound of unencumbered snoring.

That evening, Mother was silent. After that, she no longer engaged in any violence toward me, making it clear that she had been satisfied by my manly behavior. I suspect that when I acted aggressively to protect her, she stopped seeing me as the weak, little boy I had been until that point. I had not grown up completely, but she had seen unmistakable signs of me becoming a man.

No doubt that evening, the sunset that had illuminated the heavens and earth so magnificently—that bloody sunset that was as beautiful as it was tragic—had conveyed its passionate energy to all of our veins. It had flowed into Mother, into me, and even into Kameji, with all of his forlorn melancholy.

Imagining Father

1

Tangible things are not the only things that can leave deep scars on the soul of a young child. Sometimes things that do not exist—things that are absent from one's life—leave even firmer imprints on the soft flesh of the heart.

In my early youth, the thing that I missed above all others was a father. My father died soon after my birth, well before I had emerged from the blackness of oblivion into the light of consciousness—before I had even really come into being. In a sense, my father's absence preceded my very existence.

When people asked me, "Mut-chan, don't you wish you had a daddy?" I would shake my head and say, "Nuh-uh," without any expression at all. People must have thought me very unloving, even indifferent to the idea of having a father. Quite the opposite. Since I had lost my father, I was compelled to think about this thing called a "father" far more often than children whose dads were a constant part of their lives.

Mother and Grandmother always seemed to be trying to construct an image of my absent father within me. I imagine they were doing this on purpose. Even Grandfather, who barely spoke, would sometimes say, "Your daddy died so young. What a poor boy you are!" thus calling up a virtual image of my father within my imagination. From the moment the first twinkling of consciousness appeared within me—that moment we call in Japanese "a mind for things"—I became skilled in the process of

taking words and incarnating them into flesh, much as Christians believe
the word of God created mankind.

The most important source for me in the sacrament of incarnation
was the painting of my father that hung above the sliding closet door hiding the Buddhist altar. In the portrait, my father's hair was slicked back
with pomade. The painting was executed in a clumsy attempt to make the
light and shading look naturalistic. He had a forehead that was not very
wide, one of the traits of the Takahashi family. His eyebrows were thick
like Grandmother's, and his eyes were open wide as if in surprise. High
cheekbones. A prominent Adam's apple. A neck that hardly looked strong
enough to support his big head. An outer kimono that lined up with the
collar inside just a little too perfectly. On the sleeves of the kimono was
the family crest, a hanging wisteria. The artist had drawn the crest in the
folds of the kimono in a way that looked somewhat unnatural. Since the
whole portrait was done in a thin wash of ink, it had faded terribly with
time and turned the brownish color of tea. This was my father: Takahashi
Shirō, born May 13, 1906, deceased March 29, 1938, at age thirty-one.

The portrait only showed him from the shoulders up. My father
did not have a body. In a certain sense, I guess I could say the portrait
was symbolic. Since my father had been lost to me from the start, it was
strangely fitting that in the portrait he was missing everything from his
chest downward. After all, the portrait depicted him in a corporeal form
that, at least in my view, he had never even had.

The second thing that helped me construct a mental image of my
father was the family gravestone, located a little more than a half-mile from
Grandmother's home. The belt of land where she lived was called Shinnyū
and lay across the railroad tracks a little ways from the town of Nōgata.
Shinnyū, in turn, was broken into several other little neighborhoods, scattered across the countryside. There was a little song made up mostly of place
names that would help travelers remember the order of the neighborhoods:

Wada, Hachiryū, Kamenko
Eira, Baba, Saikōji
Go up, go down, Kamoda

In the neighborhood of Wada, there was a hill covered with short, leafy *kumazasa* plants, and on top of that was the graveyard where many of the local households buried the cremated remains of their dead. If you climbed the hill to the cemetery, the landscape of Wada unfolded right before your eyes. A little farther beyond that was Hachiryū and Kamenko. The other side of the hill afforded a clear view of Eira, Baba, and Saikōji, and if one were to cross the bridge over the Inunaki River from Saikōji, you would go up and down a few sloping mountains before reaching Kamoda, which was well known for its cherry blossoms. The locals had spent their entire lives there without hardly ever stepping outside the region, so from the top of the hill they could survey the stage where their entire lives had played out.

My father's situation, however, was somewhat different. He had gone to work for the Mitsubishi Mining Company after graduating from grade school. Soon afterward, he went down the river and got a job in one of the companies associated with the Yahata Steel Manufacturing plant. It was there that he died. During his life, he read widely and wildly, consuming anything he could get his hands on, so his mind stretched well beyond the boundaries of the other, more provincial villagers.

The placement of his tombstone was symbolic. The stone under which he lay occupied one corner of the same humble graveyard where the main branch of the Kōno family—the ruined family from which Mother's mother had come—had been interred. Because the Takahashis had come from Yame-gun in western Fukuoka prefecture, they didn't have a family cemetery in the area. (Come to think of it, in the song that I mentioned earlier there was no mention of Matsuyoshi, where the Takahashis had their straw-thatched home, or Ike-no-ue. Those were the two places where people from other provinces settled—separate from the old families that had lived in the area for generations.) There were no gravestones for outsiders. The right to rest in the cemetery was a privilege my father had earned by marrying the daughter of one of the local families.

At the edge of the grassy bamboo overgrowth, the sunlight poured through the bamboo leaves and illuminated the thick, shiny leaves of a star anise tree. Nearby was a patch of red earth. A thick clump of reedy plants kept growing back in this spot, no matter how often we cut them back. A group of tombstones stood atop that patch of earth and among them was the one under which father was buried. He did not have a proper gravestone. It was not a big block of granite that had been hewn by a stonecutter or carved with a posthumous Buddhist name. Someone had simply picked up a nice-sized natural stone and placed it on top of a mound of earth. That was all.

"This is the grave of the old lady from Kamenko, and this is mommy's stepfather. Over here's mommy's older sister and brother. Don't know who this one is. Then over here is your daddy and your older sister Hiromi . . . " Mother explained which grave belonged to whom, and we lit incense before the stones, squatted down, and put our hands together in respect; however, no sooner had we left the graveyard than I had already forgotten the order of the gravestones. Several times a year—at the vernal equinox, the autumnal equinox, and the Obon festival—we would come to visit the graveyard and pour a big bottle of water over the stones to wash them. I would always think of the white bones embraced by the darkness underground, and I would wonder, "Do dead people get thirsty?" Apart from these few recollections, I do not have many other memories of my father's grave.

The third source that helped me to construct an image of my father was the collection of stories Mother and Grandmother told me about him. According to them, he was a day laborer *botchan*. What this meant was that he worked from day to day, without a permanent guarantee of work or a regular salary, but he was still as generous and easygoing as a *botchan*—a privileged, innocent son from some well-to-do manor. Grandmother and Grandfather were also classic day laborers. At the building and repair facilities of the mining company, they did things like haul gravel and odds-and-ends carpentry work. In fact, many of the people at the company were paid day to day. The only well-to-do manor in the area was the household of the president of the mining company, and he alone received a solid salary.

There is an anecdote that shows how easygoing my father was. One evening he was coming home from work at the mining company when it started to rain. A friend who was walking with him tried to hurry him by saying, "Takahashi, let's get a move on."

My father, who must have been twenty-five at the time, didn't make a fuss. He simply responded, "You dummy! Even if you hurry, it's still raining up ahead," and kept walking at the same pace.

Mother would compare my personality with my father's and express her preference for his cheerful disposition at every opportunity. All the time she would tell me things like, "He didn't have a stunted, perverse disposition like yours."

Because my father was so easygoing, an uninterrupted flow of coworkers came to visit him and my mother when they were in living in Hachiman. My father once told them, "Hey, I've got an idea. Why don't you bring your dirty clothes over?"

"What are you talking about?"

"My wife's crazy about doing the wash. The more dirty clothes, the happier she'll be!"

Sometimes people told me I resemble my father. One time, Mother took a serious tone with me and said, "Mut-chan, Mommy's angry, so you'll be good, right?" I was just a little kid at the time. I shook my head and said, "Nope, I like that angry voice." Grandmother told me that a similar exchange took place between her and my father. Apparently, she would also say similar things to him when he was a little boy: "Now, Shirō, you don't like it when Mommy gets mad, do you?" My young father's eyes would grow wide, and he would say, "Yep, I do!" I wonder if our similar responses weren't the result of some sort of primitive instinct passed from father to son.

A child and its mother are connected through the accommodating tube of the umbilical cord in what amounts to a single, strange, gourd-shaped universe; however, the father represents to the child both an original reason for being as well as an independent "other." This other is the pleasant, newly shaved chin that brushes against the young son's thighs while he is carried on his father's shoulders. A father is the set of powerful thighs that lifts his son as he tucks him under his arm in the bathroom. A father is the thick fingers that slip into the son's hair and wash it a bit too roughly while holding his boy on his lap. A father is the breath that smells like tobacco, the rough heat emanating from the palm of a man's hand.

I inherited my father's looks, but that is about as far as our connection goes. Ordinarily, a small boy will learn from his father without even necessarily being aware of it; he learns through the skin that touches him. In learning from this other—the person who represents the original reason for being—the quiet process of personal development begins within the darkness of the young boy's soul.

I never had a father who could serve as a role model, so instead I tried to fill in his absence with other things. But the portrait, gravestone, and stories from Grandmother were nothing but pictures, stones, and words—things that would never transform into flesh. To construct the universe of my own self, I had no choice but to seek out someone who might serve as a father figure to me.

2

I was probably around three the first time Mother met Ōgushi Kanjirō-san, the man who would become her lover. They probably first met when Mother was living and working in an inn in Shimonoseki. Apparently, she was not immediately attracted to the Japanese button salesman living in Tianjin. He was old enough to be her father—so much older that the woman in charge of the inn would ask, "Did Hisako give you the assistance you needed?" At some point in their relationship, however, she seemed to have developed some affection for him. Perhaps this was because every three to six months he would come to stay at the hotel and would do nice things for her. He would say, "Why don't you make yourself a kimono?" and give her some cloth, or he would tell her, "You should at least put on some makeup," then send her some imported cosmetics. When I was four, Mother followed him to China to live in his household with his wife and three children. It was a year before she would return to Japan.

After she came back, Mother found a new place to live in Moji. I was about ready for the first year of elementary school when we moved. It was in Moji that I first met Ōgushi-san. I did not know it at the time, but someone had secured a house for him where he could stay when he was traveling back and forth between China and Japan. In those days, he made the trip every three months or so, crossing the straits between the mainland and Japan via the ferry between Pusan and Shimonoseki.

It happened one afternoon only a few days after my mother and I moved into our new house in Moji. I had not made any friends yet, so I was alone outside leaning absentmindedly against a telegraph pole when I happened to see a man come around the corner. He walked by the Nagase barbershop, three doors down on the right, and headed toward me. He wore a suit of white linen, carried a big black bag, and had a reddish face of ample proportions. He looked rather out of place in this dusty street alongside the sea. Hardly anyone came down our street, only horse-drawn carts laden with cases of beer. It struck me as rather comical that such a man should show up on our little street.

The man wiped the sweat from his brow; then a moment later he did it once again. It was the beginning of September, and so it was hot. I was dressed in shorts and short sleeves as I leaned against the pole. He approached. I looked at him for a moment; then my gaze fell to the ground just a little ways before his feet, unwilling to meet his eyes directly. That was how I handled myself when I was confronted by an adult. I had not been comfortable looking an adult in the eyes ever since my relatives started passing me back and forth from one pair of adult hands to another in their unending game of Heaven and Hell.

The stranger stood in front of me. My eyes were glued firmly to the ground. He smiled and spoke as if trying to lift my fallen gaze. "Hey, little boy, do you know where the Takahashi household is?"

When my last name emerged from his mouth, my fallen gaze must have wavered for a moment. I instantly had the sneaking suspicion that this man was Ōgushi-san, who had taken Mother from me only a year ago. In order to hide my consternation, I did not lift my eyes, but I played it cool and brusquely whispered, "Over there."

His eyes traveled to the door where my seemingly halfhearted words had directed him, and he looked up at the nameplate. "Ah, you're right. I see her name—Takahashi Hisako."

I kept my head lowered, but I peeked with upturned eyes as the fat hand of the man pushed the door shut behind him. I moved away from the pole where I was leaning and kicked a rock with my canvas sneakers. It went skittering in the road. A moment later, I heard Mother call me, "Mut-chaaaan . . . ! Mutsuo . . . !"

I opened the front door without saying anything or even making a sound. Silently, I proceeded to the closed door that led into the room where we ate, but I stopped short without opening the door.

"Where are you?" Mother's voice filled the room on the other side of the *fusuma*. Her question appeared to be half-directed to Ōgushi-san, as a form of apology for my not being there. I heard her footsteps approach the door and stop; then the *fusuma* slid open. In Mother's face, I could read a combination of surprise and confusion when she saw me there. The reason I had been standing there silently without answering was out of a childish desire to play a trick on her. If she had let out a cry of surprise when she opened the door, probably everyone would have laughed and my trick would have had a happy ending, but because that didn't happen, my behavior appeared to be the perverse trick of a naughty child.

"What are you doing?! Quick, get in here and say hello." Mother urged me in, trying to cover up her surprise. Spurred by her insistence, I took off my canvas shoes, eyes averted, and stepped into the *tatami*-covered room.

The surprise and confusion on Ōgushi-san's face when he saw me were even greater than Mother's. They were so pronounced that his face quickly transformed into an unhappy expression. It only makes sense that a fifty-five-year-old man would get ticked off if a nasty little six-year-old outside had played dumb and not offered his name when someone came around looking for the Takahashis.

His first words to me, however, were of a register completely opposite to what he must have been feeling. "This evening, we'll go to the bath; then we'll go buy some things to decorate your room." I could see that he was trying to conquer the unpleasant feelings that I, the interloper and his lover's son, had evoked in him. I could tell this from the fact that he did not affix a diminutive ending to my name, making it Mutsuo-kun or Mut-chan. Instead, he just called me by my regular name Mutsuo, thus showing no special affection whatsoever.

We took two washtubs and walked to the public bath. On the way there, I was filled with anxiety, thinking about nothing but which side of the bathing facilities he might take me into. Would we go in the women's side or the men's side? Until then, Mother had always taken me with her into the women's side of the bath. My hope that we might go there again was shattered when we arrived at the entrance. It stood before me like a great fork in a road diverging into two paths: one going to heaven, one going to hell.

"You're a man, so you ought to go into the men's side." Saying this, Mother, who was walking behind Ōgushi-san, pushed me toward the men's entrance. This was the first time I had passed through the garnet-colored door and entered the world where men stepped into the steamy, wooden bathhouse, their big members swinging heavily between their legs. I stood dumbfounded in the changing room as Ōgushi-san's thick fingers undid the top button on my collar. His fingers deftly moved down the row, undoing the next five buttons almost all at once as if by magic.

In the bath, Ōgushi-san taught me how to put my two hands together and squeeze them to form a "water pistol"—a stream of water that shoots out from the gap between the palms. He also showed me how to put together two of the wooden buckets used for scooping up water and seal them with a towel to make a floatation device. When I tried making a water pistol, the water came out in nothing more than a languid gurgle, and the floatation device I made quickly came apart in the water.

The strength of Ōgushi-san's thick fingers was remarkable to me. "If we clean you, fleas will come to the surface." Saying this, he started rubbing my closely shorn scalp until it grew sore. Then with the pads of his fingers, he began rubbing my neck, shoulders, arms, and legs as if kneading them. "Look! See how the grime's come out, like bugs." Just as he said this, little bits of grime now sat on my reddened skin like snippets of cotton thread or tiny little bugs, pushed out of my skin by his fingers.

Mother walked home a few steps in front of us. I am not sure if she had made them in anticipation of Ōgushi-san's arrival, but she had a matching pair of dark-blue cotton *yukata* for me and him, plus a white, splashed-pattern *yukata* for herself. No doubt the three of us presented a heartwarming vision of a family: Ōgushi-san with his plump physique and tiny, little me in our matching clothes, while Mother walked with us in her white *yukata*. We crossed the railroad tracks, passed through the central avenue, and at Higashi Daimon-chō, he bought a round plaque and some other decorations to hang in our house.

A couple of weeks after Ōgushi-san left, I came home from school to open the front door and find an envelope on the concrete floor. It was face-down so I saw the words *Takahashi Yoshirō, Pusan* on the back. I turned it over and saw it was addressed to Takahashi Hisako-sama, 2-Chōme, Minami Hon-Machi, Dairi, Moji. It was addressed to Mother. Holding the letter between the thumb and forefinger of my right hand, I spun the letter round and round as I entered the room and asked, "Say, who's this, Mom?"

She grabbed the letter from between my fingers. Then with a sternness that was almost humorous, she said, "Ōgushi-san is your father. This is his new name: Takahashi Yoshirō." Of course, he had not become my father. He was just using a secret name in order to hide the fact that my mother and he were having an affair from the postal carrier and the neighborhood.

As the letters from Takahashi Yoshirō continued to come, the war came to an end. When Ōgushi-san showed up a few months later, he looked completely different from when I had first met him. He was dressed in shabby clothing that looked like the so-called citizens' clothing that was so common during the war. In listening to him talk to Mother, I gathered a rough picture of what had happened: he, his wife, and children had fled from Tianjin and returned to their native land of Japan with nothing more than the clothes on their backs. Of course, the assets that they had built up over the course of half their lives had been frozen. He sent his wife and children back to her mother, a farmer in Saga, and now it was time for him to think about what to do about Mother and me.

He had decided that he would divert shoes from the occupation army PX into the black market. He was a businessman to his very core. Almost immediately, he managed to make some special contacts with someone in the occupation forces. Black marketeers from Korea started coming and going from our house under the veil of night.

During that time, Ōgushi-san spent a long time at our house. The neighbors greeted him as the master of the family, and he treated me like a son. When I hung my head and looked downward in my usual way, he encouraged me to lift myself up. "Mutsuo, you're a man. A man should act like a man and throw out his chest." He would also say things like, "Mutsuo, sing a song. Sing a cheerful song for us in a loud voice."

When he went to Kokura, Shimonoseki, and other places, he would sometimes take me along. Once, when we were standing in line to buy ice candy, he wiped the sweat from my brow, then immediately wiped me again. Still, when he finally handed me the ice candy, I couldn't even bring myself to thank him. That was how aloof I was, but even so, he still continued to make an effort to reach me. Later, Mother told me that he was at his wit's end trying to figure out how to deal with me and my dark personality. He even said to her, "Do you have to be the one to take care of him? Go leave him with his grandparents."

At first the trade in shoes went well, but before long the business came to a standstill. The Korean he was working with absconded with several hundred pairs of shoes. Ōgushi-san couldn't take him to the authorities without admitting his own crime. His opponent had gotten one up on him, but all Ōgushi-san could do was grind his teeth in frustration.

I slept in a four-and-a-half-mat room that looked out onto the road. He and Mother would stay up late at night in the next room, which we used for eating. They would keep the light on, and I would hear their voices whispering well into the night.

I am not sure what happened, but there was some talk of his separating from his wife. He went back to his family home and raised some money to pay off the missing shoes; then he went back to his wife and children. Mother received a whole set of household goods. There was also apparently some talk of a marriage between them, but that never came to fruition.

One evening when I went home, tired from playing, I found an unusual repast on one of the low tables where we ate our meals. The table was almost overflowing with food: sea bream that had been simmered to make a rich soup, shellfish with vinegared miso paste, vegetables cooked in broth, and even some cuts of sashimi. Such a spread was almost unthinkable in an era when most people hardly had enough to get by. Mother's voice was unusually cheerful. "Mut-chan, come here." I sat where she indicated.

Ōgushi-san was there, pouring sake into her cup. "Come on, Hisako-san. Have another drink . . ." He was already quite red from the alcohol. Although he was old enough to be her father, he still called her Hisako-san, affixing the adult suffix *–san* to her name rather than using a more diminutive or intimate expression, as one might have expected.

"No, I've had enough. You're the one who should have another."

"How about if we give a cup to Mutsuo here?"

"Come on, he's too young. He's just a boy."

"One cup won't hurt him. It's a special occasion. One farewell cup ..."

Mother didn't say anything else. She stood up and went quietly to the kitchen.

He stuck a cup in front of me. "Here, just one drink." Sensing my hesitation, he said, "You're a man, aren't you? If you're really a man, you ought to be able to handle a little sake." His big hands put the sake cup into mine and poured some of the strange-tasting liquid. I quickly gulped it down, and my head began to reel as if someone had struck me with a stick. Even when I closed my eyes, I could see lightning racing back and forth across the inside of my eyelids.

When Mother came back carrying a newly warmed bottle of sake, I pulled at her sleeve and told her in a feeble voice, "My head hurts." She laid me to sleep beside the low table. As the outside world twisted and twirled around my head, the table and the seated couple beside it spun off into the distance. When I woke the next morning, Ōgushi-san was already gone.

3

For a while, Ōgushi-san had filled in the void left by my father's death; however, soon after he left, one of my male teachers at school, Tomosada-Sensei, became another father figure to me, but in quite a different way. The first two years I was in elementary school, all I had were female teachers: Fujikichi-Sensei and Sugimoto-Sensei. When I went into third grade, I did have a male teacher, Nishida-Sensei, but he soon transferred to the high school and left us with a female teacher named Matsuo-Sensei, so I barely remember him. As a result, Tomosada-Sensei was the first male teacher I had for any extent of time.

After the ceremony welcoming us to school at the beginning of fourth grade, there was a long sorting process, as each of our names was read aloud and we were told which class we would join. I was placed in Class A, so we were the first to get our act together. We went into our new classroom and were noisily milling about, congregating in groups of our fellow classmates from the previous year, when our new teacher walked in.

Tomosada-Sensei had just returned from the battlefield. Although he was still just a young fellow in his late twenties, he seemed much more of a man than a youth to me. "I want to be your friend," he told us. "Anything . . . if you have anything at all that you want to talk to me about, just let me know. All right?"

The students raised their voices in unison, "Yes, sir."

"For instance, if you need books but your family can't afford them . . . you can come and tell me those things. I don't have much money either, but if it's only a book we are talking about, I could probably help you out."

I decided then and there to ask him to buy a book for me. I would have him buy one for me first, before anyone else asked him.

The distance between making this decision and actually making it happen, however, involved a long and extremely arduous process. Every morning, I would hide alongside the path that he would walk along to school, and as he passed I would start trailing after him. Inevitably, however, some other classmate would come up from behind and grab his attention, saying in a loud voice, "Good morning, Sensei!" thus wrecking my plan. He was also the baseball coach, so after class let out, I waited between the shrubs off the baseball diamond, but the warm-ups seemed never to end. Then when they finally did, he started practicing in earnest with the team.

One day after school, about a week after classes had started, I finally found myself alone with him. That day, we had cleaned the classroom. He would usually take the lead and set a good example, showing the students how we were supposed to clean. When it was all over, I realized that he and I were the only ones left in the room. I flushed bright red and tried broaching the subject. "Um, Sensei?"

He looked over his shoulder at me and said nothing. I realized how unpleasant and dry the words that I had just uttered were. To hide my palpitations of fear, I said emphatically, "Sensei, I want a book . . . Yoshikawa Eiji's novel *Mother Lovebird*."

"How much is it?"

"Ninety-nine yen." In those days, it was the custom to pay an extra ten percent beyond the cover price of the book as a commission to the bookstore selling it. That meant the price on *Mother Lovebird* was ninety yen.

He took the money from his wallet and handed it to me. As I took it, I did not say thanks; I just stuffed it in my book bag and dashed away. Still, my heart was pounding with excitement, and inside, I was shouting to myself, "He bought me a book! He bought me a book!"

It was not that I was especially keen to have that novel in particular. Yoshikawa's novel, which was about clan disputes in Ōkuma province in Kyūshū, had just caught my eye at the Sanwa Bookstore near school. It didn't really matter to me what the book was about. What was important to me was the special bond that would be created between us if he were to buy me something.

I do not mean to say that the book did not have any significance to me. In it, there is a scene where the young monk Suzumaru forcefully strums the strings of a *biwa* and sings the following song:

Listen to the cry
Of the mountain bird
Singing so melodiously
I wonder if it is a father
I wonder if it is a mother

The song continues:

They say it lives on fruits and leaves
This creature called the deep mountain bird
Why doesn't it, like a human child,
Long for its father's shadow
Or yearn for its mother's breast? . . .

The song is about Kumawaka, a young boy who appears as a character in the historical epic *The Chronicle of the Great Peace*, set in the fourteenth century. The song describes his powerful longing for his parents, yet it seems to suggest that his yearning for his mother is somewhat stronger: I paid special attention to the fact that he says "yearns" when talking about his mother's breast, whereas he only says "longs" about his father's shadow.

Still, part of me wonders if the person young Kumawaka was yearning for wasn't really his father, the Hino Middle Counselor Suketomo.

That is what *The Chronicle of the Great Peace* suggests. Couldn't his choice of the verb "to long for" instead of the verb "to yearn" be a sign of an even deeper yearning that he was attempting to suppress? Interestingly, Suzumaru, the singer in Yoshikawa Eiji's novel who was performing the song to *biwa* accompaniment, was thinking of his father, Sakamoto Daini, and meanwhile, his young master, Sagara Kokingo, was also longing for his deceased father. Perhaps *Father Lovebird* would have been a more appropriate title for the book than *Mother Lovebird*.

I was also a lovebird yearning for my missing father. Although he was absent from the very earliest days of my youth, I loved my father, and so I spread my tiny wings to set out on a journey to discover him. It was along this journey that I encountered Tomosada-Sensei. I had contrived the scheme to have him buy me a book in order to confirm that there was also a father figure somewhere in my teacher.

I had achieved one part of my plan, but my success was not complete. Most of the time he was at work, Tomosada-Sensei was thinking about how to get Tajima, the student at the top of the class hierarchy, away from the group of delinquent boys in town. This meant he had to spend time with Tajima's mother, who was a widow and had a reputation in town as a real beauty, and with the high school student who was the head of the gang of good-for-nothings.

It was a source of great consternation for me that Tomosada-Sensei only seemed to think about the bad boy Tajima and his slide into delinquency. I began to pretend I had a headache and play hooky. An hour after Mother left the house to go to work at the glass factory, I would eat the lunch she had packed for me and go outside and play. One day Korenaga-san, the neighbor who lived in the other half of the duplex we were renting, questioned me and told Mother what I had been doing. That night, Mother grilled me for an explanation. I lied and made the object of my jealousy the culprit: "Tajima threatened me with a knife, so I don't want to go to school anymore."

"Well, then, I'll have to tell your teacher about this."

"No, don't! Please, don't tell him!"

"If I don't tell him, you won't skip school anymore?"

"I promise. I'll go, just don't tell. If you tell on him, Tajima will kill me." I pleaded with her with all my might, terrified that the lies I had told would make my teacher lose his trust in me.

My stay of execution, however, lasted only a moment. I tricked Mother and used some of the money she had given me for errands to buy a two-wheeled toy car that you could wind up with a rubber band. She dragged me, still holding the toy in my hands, to school. My teacher was still there, even though classes had ended.

She spit out the proverb, "A lie is the first step toward becoming a thief!" then launched into her laments: "I'm all alone trying to bring up this boy. He's the only one I can rely on, and then he goes and does something like this. . . ." By the time she finished explaining the situation, her voice was full of tears.

My teacher responded, "I'm also an only child, and my mother raised me all on her own. I know what you're going through." He did not speak in a scolding tone to me but instead tried to comfort my mother.

Mother changed the subject. "He's been skipping school. When I tried to get the details out of him, he told me the Tajima boy was bullying him with a knife. . . ."

The events I most feared were unfolding before my very eyes. I looked up at my teacher's expression gingerly, but all he said was, "Oh really? I'll have to pay more attention."

By the end of fourth grade, I had learned to submit without any resistance when Tajima tried to trip me, yet it was about that time that Tajima seemed to lose his position as the main focus of Tomosada-Sensei's concern. In fact, Tajima had parted ways with the group of delinquents, and so our teacher was able to spread his attention more evenly to all of us other students.

When it came time to enter fifth grade and our classes were reshuffled, however, a new rival emerged. His name was Mizuno, and he had been in Class B during fourth grade. The cleverness and straightforwardness of this boy, with his small round eyes, surpassed any good qualities I might have had.

One afternoon during recess, we were behind the science room picking cucumbers and munching on them when the bell rang to signal the return to class. A number of us decided to ignore it and stay outside.

Toward the end of the fifth period, we, the saboteurs, returned, but the teacher made us stand in a line in front of the class.

"Why didn't you come back to class when the bell rang?"

One of us said, "I didn't hear it." All of us nodded.

Our teacher, however, did not nod. "Oh, come on. Are you deaf? Tell me the truth. If you tell me the truth, you won't get into any trouble." He stood in front of each of us in turn asking, "Did you hear the bell or not?" Each one of us answered feebly, "No, I didn't."

Then came my turn. I felt the words "I heard it" rising in my throat. "I heard it, but I didn't want to come back." If I had actually said this, I would have been a good boy—the only one among them—but in the end, I just said, "No, I didn't," like everyone else.

The teacher moved on silently past me. Suddenly, Mizuno, who was standing next to me, burst into tears. "Sensei, I was bad. I heard the bell, but I didn't come back."

"All right, then," our teacher said. "You were misbehaving when you didn't come in when you were supposed to, but I'm glad you were honest about it. You can go back to your seat, Mizuno."

I hated Mizuno for that. He had said exactly what I had been thinking. I hated him because he gave expression to what I had wanted to say but had not—no, *could* not.

Tomosada-Sensei had shown Tajima special attention, but he did not love Mizuno in any special way. No doubt all of us students were the same in his eyes. If he showed favoritism to anyone, it was probably me. Nonetheless, I was like the jealous older brother who rebukes his younger brother, recently returned from his long wanderings. I was the wicked Cain who hated his younger brother and rose up to slay him, simply because he had been so kind.

4

I suppose it was only after I graduated from elementary school and emerged from under Tomosada-Sensei's wing that I really grew close to him. Finally, I could go and visit him without thinking of Tajima or Mizuno. I would visit him once a month when I had the time, or at least once every three months when I became especially busy. We became close enough that he would give me his old shirts and underclothes to wear. This closeness continued until I graduated from high school. In a sense, Tomosada-Sensei and I developed a sort of idealized father-son relationship. Still, I continued to devote myself to my perpetual search for a father. My search was only complicated by the fact that my model for what a father should be remained Takahashi Shirō, a man who had been taken away from me by death before I could ever associate his name with the reality of his existence.

Since I was living with Mother in Moji at the time, we no longer had father's gravestone and portrait nearby; however, the memorial tablet that stood in the center of the Buddhist altar in the closet served the same purpose, even though it was inscribed not just with his name but with the name of my elder sister. The memorial tablet was nothing more than a single piece of lacquered wood inscribed with two names, yet it had a strange sense of presence about it. That sense of presence was connected to a certain bad habit of mine, and that bad habit, in turn, was linked to my propensity to steal.

The two-wheeled toy propelled by the rubber band was not the only evidence of my sticky fingers. On the other side of the corridor of bare earth that connected our front entrance to the cooking area was the shop where our neighbor Korenaga-san sold cheap confectionaries. When the sliding glass door beside the corridor was open, all I had to do to steal toffee from the glass jar in her shop was to pop across the corridor.

It was a habit for me to poke around the nooks and crannies of our house. One day soon after I entered middle school, I was looking for some change to buy some candy when I discovered two strange things in a thick, white envelope inside Mother's handbag. One was a little black booklet about the size of a matchbox. In it, there was a seemingly endless series of pictures of men and women drawn with long hair, *marumage* hairstyles, and no eyes or noses. Each of the pictures showed them coupled in strange postures. The last picture showed a woman being penetrated from behind while holding a suckling child at her breast. On this page were the words "The blessings of children." That is how the booklet ended.

The other thing was a series of printed images about the size of playing cards. There must have been more than ten of them, and together they formed a sequence that told a story. In them, a blind masseur was hired to give a geisha a massage. His hands traveled from her shoulders to her lower back and legs; then they began to crawl up again. As he closed in on her private parts, the two ended up with their bodies entangled. The masseur played the main role at first, but before long, the geisha grasped the reins of authority. In the last picture, they had finished their encounter, and the masseur stood with his bottom out, legs spread wide, and his half-withered sex in full view. His blind eyes narrowed and his mouth creased at the corners as he laughed noiselessly.

From that day onward, these two sets of strange "pillow pictures" became my companions whenever I engaged in my bad habit. I flipped through them with my left hand or I laid them out in a row on the *tatami* as my right hand conducted its onslaught on the growing flesh between my thighs. The handbag that contained the pillow pictures was kept under the Buddhist altar in the closet, so each time I stole the pictures and engaged in my bad habit I was reminded that there was some sort of connection between my father's memorial tablet and my activities. My strangely acute awareness of the tablet's presence came to represent one of the reasons that I felt so guilty about my habits.

In those days, I had a classmate named Wakamatsu. Once when we were in fourth grade, we had gone to the lumberyard behind the ice factory along the seashore, and there, between the piles of lumber, we had fooled around with one another. Since that day, we would play masturbatory games every time we met. Like a monkey sharing his discoveries, I showed him the things I had found. The pictures of the masseur and the geisha served our games especially well. We would take turns becoming the masseur and the geisha as we went at each another. When Mother was not home, we would spread the pillow pictures on the *tatami* and roll around on top of each other. Meanwhile, I kept thinking of my father's memorial tablet in the Buddhist altar inside the sliding doors of the closet.

One day, I was fooling around like this with Wakamatsu when I heard the front door open. At first I thought it was Korenaga-san, but the footsteps approached the sliding door near us, then stopped. Fortunately, I had placed a bar in the groove of the sliding door to keep other people out.

"Mut-chan? Hurry and open up."

At the sound of Mother's voice, I pulled my pants up with one hand and crammed the pillow pictures into the envelope with the other. I quickly opened the closet door, shoved the envelope back into her handbag, and closed the door again. Then, exchanging glances with Wakamatsu, I slowly removed the bar that kept the door closed.

"What were you two doing?" Mother peered in through the open door with furrowed eyebrows.

"Sorry, sorry. We were taking a nap. You're home early, Mom."

She remained silent, her eyebrows still furrowed in suspicion. When I saw Wakamatsu off, I went outside and did not return until sunset.

Mother seemed to have figured out what I was up to. The next day, the pillow pictures had disappeared from her handbag. That was proof she knew what was going on.

I looked everywhere for the envelope—in the trunk, in the boxes where we kept our clothing, in the openings of our bedding, in the drawers for the tea utensils, and in the box where Mother kept all her important documents. Finally, when I stuck my hand into the scraps of cloth we kept in our big tea canister, my fingers encountered the familiar touch of the envelope. When I pulled it out, however, I saw that the envelope I had found was narrower and longer than the one I had seen before. I turned it upside down, and a piece of paper folded into thirds slid out. As I spread it out, I saw the following words written skillfully in pen:

After the tragic loss of the Heike clan at the Battle of Dannoura, where they sunk into the sea and disappeared among the seaweed ...

Clearly, it was not a letter. With difficulty, I tried to decipher the pseudo-classical Japanese text. What I could make out was this. A woman by the name of Kenreimon'in from the Heike clan was saved by a man named Kurō Hōgan Yoshitsune, even though she wanted to die. Yoshi-tsune made advances, and although she refused him at first, she felt as though she had no choice but to accept his affections. In the end, however, she became enthusiastic about their relationship. From there on out, it was exactly like the story of the masseur and the geisha.

The story depicted her shift from refusal to acceptance in subtle terms: "In her excited state, she cried out 'Ah, ah' in exaltation, and gradually, she opened to him." Then, the following day, after she had shifted into the role of principal actor, the narrative stated, "As they heard the crows calling at dawn, she felt her heart and body melt and rush into their new struggle with the force of a waterfall. When he showed signs of already wanting to leave, she drew her knees together so he could not escape."

What surprised me the most, however, were the words I found at the very end: "Copied by Shirō, 1926." In that instant, I felt as if I were transported to some high, radiant place I had never known before. There, in that place where the air was so thin and hard to breathe, I met my father for the first time. I had never seen my father's handwriting before. Through the watery surface of those virile letters I was seeing for the first time written in pen, I was able to form a clear vision of my father. In 1926, my father was only in his teens as he sat facing his desk, diligently copying this erotic book. It was not in my imagination that I saw him—it was as though I was seeing him through the rippling waters of a vision. At that moment, the image of me engaging my bad habit was superimposed on the image of my father, and like two photographic negatives, the images fit perfectly. In that moment, the virtual image of my father that had proved so elusive suddenly became real. For the first time, I had a father who belonged to me.

Communities outside the World

1

The first time I was ever visited by a sensation of something "outside this world" was probably when I was in a train. I am not sure where I was going. Perhaps I was in the train going with Grandmother to visit my aunt in Yame-gun, or perhaps I was on my way to Shimonoseki to go meet Mother, accompanied by my young relative. In any case, I do remember that I had propped my chin on my hands, which were placed against the glass window, as I gazed absentmindedly out the window. The landscape approached us with great speed from the front of the train and quickly retreated to the back.

"If you keep looking out like that the whole time, you'll get sick to your stomach and throw up."

But I continued to look outside anyway. All sorts of things went by—telephone poles, stands for drying rice, clumps of trees. The train was swallowed up in the darkness of a tunnel then spit out again. There was an interruption in the regular rhythm of the track; then we crossed a metal bridge.

All of a sudden, the train jerked and came to a halt. The conductor, who was wearing a railway uniform and cap, came around to where I could see him, made a strange face, and shouted, "Shingooo-machiii!"

What he was saying was "waiting" (*machi*) for a "stoplight" (*shingō*), but to me it sounded like he was saying, "the town of Shingō," since the word *machi* also means "town." I looked around hoping to see the landscape of a town. I looked for an ophthalmologist's sign shaped like an eye with creased eyelid. I looked for a Japanese-style inn with water spread in front to keep the dust down and a dark, glass door to mark the entrance. I looked for a little girl wearing the brightly colored kimono you might see at the Seven-Five-Three Festival. Most important, I looked for the quaint station you would expect to see in a tiny town. I didn't see any of these things, however. The only things that greeted my eyes were the cliffs created when the engineers cut the hills away for the train tracks and dark, unpopulated rice fields that the farmers had created among the hills.

I quickly rushed over to the opposite side of the train to look, but there was no town there either. Meanwhile, the train shook again and started to move. The illusory town of Shingō retreated into the distance where it would remain forever. Even if I were to get on the same train again, we would never stop there again.

The town of Shingō was a strange place indeed. It was nowhere, but it was everywhere at the same time. Every time the train stopped and the conductor came round to shout "the town of Shingō," whatever was in front of me—the middle of the mountains or the seashore—would immediately be transformed into the town of Shingō. I would look for signs of the town, but strangely enough, there was nothing there but reddish cliffs alongside the tracks or the seashore with lapping, white waves. Nonetheless, the conductor's solemn declaration led me to think this must undoubtedly be the town of Shingō, and I conjured up visions of a town located there in the middle of nowhere. That was how I learned there were places outside this world we cannot see with our eyes alone.

It was the town of Shingō that first taught me there were places outside this world, but it was Otama-san who lived by the Kanroku Bridge who taught me there were people outside the world, too. The Onga River flowed parallel to the eastern edge of Nōgata, and the Kanroku Bridge crossed it near the southern edge of town where the rows of houses ended. On the other side of the bridge, there was a road that led to a cluster of houses known as Tonno. The houses were at the foot of distant Mount Fukuchi, which was shrouded in pale-blue mist. I sometimes went with Mother when she went to visit one of her female relatives in Tonno. As we crossed Kanroku Bridge, she would close her decorative parasol then point with the tip at the riverbank below.

"Down there below the bridge is where Otama-san lives."

The parasol in her right hand pointed down where the horizontal beams of the bridge passed from pillar to pillar. Someone had hung straw bags, the kind that originally held coal, between the pillars to form a makeshift shelter. In front of that was a bunch of fava bean flowers, which always looked to me like the faces of little puppy dogs.

"Down there with the flowers?"

"Yeah, Otama-san must have planted them to harvest and make into soup."

Stirred by the wind and bathed in the shallows of the Onga River, which flowed listlessly by that late spring day, the fava bean flowers gave the shelter the impression that someone was indeed living there. Still, Otama-san, the woman who had allegedly planted them, was nowhere to be seen.

"Where is she?"

"She's probably gone out to beg."

According to Mother, Otama was originally the daughter of a well-to-do family in Nōgata. When she got to be of marriageable age, she became the wife of a wealthy farmer in Tonno and gave birth to a lovely little boy. Her husband was kind, she had plenty of money, and she had male and female servants to wait on her. She lived a life free of want and should have been entirely happy. Suddenly, however, she lost her senses and began living under Kanroku Bridge. The change was so sudden that people said it was as if she had been "possessed by a fox."

Her husband and other relatives set out to Kanroku Bridge to bring the madwoman back. She did not resist as they took her back to where her husband and son lived, but only a few days would go by before she was back at her sunny spot below Kanroku Bridge, ripping the undergarments of her kimono into long strips and twisting them to form string.

No matter how hard they would try to keep her at home, no matter how strictly they kept watch over her, Otama-san would always find a way to escape—sometimes simply disappearing "like a ghost." No sooner had she disappeared than she would reappear at the Kanroku Bridge. Mother told me that not a single person had ever seen Otama-san escape along the road from Tonno to the bridge. As she said this, she made a scary voice.

Naturally, people teased Otama-san's son. They bullied him, calling him "the crazy lady's son" and "beggar boy." By the time I went to the bridge, however, he had grown up. His father had passed away, and he had taken charge of his father's household. He had taken a bride and had a good reputation in town. Still, he thought of his mother. I was told he went over and over to the bridge to try to bring his mother back, but eventually he gave up completely. Three times a month—every ten days—he went early in the morning and put a basket full of uncooked, polished rice next to the bridge. At the end of the Obon season, he also left her a kimono and a sash. He could tell his gifts had reached her when he saw the smoke rising from the fire at the base of the bridge where she cooked the rice every morning or when he saw the kimono and sash hanging on her clothesline between pillars. Still, one wonders if she was ever aware the gifts were from her own son. . . .

"After all, she is crazy," Mother said.

"Isn't she back yet?"

"She's gone out begging. She probably won't be back anytime soon." When Mother said the word *begging,* she knitted her eyebrows slightly.

"What does *begging* mean?"

She was silent for a moment. "It's when you don't work. Instead, you bow in front of people and get money from them."

"Does that mean they're bad people?"

She paused again. "They're not bad people, but they don't like to work, so they just act lazy and end up not doing anything at all."

I remembered the people I had seen on the day of the festival at the Taga Shrine. They sat on the bridge to the shrine, the steps, and the gravel road, dirty and mumbling to themselves. They were the ones who lowered their heads in front of the dressed-up people who were dragging dressed-up children by the hands. They were the ones who crouched on the ground before the drunkards, the firemen, and the ladies of the Housewives' Association for National Protection as they shuffled by. They were the ones who bowed when the slightest bit of change was thrown their way. I couldn't believe that these people, who suffered so much, were lazy.

"Are they begging because they want to?"

"Of course they are. If they didn't, why'd they throw away perfectly good positions in society and run away from home?" Her answer made it clear she was thinking of Otama-san in particular.

"So does Otama-san also sit there on the stone steps during the Taga festival?" I looked back through my memories to see if I could remember anyone who matched Otama-san's description sitting on the steps the day of the festival.

But Mother said, "Otama-san's crazy, but she's still proud and won't come beg at the festival."

There was some part of Mother that seemed to sympathize with Otama-san—or, rather, I wonder if there wasn't some part of her that wanted to be like her. If Mother went crazy, then it would have been much easier to resign herself to her difficult lot in life. I suspect Mother thought, "It would be so much easier if I were just a little bit crazy and could escape to someplace outside the world . . ." If that was not the thought that was running through her mind, I am not sure what to make of her next utterance, which she delivered with a shadowy smile: "What would you do if—just if—Mommy were to become like Otama-san?"

I clammed up, not knowing what to say.

Seeing that I was at a loss for words, Mother retracted her startling words. "I'm just kidding. But if you don't listen carefully to what I've got to say, who knows? Maybe I might end up like Otama-san someday."

Mother opened her decorated parasol and began walking. Walking briskly behind her, I was still preoccupied with thoughts of Otama-san. "Isn't she back yet? Otama-san, I mean."

"She'll probably be there when we go home from Tonno." But when we crossed the bridge on our way back from Tonno, Otama-san was still nowhere in sight. I suddenly remembered the town of Shingō. No doubt that was where she had gone. The illusory town that was everywhere and that was nowhere at the same time—that was where Otama-san had to be.

But no, that wouldn't explain everything. Otama-san lived at the Kanroku Bridge. Didn't that mean that the bridge that Mother and I had crossed just a moment ago was *itself* the town of Shingō—the place that was everywhere and nowhere at the same time? Or maybe it was even simpler than that. Perhaps Otama-san herself was an inhabitant of the illusory town of Shingō.

Mother, Grandmother, and all the other adults talked about Otama-san as if they had seen her with their own eyes, but I couldn't help wondering if anyone had ever seen her for real. Someone who was everywhere and also nowhere—that fit her description perfectly, didn't it? If so, there was no guarantee that we might not also end up like her. However, Mother didn't say a thing as we crossed the long bridge into the sunset and entered the town before us.

2

Not long after that, Mother went to the town of Shingō and became another Otama-san. It was during the spring when I was four that Mother chased after Ōgushi-san to China, a place entirely unknown to me. No one told me where she had gone. It was only three months after her disappearance that the package arrived from Tianjin and Grandmother opened her mouth, which had been so firmly shut until that point.

"Your mommy's gone off to China. She's become Chinese."

The unfamiliar word *China* Grandmother had used had the same mysterious ring to it as *the town of Shingō*, and the word *Chinese* made me think of Otama-san. It was clear that my grandmother thought little of my mother for butting into someone else's marriage, and it was for that reason she no longer belonged to our world.

When my aunt came from Yame-gun to stay with us, suddenly there were two people to criticize Mother. Grandmother said to my aunt, "Hisako-san's gone and become an *odekake-san*." She used the euphemism *odekake-san*, which literally meant "someone who's left the family," but it was used in popular parlance to refer to a mistress.

"Calling her an *odekake-san* is too polite. A 'mistress' is what she is. Simply put, she's the lowest of the low."

"What could she be thinking? She's living under the same roof as the man's wife!"

"That's proof right there she's a nonperson."

"No ordinary person could do such a thing."

"She's not even human."

Grandmother turned to look at me. "And just think, she's got this child right here."

"What of it? A nonperson, I tell you."

Although my aunt was born the same year as Mother and was in reality her sister-in-law, there was no affection between them. She just kept on calling Mother a nonperson over and over again. This phrase was unfamiliar to me, but it was clearly something terrible. It was much later that I learned it was a terribly discriminatory term used for criminals or social outcasts, whom most of society treated as the lowest of the low.

A few months later, I was two doors down on the right, lounging in the sun on the veranda of the *hondō* where Granny Tejima did her praying. Suddenly, the *shōji* slid open and the little old lady inside peered out.

"Mut-chan, did you know that your mother in China's got alopecia?"

"*Alopecia?*" I repeated the unfamiliar and difficult word.

Granny Tejima started running her fingers through an invisible head of hair in the air. "Your mommy's hair is gonna fall out. What would you do if her head became all bald like a priest's?"

I didn't know what to say.

"She's living in the same house with another man's wife, so she'll probably have all kinds of worries. When she goes outside, I bet she's got to put the hood of the rickshaw down, even in the day."

Her rich head of hair was going to fall out, and she was going to look like the dead priest from Shinshōji . . . ? No, such a thing was unthinkable.

"Liar! Mommy's not going to become a boy. I mean, she's sent me all those presents and things." Somehow the gifts represented to me a symbol of her femininity.

However, Granny Tejima's eyes, which were as sharp as needles, grew even sharper. Surrounding them was a network of small wrinkles. "I'm not lying. She won't tell other people, but she told my Tamie in a letter. She said she'd rather die, but then she thinks about you and realizes she can't let herself die. That's what she wrote all right."

Tamie-san was Granny Tejima's granddaughter, and Mother loved her like a little sister. If she had written that in a letter to Tamie-san, then there's no way it could have been a lie.

I tried imagining Mother as a priest rocking along inside a dimly lit rickshaw, wearing the same clothes she was wearing the last time I last saw her—her coat of iridescent material over a *yagasuri* under-kimono decorated with stripes. Did she have to become a priest because she was "no longer even human," as my aunt had said?

I thought about Pana-chan's father. Pana-chan was a little girl I used to play with as a friend. She lived in the cluster of houses that belonged to the Korean families on the other side of the graveyard above Grandmother's house. Her real name was Hanako, but her mother, who was not able to say certain sounds very well, pronounced it "Panako," with a *P* sound at the beginning. As a result, everyone knew her by that name, which was then shortened to the nickname Pana-chan.

On afternoons when Grandmother didn't go out to work, Pana-chan and I would spread a straw mat on the dirt in front of the house and pretend to cook, using persimmon flowers and water chestnuts we would collect from our surroundings. Usually before Grandmother came back, we would hear Pana-chan's mother come home and call "Pana! Panako!" Still, there were times Grandmother would come home first and find us surrounded by rice and hot steaming dumplings fashioned out of sand. On those occasions, I could see the displeasure in her face.

"It's 'cause of Pana-chan's father. He was taken away by the police."

One evening, when Pana-chan's father had just come home from the coal mines and was washing his feet at the front entrance of his house, a policeman walked in and arrested him. When I asked Grandmother why, all she said was, "They took him away 'cause he's lazy and a good-for-nothing."

Perhaps her father had some connection to the anti-Japanese resistance. Escaping from the heavy pressure of His Majesty's Japan and restoring the nation of the Korean people—in Grandmother's mind, wanting to do that might well have qualified him as a "lazy good-for-nothing." Grandmother did tell me that someone had seen him in Kami-yamada. His hair had been shorn, and he was clad in overalls and swinging a pickax, laying rails to a mining site.

"If you do something bad, you'll become a nonperson. And if you become a nonperson, they'll shave your head like a priest." Did that mean that Mother had done something bad and become a nonperson, and that was the reason that she had a bald, priest-like head?

There were some indications that Grandmother seemed to think that Koreans were nonpersons by their very nature. She referred to

Pana-chan's mother and the other people who lived on the other side of the graveyard in the houses alongside the sloping road as a "bunch of nonpeople even among nonpeople." I could not help noticing how poor their houses were. The roofs were little more than rusty sheets of metal weighted down with rocks to prevent them from being blown away. I would see them emerge from these houses with tubs balanced on their heads. They would speak in their mother tongue, full of plosive sounds like the rapid fire of a machine gun as they would walk together to beat their laundry at the water's edge.

In Grandmother's eyes, another group that was innately nonhuman like the Koreans was the *eta-goro*. According to her, the *eta-goro* were non-human because they would do dirty work like "skin horses and animals and change the teeth on the bottom of your wooden clogs." Elsewhere in Japan, the group to which she was referring was known by the discriminatory word *eta*, which means "full of filth," or *burakumin*, meaning "people of the outlying settlements." They were the untouchables who did jobs that others considered impure and defiling, and for that reason they were segregated from others and treated very badly. In our area, they lived together on the farthest outskirts of Nōgata, in a small community called Hyappyō. They would come to Shinnyū as hired hands to help out with the harvesting of the barley or the rice fields, but they were not allowed to cross the thresholds into people's houses. When it was time for them to eat, they would spread a mat in the yard and eat separately from the other villagers. When they were done eating, the bowls and cups they had used would be smashed to bits right before their eyes.

"Be sure not to make a mistake and wander into Hyappyō," Grandmother warned me. "If you ask them the way on the road, they'll say this and that, but you won't understand a thing. They make all kinds of mistakes with their words." The irony was that Grandmother was speaking in such a heavy dialect that people from other parts of Japan would probably think the same thing about her.

A few months after I heard about Mother's sickness from Granny Tejima, I went on a pilgrimage with Grandmother to the nail-pulling Jizō at Naka-aruki. We were walking back afterward with an elderly lady from the small settlement of Shimono when we got lost in the mountain roads.

We walked a long ways through the woods, stepping through the summer leaves that had been blown from the trees. Eventually we came to a tranquil cluster of houses tucked silently away in the hills. We heard the lowing of a cow coming from the depths of the settlement, which seemed to be devoid of people. The old lady from Shimono whispered in a worried voice, "Mut-chan, this is Hyappyō."

I got the impression that together with these two old ladies I had wandered into an illusory town of nonpersons that was both everywhere and nowhere at once. If so, it would only make sense that Mother, who had become a nonperson as well, might be here, too.

All of a sudden, there was a woman standing right in front of us. She was of a rather small stature and had a towel wrapped around her head. She was wearing rather simple work pants that were bunched at the bottom, yet she had a face that looked quite elegant. Other than the fact that she looked like she was about thirty years old or so, there was nothing about her that resembled Mother, but even so, I could not help but check to see if there was any sign of hair underneath the towel.

The old lady from Shimono bowed her head. "Sorry for asking, but which way should we go to get to Shinnyū over in Nōgata?"

"If you take this road straight, you'll end up right in Shinnyū."

She hadn't said "this and that" at all. She had gotten straight to the point. Why would such a ladylike, kind person be considered a nonperson? Had she done something bad like Mother and been cast out so that she was forced to join a community of nonpersons? And why was that quiet, peaceful place, surrounded by hills and forest, shunned by everyone in the rest of the community? To me, it felt as if this place, just like the woman standing before me, had left the real world behind, abandoning the world for an illusory space that was both outside the world and nowhere at the same time.

3

A year later, Mother came home on the ferry from Pusan to Shimonoseki. As she leaned back on the wicker chair by the bay window on the third floor of the hotel, I saw that her hair was as black and rich as before, and

I was on the verge of believing that everything Grandmother and Granny Tejima had said was a lie. Still, there was proof that Mother had become Chinese—she was wearing a Chinese-style dress with a navy-blue clover pattern, and on the ring finger of her right hand holding her cigarette was a ring inlaid with a deep-green piece of jade. Maybe Mother had become a nonperson and lost her hair, but if so, it had grown back. It was impossible for me to miss the fact that although I had longed for Mother so much, she was no longer quite the same woman she had once been.

Soon afterward, I moved with Mother to Moji, and it was there, when I was in second grade of Citizens' School, that the war came to an end. The end of the war turned all of us ordinary Japanese who had previously been part of society into outsiders. Conversely, the people who had previously been on the fringes of society were now able to walk in triumph down the main avenues of society.

The winter after the war ended, Mother took me to Shimonoseki, where I saw a strange sight in front of the train station. There was a row of Koreans that stretched on and on for nearly a mile along the road through the burned-out ruins of the city. The row of people went down the sloping hill, stretching so far that I lost track of them in the distance. They were squatting alongside the road, holding glass-lidded boxes containing cakes stuffed with sweet bean paste, rice balls coated with beans, rice dumplings coated with soybean flour, sweet potato treats, and other goodies.

The vendors lining the avenue of makeshift stalls did not seem to really care whether or not they sold any of their goods. Even though the penniless passersby might look at their goods covetously, no one had enough money to buy them. The vendors just sat there all day long, as if enjoying the expressions on the faces of their former assailants who were now timidly casting glances at the products, then slinking off without buying anything.

Could that have been a form of vengeance? Was it for the sake of revenge that the vendors squatted there all day long in such an uncomfortable position, holding their boxes full of goods? When they grew hungry, they lifted the glass lids of their boxes, pulled out some of the goodies inside, and sunk their teeth into them as if they were the most delicious things imaginable.

But my first encounter with the black market showed me something that was relatively primitive compared to what would came later. In the twinkle of an eye, black-market stands started appearing everywhere—in front of train stations, in vacant lots, along the rivers, in the plazas, in the burned-out ruins. . . . They began here and there with rows of two or three stalls constructed of rough, unplaned boards. The stalls multiplied like bacteria, and if they found even the slightest opening, they would extend into it like a starfish sprouting new legs.

When the social order was swept away at the end of the war, the people who had once been chased into the blackness at the edges of society had taken up a role at the center of society, ushering in an era in which the black market supported the social order. There, they made the flower beds bloom with black blossoms. Everyone said that it was an era of physical privation, but in the black market, you could find anything. The products ranged from daily necessities to luxury items. There was food from the seas, food from the mountains, and food from the fields. There was nothing that these markets did not have. The only thing missing was the money to buy their products.

In the black market of Moji, it was the Koreans and the crooked peddlers who made their influence felt the most. And no doubt the street vendors selling ointments, banging on pots, and using herbs for healing were from the village of nonpeople. The vendors all seemed to be unusually animated. The black market was a place where ruddy-faced vendors would stand tall and greet their jittery customers, who by contrast had pale, pasty complexions. Even though the customers had faces devoid of color and seemed quite nervous, there was a strange sense of freedom in the black market. That was the reason there were so many people walking around these stands, even if they were adults without any money or reason to be there. On the way home from school, I too would get lost in the maze of stalls, which boiled with a strange heat. I would often spend hours just wandering there.

I bought something to eat there just once. When I was in second grade, I was going home from school one day when I ran into Mizuno from Class B in front of the Shōchikuza Movie Theater. He had just come out from a film.

"You oughta try watching that movie. It's super interesting. They actually have intercourse in the movie!"

"You're kidding. There's no way they'd do it in a movie."

"Think I'm lying? Watch it yourself. They really do it."

After Mizuno left, I looked at the stills from the movie displayed in the window. They showed a foreign man and woman with expressions that were so dramatic that they were almost irritating. The couple was shown in a range of positions, both seated and standing, but there were no photos of them having "intercourse." I went home, pilfered one and a half yen from the drawer of Mother's makeup stand, and ran back to the movie theater. Once I got there, however, I found a sign on the ticket office that said the entrance fee was two and a half yen. I was disappointed, but there was no way that I was going to pass up a scene of intercourse.

I peeked into the entrance. The girl who was collecting tickets was seated on the left-hand side and straight ahead was the curtain that separated the hallway from the seats for the moviegoers. Hanging from the ceiling near the curtain was a framed movie still of an actor and actress who rivaled one another in beauty and splendor.

Right then, a group of four or five *yakuza* came in and started talking to the ticket taker as they stood there. I walked in from the front entrance, pretending that I wanted to get a better look at the movie still by the curtain. In a moment when I thought no one was paying attention, I slipped through the curtain.

The movie was *Pépé le Moko*. I kept watching, but as the film reeled past, the scene of intercourse that Mizuno had mentioned didn't appear on-screen. What did, however, was a scene of Pépé lying in his bedclothes on the bed, and a woman, also in her bedclothes, on top of him. Even I, still a little boy, knew that was not intercourse.

When I left the darkness of the movie theater, the light was so bright that it hurt my eyes. At the same time, however, the pain was also pleasurable. I plunged right into the bustle of the black market and used the one and a half yen that had grown damp and sweaty in my hand to buy some buns stuffed with bean paste, which I promptly gobbled down. The outside of the buns probably contained more mugwort than imported American flour, and the bean paste at the center of the bun was not sweet at all, but even so I was filled with a sense of ostentatiousness at pilfering Mother's money, sneaking into the movie theater, emerging from the blackness, and eating black-market food. I felt as if I had passed through the Eleusinian mysteries, and coming from the blackness into the light I had experienced some of the same unfairness as those compatriots in the black market. My undeveloped, youthful soul felt a strong affinity for what was outside my world in the realm of the other.

There were people my own age who belonged to that other world, such as the homeless boys camped in front of the Moji train station. I would see them every time I went to school or came home again at the end of the day. They ranged from seven to fifteen years old and were dressed in rags, but since they belonged to that community outside of society, they struck me more like adults than children. They set up shoe-polish stands in a row in front of the station, and they called out to potential customers in adult language. When people ignored them and walked on by, they would curse at the passersby with expressionless faces; then one boy would quietly pass a cigarette to the others. When I stopped and stared at them, they would kick gravel in my direction.

Once, when I was in fourth grade, I had a black-and-white spotted puppy, but it suddenly went missing. Two or three days later, one of my neighbors told me he had seen my puppy near Moji Station. He said the homeless boys in front of the station had been playing with it. I begged Mother to go talk to the boys.

I went with her to the station but watched from a distance as she went among the group of boys, squatted down, and had a long talk with them. It was probably about thirty minutes later that one of the boys held out the puppy and Mother took it in her hands. As she walked back toward me, she looked back over her shoulder over and over and nodded to the boys.

The boys shouted in unison, "Lady, don't forget our request."

"I promise."

Her eyes were overflowing with tears as she reached me. At first the boys had told her it was their dog all along, but when Mother said, "That's our pet dog," they finally told her the truth. In exchange for giving back my puppy, they had begged her over and over that if she found another cute dog, she would bring it to them.

I looked over in their direction. The boys were huddled underneath the eaves of the sheet metal roof that stuck out from the makeshift building that was the station. They were waving at us. For the first time, the boys looked unpleasantly small and uncomfortably cold to me.

Nonetheless, the appeal of the communities on the outside of society grew stronger day by day. When I was in fifth grade, the day before my class was set to go on our winter field trip, I gave Tomosada-Sensei a note that said I would not be going. The morning of the excursion was overcast. After Mother left to go to the glass factory where she was then working, I wrote a note and left it on the table.

"I'm going out for a while for *mushashugyō*." The word *mushashugyō* refers to the period of training that a samurai undergoes as he wanders around the countryside and practices his skills in the martial arts. I wanted to go out and see the world, but I did not have the words to say that. The word *mushashugyō*, which I had heard in old stories, was the only word in my vocabulary that I could use to translate my desire to experience what lay outside of society.

I walked beneath the sky, which was covered with clouds that seemed pregnant with light. If I was going to go to the fringes of society, then it only made sense that I should go somewhere I had never been before. Perhaps I should cross the straits between Moji and Shimonoseki, then start walking along either the San'in highway or the San'yō highway through Honshū. I knew that somewhere beyond that was Tokyo, the place the adults had been talking about when I was three or four and they had lifted me up, asking, "Can you see Tokyo? Can you see Tokyo?"

However, my straw sandals did not carry me far enough to experience a proper period of courageous *mushashugyō*. Instead, they carried me down the Tsukushi highway, which was already familiar to me. I passed through Kokura, then Yahata, until Kurosaki, where I bought some candy alongside the road. I only had three and a half yen left. But the time I passed Orio, it was clear that my feet were carrying me in the direction of Grandmother's house. From Orio, I walked along the Chikuhō railway line until I came to the town of Nakama.

At Nakama, the rails divide into the Chikuhō line and the Katsuki line. I chose the wrong path, and after three hours, I reached Katsuki station. I thought I would stay in the small, bleak waiting room until dawn the next morning, but the young railway worker from the station who came to sweep the floor came and peered into my face suspiciously.

"Hey, kid, where're you going?"

"To my grandma's in Nōgata, but I got lost."

"Lost? I'll say. This is Katsuki here. You mean to tell me you got on the Katsuki line?"

"I don't have any money, so I walked."

"You say your folks don't have any money?"

"Yeah, that's why I walked."

The railway worker mumbled to himself that there are some horrible parents in the world, then withdrew into the stationmaster's office. A moment later, he came out again with a ticket to Nōgata in his hand.

"In twenty minutes, there'll be a train to Nakama. Change trains there to get to Nōgata."

It was one in the morning by the time I arrived at Nōgata. Flurries were dancing through the sleeping town, but before the snowflakes even reached the ground, they disappeared into the darkness, melting above the earth. When I reached Grandmother's house and tried the door, it slid open immediately. It seemed she had just gone to bed. She and Grandfather were sleeping in their futon, head to foot like usual. I slid under the covers and promptly fell asleep next to them as I had done in the old days.

The next afternoon, when Grandmother and I came back from picking garlic chives in the fields, I found Mother waiting on the packed earth near the entrance to the house.

"Mutsuo."

I didn't know what to say.

The warrior who had intended to wander through the provinces on a voyage of austerity and training rushed into his mother's open arms and began sobbing pathetically. On the train on the way home, I did nothing but press my face against the windowpane and gaze at the landscape outside. I kept hoping the train would shake to a halt and make the town of Shingō appear. If it did, then perhaps I could run off and disappear into the town that was nowhere. That, however, was about the only time I remember that the train kept on running smoothly without any stops whatsoever.

It appears that my *mushashugyō* excursion had caused quite a furor at school. People told me that someone had posted on the announcement board just inside the front gate of the school a notice about my disappearance along with a request for help to go out looking for me. The teachers had also called an emergency meeting to talk about me. I felt embarrassed and feigned illness so that I did not have to go to school for four or five days.

When Tomosada-Sensei came to the house to check up on me, I buried myself under the covers so that only my eyes were peeking out. Next came Mizuno, who was the official class leader, but I still remained hidden deep under the covers. In hiding myself from the world, I was able to put myself at ease, almost as if I had managed to slip into the mysterious town of Shingō outside of society. In my comfortable cave beneath the covers, I went back through my mistakes and thought about where I had gone wrong.

4

The homeless children in front of the train station vanished, and the black-market stalls began to transform into proper streets full of shops. Society was reasserting its order once again. I had entered middle school and was in my second year there. My interest in what lay outside the world seemed to have turned inward. Or to put it in a better way, it seemed that I was now more interested in showing what was inside of me to the world outside. It was about that time that I began writing poetry, and I poured an increasing amount of my time into this pursuit. My interest in writing poetry became a bad habit that was equaled only by another bad habit—the one that had to do with the flesh.

Early in the summer of my second year in middle school, a new school building was completed for us. While it was being constructed, we had classes in the elementary school a little more than five hundred yards down the road. When the new building was done, we students helped to move, putting desks on our shoulders and carrying chairs by hand to the new location. We were about halfway along when a siren went off to announce the funeral of the former Empress Kōgō. We placed our tables and chairs on the road to revere the memory of the unhappy lady who had once been the mother of the nation.

The moment of silence lasted for about a minute. Once again, we put the desks over our shoulders, picked up the chairs, and set off for the new building. We entered the new classroom, put each of the desks and chairs where they belonged, then started cleaning. Not realizing what a big task it would be, I climbed onto the windowsill and began wiping the glass clean.

I breathed on the window, then used a dry rag to wipe the cloudy portion of it. I breathed again, then wiped again. When I had finished two windows, I jumped back down to the floor. I immediately experienced an overwhelming attack of vertigo, so I sat in the chair beside me and lay down on the desk in front of me.

A few moments later, when I lifted my head, I realized that my relationship with the world around me had clearly changed. The voices of all the friends surrounding me had become irritatingly distant, rather like the chirping of the birds heard in the morning while lying in bed or like the voices of the vendors outside heard while half-asleep during a noonday nap. A misty sheet of silk had settled over my hearing.

The next morning, Mother took me to an ear and nose specialist.

"What happened?"

"Yesterday at school when I was wiping the glass window, I got down, and suddenly I had trouble hearing."

"You've gone hard of hearing."

The doctor looked like he was in his thirties, and he already had a chubbiness about him that made him look slovenly. On the other hand, he had a rosy complexion. He delivered his diagnosis as he played with his mustache—little more than a patch of hair beneath his nose. He had not even examined me.

My treatment started that day. I was prescribed a primitive form of physical treatment that involved blowing air up my nose so that it would come out my ears. We kept this up for a couple of months, but there was no sign of improvement. We tried changing doctors, but still I did not improve.

As this was going on, I realized that it was not just my hearing that was being affected. A gauzy mist had started falling over my eyesight as well. We went to an eye doctor, but apart from the fact that my eyesight had fallen from 1.2 to 0.8, the doctors could not point to anything in particular. I began to wonder if it was something greater than a problem with my eyesight or hearing. Perhaps some sort of gauzy membrane had fallen over my entire existence.

I went for a complete physical at the Moji Citizens' Hospital, the only comprehensive public hospital in town. They found no abnormalities in either my eyes or ears. My brain seemed to be functioning normally, and there was no failure in my internal organs. A young doctor of internal medicine looked through an eyepiece into my eyes: "There's nothing out of the ordinary that we can detect."

But that in itself was a firm declaration of abnormality—an abnormality that could not be treated and healed. If I had something wrong with me that medicine could diagnose and treat, that would mean that I was normal but simply had a tiny little flaw; however, my abnormality was something that stubbornly resisted medical diagnosis and treatment. Wasn't that the most extreme type of abnormality of all?

I left the hospital and walked down the sloping street underneath the autumn sky. Its clarity stood in stark contrast to my own existence, which had been shrouded by some sort of strange membrane. As I walked down the street, I thought of the town of Shingō. That day when I finished wiping the windowpanes and jumped down, perhaps I hadn't landed on the floor. Perhaps I had landed in the dizzying, illusory town that was everywhere but nowhere at all, and I had been living since that moment inside the vacuum-filled capsule of the town of Shingō, kept at a distance from everything surrounding me.

The thought made me strangely listless and happy. As I walked down the sloping street, I felt like a ghost. On one side of the road, there was a bunch of cosmos fluttering in the wind. There was no doubt that those flowers were real. Similarly, I as a boy—the version of me that had existed right until the moment I climbed onto the window ledge—was also real. That much was certain, but I couldn't help feeling as if the person that I used to be was now shining somewhere out in the distance. By contrast, the person that I was at that moment—the part of me that was looking across the distance at my shining era of youth—had started to seem strangely like an illusion.

I went down the hill into town, but as I proceeded with uncertain footsteps, I found myself surrounded by a wave of people moving along energetically. I heard the beating of drums near and far, and there were fireworks going off at regular intervals. It was the day of the big autumn Palace Festival of Yanagi-no-gosho in the neighborhood of Dairi.

In the twelfth century, the infant Emperor Antoku and his retinue had stopped there on his long journey after the collapse of his capital. The old name for Moji had been Yanagi-no-ura, meaning "behind the willow tree," and people borrowed that name and started calling the area where the shrine was *Yanagi-no-gosho*, meaning "the palace at the willow tree." In fact, it was also said that Dairi, the neighborhood where it was located, came from the word *dairi*, meaning "imperial palace," the august residence of the emperors. The two were written with different characters, but the pronunciation was the same.

The Dairi festival was pretty small compared to some of the other local festivals, including the Festival of the Previous Emperors, which took place at Akama Shrine on the opposite shore of Shimonoseki, but the Dairi festival was no less distinguished in terms of its history. In 1185, when the Taira clan was defeated in the straits between Moji and Shimonoseki in the large naval battle that concluded the Genpei War, the woman who was caring for the infant Emperor Antoku jumped into the sea, holding him in her arms. In order to console the spirit of the emperor who had died at such a young age, the Palace Festival was held in Dairi in the spring and autumn. The priest from the local shrine dressed up as a member of the court and rode a sacred horse, giving the festival a whiff of courtly elegance.

In short, the festival was held to celebrate the death of the infant emperor at sea. When it came time for the portable shrines from every neighborhood to be pushed onto the festival grounds, the festival took on a more bloody aspect, as if its purpose was to gain vengeance for the young life lost at sea. The portable shrines slammed into one another, and the young men who were riding on top, clad in pure, white-bleached cotton loincloths, flashed their drawn blades and jumped from their shrine onto the roofs of the others. In the wild years that followed the end of the war, who knows how many young men fell to the ground, with their white cotton loincloths dyed red with blood?

All around me, a group of people had gathered and were shouting, clapping their hands, brimming with enthusiasm. They surrounded me and jostled me about furiously, but at the same time their frenzied commotion seemed strangely far away from me. The wave of people swelled with each passing moment, but there, in the center of it, I alone was sealed in a vacuum.

More than ten years later, I was in an underground labyrinth in Shinjuku when I had exactly the same experience all over again. I turned that experience into a poem:

> Put me on the portable shrine,
> And carry me to the bustle of daytime
> To the crowd that stinks of the animals' pen
> Of sweat, of grime, of vomit, of shit
>
> To the commotion of the day of triumphal return
> The clamor of the day of retribution
> The frenzy of the day of the festival
> The shouts of the day of anger
>
> So ignorant, brutal, lascivious
> This gathering, which is of love
> The flesh of so many loving one another
> Fumbling and touching everywhere
>
> I have paled to the color of the continent
> Have drowned in the sweat of death
> On my shrine, into the surging crowd
> Go forth, scatter, and disappear!

The masses will rip open my chest
Pull out my heart and my liver
Pluck out my eyes, rip off my sex
I will be lost as they wander away

The shrine will be crushed and fall apart
Blood will stain the flagstones
I will be with the crowds carrying me away
I will be everywhere

The crowds were moving. The crowds were certainly real as they continued their ceaseless motion. There was no doubt about that. They existed, sure and steadfast, unbroken and unflinching. By contrast, I was the only person who was not really present, even though I stood in the middle of the crowd. As I looked out across the crowd, the adolescent part of me that was not really there seemed to catch a glimpse of a shining, lost myth of youth that had retreated far into the distance. That, I realized, was the real me. Off in the distance, that shimmering spot far away was the place where I really was.

Afterword to the English Translation

MORE THAN FORTY YEARS LATER . . .

I wrote *Twelve Views from the Distance* in 1969, when I was thirty-two years old. Using that year as my vantage point, I gazed across the distance of time onto the panoramas of my childhood, examining the years between 1937 and 1952 through twelve different windows. That was what I had in mind when I gave the work this title. Since I first wrote the book, more than forty years have gone by, depositing us in the year 2012. The events that transpired in and around the year I wrote this book have also retreated into the past, becoming two-dimensional panoramas in the distance, rather like the past events I describe in this book. Perhaps it would make some sense for me to say a few words about that distant two-dimensional landscape—in other words, the events that surrounded the writing of this book.

The inspiration for this book came when I was sharing my memories of my youth with the head of the advertising agency where I worked at the time. My boss was an excellent editor who had experience ushering a number of aspiring authors to maturity. He had always shown a great deal of interest in my stories, and one day he told me, "It would be a shame if all you did was talk about these things. You ought to write this down and serialize it in a magazine." He even made arrangements for me to publish my reminiscences. He had recently become a consulting editor for a cooking magazine called *My Cook* (*Mai kukku*) and thought that might be a perfect place to start. "You can have twelve installments. What will you do for a title?" he asked. *Twelve Views from the Distance* was the first thing that leapt from my mouth. I decided, however, that I would not be too closely bound by that title. Each time I sat down to write an installment, I wrote rather freely.

I was right in trying this relatively free approach. I was able to write smoothly, without any difficulty. It was amazing to me how easily the old memories from my youth came flooding back, one after another, as soon as I had decided on the theme for the month's installment. Later, an elderly friend of mine asked me, "Why is it that you are able to remember your infancy in so much detail?" I told her that perhaps it was because they were such unhappy years. Later, however, I reconsidered, realizing that it was just a commonplace notion that we were all unhappy during the years surrounding World War II. In fact, I realized that I was probably happier than many of my contemporaries who had lived in relative security. Before I published the book, I had the novelist Mishima Yukio look it over for me. I still find his reaction interesting. He told me, "My goodness, I didn't realize that you grew up in such a terrible environment. I thought that you grew up in some happy household, the apple of your parents' eyes. In any case, the suffering of your youth doesn't seem to have stayed with you in any way." As everyone knows, later that same year, on November 25, Mishima killed himself in a dramatic public act of suicide.

One of the strongest reactions to this book came from my own mother. When I wrote it, I never intended to make her look bad, but she seemed to receive quite a shock when she read it. She realized that, even though I was no more than a little boy, I had managed to figure out the secrets she had tried to keep from me, and to make matters worse, I had written them all down as an adult. She telephoned my sister Miyuki, who had moved from Kita-Kyūshū to Gotō, Nagasaki prefecture where she lived with her husband, and said, "I want to sue Mutsuo for slander, but what do you think? This month, he sent me double the amount of money he used to send in the past, so maybe I should just sit back and wait and see what happens." My sister immediately called and pleaded with me, telling me how much she would hate for there to be a lawsuit in the family. "If it's true that you sent her twice the money this month, then please keep paying that amount in the future." I did not always follow her advice to the letter, but I did increase the amount I was sending her little by little, and apparently she eventually stopped talking about bringing a lawsuit against me.

My mother grew ill in her midseventies. My sister and I decided that she should move in with my sister in Gotō and I would pay for the extra costs. In the end, she wound up in a private room in a Catholic hospital, where all the doctors and nurses were nuns. My sister pulled up a bed alongside hers and nursed her through her final days. I think that one effect of that closeness was that it revived the kinship that had not existed between my mother and my sister for fifty years. Everyone said afterward that her death was a peaceful one, full of gratitude for the care her daughter and son had provided. Her funeral was held according to her own religion (not Christianity), and knowing that I would be treated as an outsider, I elected not to go, even though I deeply mourned her passing.

With my mother's death, the story that began in *Twelve Views from the Distance* came to a close. Now that forty-three years have passed since I first wrote this book, I realize I am glad I wrote the book when I did. Back then, I was able to pull the memories forth almost as if I were unreeling a spool of thread, but if I sat down to write it again today, I am not at all sure I could do it. Moreover, in that time Japan has changed so much as to be almost unrecognizable. The landscapes and social structure of the nation have changed, and people's hearts have as well. If I had not sat down to write this book when I did, there is no doubt I would not have been able to return and reexperience the Japan that had just barely managed to hang on through the earliest days of my life.

Glossary

amado: literally, "rain doors." In traditional Japanese architecture, *amado* are sliding wooden doors on the outside of a house that protect it from cold, the elements, or intruders. People would often slide them to the side during the day in order to let in light and warmth from the outside.

Amida: the Buddha (enlightened being), who is often believed to come to get people on their deathbed in order to release them from the cycle of rebirth and take them to the Western Paradise.

Banzai: literally, "ten thousand years." During World War II, soldiers were educated to shout "His Majesty, Banzai!" while charging into battle.

bentō: a Japanese-style boxed meal. A *bentō* box typically contains a large compartment of rice plus smaller sections of bite-sized portions of other foods.

biwa: a stringed instrument held vertically on the lap and played with a large, pointed plectrum.

bunraku: a form of Japanese theater from the seventeenth century with large, articulated puppets onstage instead of live actors. Because it was so popular, much of the great theater written in Japan from the seventeenth century onward was written for the *bunraku* stage.

-chan: a diminutive suffix attached to a name, usually to show affection or endearment. It may be affixed to just the first syllable or sound of a person's name. The name Mutsuo might become Mut-chan or Haruko might become Haa-chan. In southern Japan, where Takahashi grew up, this word was sometimes pronounced *yan*.

The Chronicle of the Great Peace (*Taiheiki*): a semifictional history of the era of the northern and southern Courts (1331–92). The text was read aloud and therefore has many oral elements, including songs.

Citizens' School: in 1941, the Japanese government changed the system of grade school and gave it this new label. In the new system, elementary school lasted for six years, and high school lasted for two years.

daikon: this word simply means "radish," but the kind most common in Japan is a mild, white radish often as long as two or three feet in length. Because *daikons* keep for a relatively long time before spoiling, they were a good product for poor, prewar families without iceboxes.

Empress Kōgō (1884–1951): the wife of the Emperor Taishō, who reigned from 1912 until 1926. She was the mother of the Emperor Shōwa (often known in the West by his given name Hirohito), who was on the throne from 1926 to 1989.

Enma-san: according to traditional folklore, Enma-san was the judge who determined how long people would stay in Hell, which was a frightening place full of mountains of needles, pools of blood, and demons with torture devices.

Fudō Myōō: the Buddhist deity known in Sanskrit as Acala. He is believed to protect Buddhism and its believers by destroying delusion. He is often depicted with a muscular body surrounded by a halo of fire, carrying a sword in one hand and a rope in the other.

furoshiki: a fairly large square of cloth used to wrap packages, lunch boxes, or other things. After a special celebration in Japan, hosts will often offer small gifts, such as *furoshiki*, as a thank-you gesture to their guests.

fusuma: a sliding door made of solid wood covered with paper. In traditional Japanese architecture, *fusuma* typically divided rooms inside the house or served as closet doors.

hiragana: the set of phonetic Japanese syllables most often used in modern Japan to write Japanese words.

Inari: the Shintō fox god associated with harvests.

ink stone: a stone used in calligraphy. People place a small puddle of water in an ink stone and rub an ink stick in it to create the dark ink used in East Asian calligraphy.

jikatabi: work shoes typically made of canvas with thin, flexible rubber soles. The big toe has a separate compartment from the other toes, ensuring better balance and footing while working on carpentry or building projects.

jinbei: casual summer clothing consisting of a pair of long shorts and a thin, short-sleeved top that closes in a crisscross fashion across the chest. *Jinbei* are usually worn only by men.

Jizō: the Buddhist bodhisattva known in Sanskrit as Ksitigarbha. He serves as a guide to lost souls and a protector of children. He is most often depicted in Japan with the shaved head of a priest, holding a jewel of wisdom in one hand and a staff in the other.

kanji: Sino-Japanese characters used for writing. Japanese children typically begin learning *kanji* after learning the phonetic *hiragana* and *katakana* scripts.

Kannon: the Buddhist bodhisattva of mercy known in Sanskrit as Avalokiteshvara. Kannon figures appear in different guises: sometimes male, sometimes female, sometimes with eleven heads to see in many directions, and sometimes with a thousand arms to reach out and help all living beings in the universe.

kappa: a mischievous and often cruel water sprite in Japanese folklore. In many stories they kidnap children to eat, and they often pull out and eat the rectums of their victims to try to get a mystical jewel supposedly hidden inside.

kasuri: a weaving technique that uses threads of different colors to create patterns in the woven cloth; sometimes called "splashed pattern" or "flying white."

katakana: the set of phonetic Japanese syllables most often used in modern Japan to write words borrowed from foreign languages.

Kintarō: a folkloric hero who used his supernatural strength to vanquish ferocious demons.

Kishimo: according to Buddhist legend, Kishimo was a frightful demon who killed the children of other people until the Buddha hid Kishimo's child to show her how painful it is to lose one's own child. After this experience, she repented and became a guardian of children.

kumazasa: a type of short, leafy, striped bamboo (*sasa*) known in Latin as *Sasa albo-marginata*.

marumage: a traditional, rounded Japanese hairstyle worn by married women.

masu: a small wooden box used for measuring liquids, rice, grain, beans, and other items. Often, *masu* are used to serve sake. Modern *masu* are approximately six fluid ounces.

memorial tablet: a lacquered piece of wood carved with the name of a deceased loved one. It is most often kept on a small Buddhist altar within the household.

mirin: sweet rice wine used for cooking.

Mount Kōya: the center of the Shingon (True Word) sect of esoteric Buddhism. Located in modern Wakayama prefecture, the mountain is covered with Buddhist temples.

Namu Amida Butsu: a Buddhist mantra that roughly means "All Hail to the Buddha Amida." Followers in the Pure Land Sect of Buddhism believe this incantation will allow one to be released from the cycle of suffering and rebirth.

Nee-san: this word means "older sister" but is sometimes used like "Miss" in English when addressing women older than the speaker.

Nezumimochi: a Japanese privet tree, *Ligustrum japonicum*.

Obon: the Festival of the Dead that takes place in July or August. Schools and businesses typically give a vacation of several days at this time of year, and people go home to visit their families and make pilgrimages to family graves.

Ogawa Mimei (1882–1961): a Japanese author well known for his tales for children.

Onoe Matsunosuke (1875–1926): a film actor who starred in more than a thousand films, including many ninja and samurai movies, during the early era of Japanese cinema.

pillow pictures (*Makura-e*): a euphemism for pornography.

postal savings account: in addition to delivering letters and packages, the Japanese post office performs the same functions as a bank, and many people in Japan have savings accounts at the post office.

ramune: a popular carbonated drink. It comes in a bluish-green bottle with a marble stopper, which is held in place by pressure from the carbonation inside.

samisen: a three-stringed instrument played with a plectrum.

-*san*: a suffix attached to names to mean "Mister," "Miss," or "Missus." It shows respect toward the person to whose name it is attached. In southern Japan, where Takahashi grew up, this suffix was sometimes pronounced *shan*.

Sanbo Kōjin: a god who protects the Three Jewels—the Buddha, Buddhist law, and the monastic community. He is typically depicted with a threatening expression on his own face and a crown topped by three heads. He is also worshipped as the god of the kitchen.

sasa: a type of grass related to bamboo that grows thickly and close to the ground.

sen: a unit of money that corresponds to 1/100th of one yen. During the prewar and immediate postwar era, a *sen* had measurable value, but in contemporary Japan a *sen* has become so small that the government no longer issues coins for anything less than a yen.

Sensei: a word that most often means "teacher," but it can be affixed not just to the surnames of teachers but also to writers, doctors, and others who stand in positions of social or cultural authority.

Seven-Five-Three Festival: a festival held on or about November 15 to celebrate children who are seven, five, and three years old. On the day of the festival, children dress up in fancy kimonos and make pilgrimages to the local Shintō shrines to wish for longevity and luck.

Shakyamuni: The Japanese name for the historical figure Siddhartha Gautama, who lived in ancient India and delivered the teachings that evolved into Buddhism.

-shan: a childish variant of the suffix *san* used in southern Japan.

shibugami: Traditional Japanese paper that has been strengthened by adding the juice of an astringent persimmon.

Shinchōsha: a prominent Japanese publisher.

Shintō: the indigenous system of Japanese religious practices, which revolves around a large number of deities, many of whom have to do with aspects of nature. In the chapter "Princes and Paupers," Takahashi mentions the deities Izanami and Izanagi, who according to Shintō folklore were the first deities to descend from the Field of Heaven to the islands of Japan. Shintō deities are worshipped in shrines (*jinja*), while Buddhist deities are worshipped in temples (*tera*), but there is much intermingling of Shintō and Buddhist deities in folk religious practices, such as those practiced by Granny Tejima in this book.

shōji: a sliding door made of a wooden lattice affixed with paper or frosted glass, which allows light to pass into the room. If used on the outside of the house, there would typically be another set of solid wooden doors on the outside to protect the *shōji* from the elements and to protect the house.

soba: buckwheat. In Japan, soba husks are often used as stuffing inside pillows.

sōmen: a thin, white noodle usually eaten cold during the summer.

tabi: ankle-high socks with a separation between the big toe and the other toes.

-tan: a suffix appended to names in the south of Japan to show respect tinged with familiarity.

tanuki: a Japanese raccoon dog. In folklore, *tanuki* are tricksters and supernatural shape-shifters that often play cruel and sometimes murderous tricks on humans.

tatami: a matting of finely woven straw, common as flooring in Japanese-style houses. Cool in the summer and warm in the winter, it is firm and comfortable. The standard size for *tatami* mats is approximately 36 by 71 inches. Japanese often describe the size of a room by stating how many mats cover the floor. A four-and-a-half-mat room is a common size for a tiny room, but many more comfortable living quarters have rooms that are six or more mats in size.

tobukuro: traditional Japanese houses often have wooden lattice doors covered with paper or glass (*shōji*) that separate the interior and exterior of the house. Because such doors are not effective against cold and rain, there was often another set of wooden *amado* (rain doors) on the outside. When people did not need the outer *amado*, they would slide them into the *tobukuro*, a big door pocket built into the side of the house. When nighttime came, rain would fall, or the residents would go away, they would slide the *amado* out again from the *tobukoro* to protect the house.

udon: a thick, wheat-flour noodle sometimes served in soup and sometimes plain with a dipping sauce on the side.

Urashima Tarō: the protagonist of a popular folktale. After rescuing a turtle, who turns out to be the daughter of an underwater Dragon King, the turtle takes Urashima Tarō to the king's underwater palace made of precious substances. When he returns to earth, he finds that a vast amount of time has transpired.

-yan: a diminutive suffix appended in the dialects of the south of Japan to the names of puckish boys a bit on the wild side.

Yoshikawa Eiji (1892–1962): a popular author of historical fiction. His novel *Mother Lovebird* (*Hahakoidori*) was first serialized in 1937–38.

yukata: a thin kimono shaped like a bathrobe and often worn in the heat of summer or when resting in the evenings.

English Translations of Takahashi's Writing

POETRY

Poems of a Penisist. Translated by Hiroaki Sato. Chicago: Chicago Review Press, 1975. Reprint, Minneapolis: University of Minnesota Press, 2012.

On Two Shores: New and Selected Poems. Translated by Mitsuko Ohno and Frank Sewell. Dublin: Dedalus Press, 2006.

We of Zipangu: Selected Poems. Translated by James Kirkup and Tamaki Makoto. Todmorden, U.K.: Arc Publications, 2006.

Sleeping, Sinning, Falling. Translated by Hiroaki Sato. San Francisco: City Lights Books, 1992.

A Bunch of Keys: Selected Poems. Translated by Hiroaki Sato. Trumansburg, N.Y.: Crossing Press, 1984.

FICTION

"Zen's Pilgrimage: Introduction." Translated by Jeffrey Angles. *Harrington Gay Men's Fiction Quarterly* 2, no. 3 (2000): 53–76.

"Zen's Pilgrimage: Conclusion." Translated by Jeffrey Angles. *Queer Dharma: Voices of Gay Buddhists* 2: 198–222. Edited by Winston Leyland. San Francisco: Gay Sunshine Press, 2000.

"The Hunter." Translated by Stephen Karpa. In *Partings at Dawn: An Anthology of Japanese Gay Literature,* 257–95. Edited by Stephen D. Miller. San Francisco: Gay Sunshine Press, 1996.

"The Searcher." Translated by Stephen D. Miller. In *Partings at Dawn: An Anthology of Japanese Gay Literature,* 207–19. Edited by Stephen D. Miller. San Francisco: Gay Sunshine Press, 1996.

Translator's Acknowledgments

In working on this translation, I have become indebted to many people. Most important, I thank Takahashi Mutsuo for his generous permission to publish this book and for the many forms of friendship and assistance he has provided since I first met him in 1996, when I was a student, writing a master's thesis about his poetry. Since I began this translation in earnest in 2006, I have asked him about small details contained in this book on many occasions. In all cases, I was astounded by his crisp and vivid memories of his youth in rural Kyūshū. Even sixty years later, he still recalls the details of the color on the glass pebbles his friend showed him on the seashore and the melodies he sang with his elementary school playmates. More than once I was lucky to hear him sing some of the many songs he describes in this book. I also thank Hanzawa Jun for the many splendid meals he prepared when I visited the sensuously lush, antique-filled home he shares with Takahashi.

I am immensely grateful to the National Endowment for the Arts, which gave me a generous grant in 2008 that not only made the translation of this book possible but also convinced my colleagues at Western Michigan University of the value of this project. The NEA's support has played a critical role in encouraging translators to pursue projects that might otherwise never see the light of day.

Earlier in 2008, the PEN American Center gave me a grant for this project. The letter announcing that I had received its award arrived when I was a fledgling assistant professor saddled with the responsibility of producing a certain amount of writing to gain tenure. Strapped for time, I had been wondering whether or not to abandon translation altogether, questioning whether the vast amounts of time, knowledge, research, and dogged perseverance required to complete a good translation weren't better spent on other pursuits. The PEN American Center grant, however, gave me the confidence and resolve to continue. It is no exaggeration to say that the grant changed my life; its support gave me the confidence to stand by my belief that it is only through translation that languages, literatures, and cultures evolve. Translation has the power to introduce new ideas, expressions, and concepts into a language or culture; it has the potential to reshape power and knowledge, thus changing the ways the world is understood.

Early versions of portions of this translation appeared in *Japan: A Traveler's Literary Companion, The Literary Review, Southern Review,* and the online journals *Cerise Press* and *Asymptote.* I thank the editors for their support and for their willingness to allow me to reprint those portions here.

Mutsuo Takahashi is one of Japan's most prominent living poets, with more than three dozen collections of poetry, several works of prose, dozens of books of essays, and several major literary prizes to his name. He is especially well known for his open writing about male homoeroticism. Five anthologies of his poetry have been translated and published in English, including *Poems of a Penisist* (Minnesota, 2012); *A Bunch of Keys*; *Sleeping, Sinning, Falling*; *On Two Shores*; and *We of Zipangu*. He lives in the seaside town of Zushi, south of Yokohama, Japan.

Jeffrey Angles is associate professor of modern Japanese literature and translation studies at Western Michigan University. He is the author of *Writing the Love of Boys: Origins of Bishōnen Culture in Modernist Japanese Literature* (Minnesota, 2011) and the prize-winning translator of *Forest of Eyes: Selected Poems of Tada Chimako* and *Killing Kanoko: Selected Poems of Hiromi Itō*.